INTERNATIONAL DISABILITY LAW

This book provides a concise guide to international disability law. It analyses the case law of the CRPD Committee and other international human rights treaty bodies, and provides commentaries on more than 50 leading cases. The author elaborates on the obligations of States Parties under the CRPD and other international treaties, while also spelling out the rights of persons with disabilities, and the different mechanisms that exist at both domestic and international levels for ensuring that those rights are respected, protected and promoted. The author also delineates the traditional differentiation between civil and political rights on the one hand, and economic, social and cultural rights on the other. He demonstrates, through analysis of the evolving case law, how the gap between these two sets of rights is gradually closing. The result is a powerful tool for political decision-makers, academics, legal practitioners, law students, persons with disabilities and their representative organisations, human rights activists and general readers.

Coomara Pyaneandee has been a practising barrister for 17 years and is the current Vice-Chairperson of the UN Committee on the Rights of Persons with Disabilities. He holds an LLB and an LLM in Public Law from the University of London. His main areas of practice include disability discrimination, protection of women and children from domestic violence and workers' compensation.

INTERNATIONAL DISABILITY LAW

A Practical Approach to the United Nations Convention on the Rights of Persons with Disabilities

Coomara Pyaneandee

Routledge
Taylor & Francis Group

LONDON AND NEW YORK

First published 2019
by Routledge
2 Park Square, Milton Park, Abingdon, Oxon OX14 4RN

and by Routledge
711 Third Avenue, New York, NY 10017

Routledge is an imprint of the Taylor & Francis Group, an informa business

British Library Cataloguing-in-Publication Data
A catalogue record for this book is available from the British Library

Library of Congress Cataloging-in-Publication Data
Names: Pyaneandee, Coomaravel, author.
Title: International disability law : a practical approach to the United Nations
    Convention on the Rights of Persons with Disabilities/by Coomaravel
    Pyaneandee.
Description: New York, NY : Routledge, 2018. | Includes bibliographical
    references and index.
Identifiers: LCCN 2018007734 | ISBN 9781138593466 (hbk) |
    ISBN 9781138593473 (pbk) | ISBN 9780429951855 (epub) |
    ISBN 9780429951848 (mobipocket)
Subjects: LCSH: Convention on the Rights of Persons with Disabilities and
    Optional Protocol (2007 March 30) | People with disabilities—Legal status,
    laws, etc. | International law and human rights.
Classification: LCC K637.A42007 P93 2018 | DDC 346.01/3087—dc23
LC record available at https://lccn.loc.gov/2018007734

ISBN: 978-1-138-59346-6 (hbk)
ISBN: 978-1-138-59347-3 (pbk)
ISBN: 978-0-429-48942-6 (ebk)

Typeset in Bembo
by Apex CoVantage, LLC

To my Mum and Dad

CONTENTS

CASES

CESCR

CEDAW Committee

Other Domestic and International Case Law

FOREWORD

As Vice-Chairperson of the Committee on the Rights of Persons with Disabilities, I draw my background from civil society organisations. As a disabled person, I experience the daily reality of discrimination. We are now moving into the second decade of the adoption of the CRPD. It is time for us to reflect on the past and prepare on the future. A new era of struggle against discrimination has started. By now, 177 countries in all parts of the world have ratified the Disabilities Convention. Yet, the challenge for human rights activists and, in particular, disability activists is as daunting as it was three decades ago. The expression of words is one thing but its translation into action by states is another. We must therefore continue to be proactive, vigilant and take the lead to continue to overcome the temptation of deliberate acts and omissions which marginalise our rights. With easy access to modern technology and social media, our voices can in relative terms be made resounding compared to my young days, when I had the feeling I was shouting in the desert.

Turning to the present publication, I salute its contents all the more because it has come out at the right time. All the subjects discussed in the 11 chapters have been analysed objectively, albeit from an insider's perspective. My colleague and friend, the author, has throughout the process exposed the reader a fresh and practical perspective of the disability rights Convention. Given the eloquent way he often expresses his dissenting views, I imagine that his job has been very challenging. His experience as a practising lawyer is also very revealing when one reads between the lines. His writing skills and presentation of the core legal elements of the Convention in the promotion of a human rights model of disability reflects the person I have known for a number of years.

The extensive reference to the case law of the Committee and its comparison with other human rights treaty bodies are useful analytical materials to construct upon for future guidance. Extensive references to disability-based discrimination, law policies and practices are eye-openers for the readers to think out of the box. For instance, the chapters on the right to life (Chapter 6) and freedom of expression (Chapter 7) illustrate clearly how the CRPD contributes to the advancement of truly inclusive societies. The exposure of the case of *Noble v. Australia* (miscarriage of justice towards persons with intellectual disability) and *X v. Tanzania* (person with albinism having his arm chopped off) warn the reader of the real threats and dangers ahead if we are not mindful of where persons with disabilities position themselves as the largest minority in the world in the twenty-first century. Exploitation, oppression and marginalisation, cruelty, in particular to women and girls with disabilities, are still real today.

The book also sums up in simple terms the complex terminological jargons which are frequently used in international public law discourse. In this regard, the author lives up to our expectations in the sense that the modern understanding of the concept of accessibility close to his heart to a very great extent educates the reader as to how he/she can be an active participant in removing physical social and psychological barriers which have been continuously built by society.

The author analyses extensively the socio-economic and cultural rights of persons with disabilities and concludes that independent living and being included in the community ought to be our ultimate aim. In this respect, his work is also normative in substance. It is true to say that the beginning of the twenty-first century has witnessed the gradual collapse of traditional theories on the gap between civil and political rights on the one hand and economic, social and cultural rights on the other. I agree that the CRPD's contribution to that end has been enormous. While my personal dreams have been translated into real living experiences, I hope that this book will serve to convert dreams into real changes in society.

Dr Damjan Tatic (PhD)
Vice-Chairperson CRPD Committee

PREFACE

It is high time all the rights and obligations of persons with disabilities and all stake-holders be analysed and compiled in one publication. There are several motivations behind this work. First, there is the need to explain in plain language, and in all possible formats, the technical concepts which form part of our rich and evolving disability law and policy. Second, persons with disabilities and their representative organisations must be equipped with the tools to understand and master the basics of their rights and states' obligations towards them. This is crucial for both the self-empowerment of persons with disabilities and to facilitate their advocacy work. Third, this book serves as a reminder for States Parties to the Convention on the Rights of Persons with Disabilities (hereinafter the CRPD or the Convention) that persons with disabilities are, first and foremost, rights-holders. Therefore, there is an obligation on States Parties to promote, protect, respect and fulfil these rights under international law. It is also hoped that States Parties will take maximum advantage of the present work in implementing legislation and policy.

Finally, as we welcome the second decade of the adoption of the CRPD, it must be noted that millions of persons with disabilities worldwide do not yet have access to basic services, and that they are still the subject of pity and charity. Yet the charitable model of disability has been combated in all its forms during the past decades by disability rights activists. Many of them are no longer amongst us, and the best way to pay tribute to them is by building upon their work. My modest contribution to this rich legacy is the present work.

The struggle of persons with disabilities for equal recognition and non-discrimination continues. Simply by being aware and conscious of our rights and states' obligations, we take one step forward together towards achieving that goal. This book seeks to promote and defend the human rights model of disability. It also attempts to maintain a practical approach to issues that affect the daily living conditions of persons with disabilities. With these goals in mind, throughout this work, we remain close to the hearts and minds of persons with living experiences of their disabilities. This is not a coincidence, given that we draw our strength and inspiration from civil society and disability rights movements. We are always mindful that we do not suffer from disability, but rather from all forms of discrimination which are sometimes oppressive and tyrannical.

It is hoped that this book will be of value to students who have embarked upon disability legal studies or studies in related fields. It will also be a useful guide for readers who have an interest in public international law, politics, economics and social affairs. The chapters have been arranged in a manner conducive to arousing and satisfying the readers' curiosity. Comments and criticisms of the work are welcome, irrespective of their tenor and form, as this is the only way we can hope to improve in future editions.

ACKNOWLEDGEMENTS

The support of all the professionally dedicated members of Coomara Pyanean-dee Chambers has been unfailing throughout the conceptualisation of this work. Although I would have wished to spend more time with my private practice and socialise more with members of the chambers, unfortunately, it had been a very difficult year.

I would like to share with the reader the fact that the idea of this book was first discussed with my father; a man who only started formally educating himself in Tamil language at the age of 40. He was very enthusiastic and was looking forward to its translation into Tamil. Unfortunately, he passed away at the very time when the sample chapters were submitted for peer reviewing. In the realm of uncertainty and in the colourless world of blind persons, we express thanks and gratitude when we run out of words. We reconcile ourselves in plain simplicity and say thank you. I accordingly thank him for everything and especially his dedication, conviction and determination and, more importantly, his ideal of the advancement towards truly inclusive societies. While now alone, my mother, Ambigay Pyaneandee, as ever determined and confident with pride, shall forever continue the battle with the unending support of my two sisters, Sheila and Toolsee, and myself.

My very dear friend, Dr Maeve Hosier, who showed a keen interest in human rights and disability discrimination immediately welcomed the initiative and kindly agreed to be the editor for the book. She polished all the chapters in native English and shared a lot of valuable suggestions. I feel greatly indebted to her for having devoted time, energy and patience to edit the entire manuscript.

My special thanks equally go to my young and dynamic junior researcher who played a key role in gathering, reading, summarising and analysing the materials. In so doing, Neel Raamandarsingh Purmah has quickly learnt to work with the strictest academic rigour.

By mid-October 2017, in the tropical warm summer of Mauritius, I announced to Maeve and Neel my willingness to target the general reader. I therefore had recourse to Professor Serge Rivière, a longstanding friend whose life and the literary world are so compounded that the divorce between the two is simply not imaginable. He also read the manuscript and made interesting suggestions. All the way through, he was faithful to the cause of the general reader from a non-lawyer perspective.

My secretary and personal assistant, Ms Sophie (Shritasing Shibnaut), and my long time collaborator Chet Bundhoo have been coordinating both my professional and personal commitments with wisdom and excellence. They both deserve the credit for being able to submit the manuscript on time.

I would also like to express my deepest gratitude to Dr Damjan Tatic, the co-Vice Chairperson of the Committee on the Rights of Persons with Disabilities, who endorsed its contents and kindly agreed to write the Foreword.

Finally, I would be guilty of serious omission as a parent if I were to forget my two turbulent and lovely teenage children, Eassen and Nirvana. They have very often distracted me while I was in the middle of the most important paragraphs. These constant and unpredictable knocks on my office door, which I understand were very innocent, but whose pattern leads any reasonable person to believe that it was intentional! However, the pleasure of being called 'Dad', and their encouragement to the cause we all defend, remind me of my own teenage years.

ABBREVIATIONS

CAT	Convention against Torture and Other Cruel, Inhuman or Degrading Treatment or Punishment
CEDAW	Convention on the Elimination of All Forms of Discrimination against Women
CEDAW Committee	Committee on the Elimination of Discrimination against Women –
CERD	Committee on the Elimination of Racial Discrimination
CESCR	Committee on Economic, Social and Cultural Rights
CRC	Convention on the Rights of the Child
CRC Committee	Committee on the Rights of the Child
CRPD	Convention on the Rights of Persons with Disabilities
CRPD Committee	Committee on the Rights of Persons with Disabilities
DPO	Disabled Persons' Organisation
ECOSOC	UN Economic and Social Council
ECSR	European Committee on Social Rights
HRC	Human Rights Committee
ICCPR	International Covenant on Civil and Political Rights
ICERD	International Convention on the Elimination of All Forms of Racial Discrimination
ICESCR	International Covenant on Economic, Social and Cultural Rights
ILO	International Labour Organisation
NGO	Non-Governmental Organisation
NHRI	National Human Rights Institution
OHCHR	Office of the United Nations High Commissioner for Human Rights

UDHR	Universal Declaration of Human Rights
UN	United Nations
UNESCO	United Nations Educational, Scientific and Cultural Organization
UNICEF	United Nations Children's Fund
WEI	Women Enabled International

INTRODUCTION

The United Nations Convention on the Rights of Persons with Disabilities (hereinafter the CRPD or the Convention) is the first international human rights treaty which comprehensively codifies and consolidates the universal rights of persons with disabilities. Following three decades of relentless struggle, on 13 December 2006, the world finally came together to adopt the Convention. The CRPD had its origins in the UN General Assembly in 2001, when the Mexican Prime Minister, Mr Vicente Fox Quesada, proposed the establishment of an ad hoc committee to consider proposals for 'an international convention to uphold the dignity and rights of persons with disabilities'.[1] The CRPD was opened for signature on 30 March 2007 and it became the first treaty to codify the economic, social, cultural, civil and political rights of persons with disabilities. It integrates established concepts relating to disability into mainstream disability law and policy.

The Optional Protocol to the CRPD provides a monitoring mechanism for alleged violations of the rights enshrined in the Convention. It serves as a vehicle for assisting individuals or groups who have exhausted domestic legal remedies to lodge complaints against a State Party. The Committee may also initiate an inquiry procedure in the case of serious allegations against a State Party, as occurred recently in relation to the United Kingdom.[2]

Since 2008, the CRPD Committee has been proactive in defending, promoting and enhancing the human rights model of disability. The CRPD rests upon two fundamental principles, namely that persons with impairments are rights-holders, and that disability manifests itself only when persons with impairments encounter social, economic, environmental and other barriers. Such barriers must be removed in order to ensure the full inclusion and effective participation of persons with disabilities in both political and public life. In accordance with the human rights model of disability, persons with disabilities do not suffer from 'disability', but rather they suffer from 'discrimination'. This rights-based model helps us to understand the contribution of the CRPD at both a domestic and an international levels. For example, in the UK, the concept of 'reasonable adjustment' has been instrumental in securing rights for persons with disabilities within the workplace, in line with the employer's duty to make reasonable adjustments.[3] At international level, the CRPD has continuously challenged domestic legislation, policies and practice which are based upon the premise that persons with disabilities are 'medicalised' and perceived to be in need of constant medical care. From this perspective, there is an assumption that persons with disabilities suffer from a medical condition which needs to be cured or attended to. The increasing number of ratifications of the CRPD by States Parties signals a rejection of this model.

To date, a total of 177 countries have signed and ratified the CRPD, and 92 countries have signed and ratified its Optional Protocol.[4] It can safely be stated that, in general, the human rights model of disability, as enshrined in the CRPD, has gained support in many parts of the world. As will be seen in Chapter 1, the CRPD Committee has already reviewed the reports of 69 countries out of the 177 states who are party to the Convention. These reports set out the steps taken to give effect to States Parties' obligations in conformity with the Convention.[5] The Committee has issued Concluding Observations and Recommendations in relation to these country reports, which pave the way for a better understanding of the fundamental rights and freedoms of persons with disabilities.[6] As a consequence, concepts such as 'reasonable accommodation' (Article 5(3) CRPD), 'accessibility' (Article 9 CRPD) and 'universal design' (Articles 2 and 4(1)(f) CRPD) which promote the right to independent living and inclusion in the community, are now better understood. These concepts have constantly been analysed by the Committee and are being used at domestic level for the implementation of legislation and policy around the globe. Moreover, the obligation of States Parties to listen to people with disabilities, in accordance with their rights, and to consult with them and their representative organisations regarding the formulation of legislation and policy, is gradually becoming a reality, albeit in an incremental manner.[7]

At the level of the UN, the CRPD has made a major breakthrough which has positively impacted upon the lives of persons with disabilities globally. It has built upon the experiences of existing international human rights covenants, such as the 1948 Universal Declaration of Human Rights (UDHR), the 1966 International Covenant on Civil and Political Rights (ICCPR) and the 1966 International Covenant on Economic, Social and Cultural Rights (ICESCR). The CRPD Committee has highlighted the lack of a disability legal perspective in such covenants. For instance, in relation to the principles of equality and non-discrimination which are entrenched in all international covenants, the CRPD Committee has assumed a leading role in extending the application of these concepts to new categories of situations. The application of the principles of equality and non-discrimination to novel situations thus marks a decisive paradigm shift in the way in which disability-based discrimination instruments are interpreted. This evolutionary approach within the mandate of the CRPD calls for a deeper understanding of the traditional classification between civil and political rights on the one hand, and economic, social and cultural rights on the other.

For historical reasons, the world has given greater importance to civil and political rights than to economic, social and cultural rights. From an international perspective, it may be said that civil and political rights define and regulate individual or group rights vis-à-vis the state. During the period of the Second World War, the lives of millions of people were threatened. People were tortured, arbitrarily deprived of their liberty, and their freedom of expression was curtailed. As a result, in the post-war period, civil and political rights were the immediate priority to be addressed by the international community via the mechanism of the United Nations. There was also an emotional response to the events of the Second World War, which resulted in a desire to redefine the value of human life. On the other hand, economic, social and cultural rights focused on the wellbeing of citizens. The obligation of states to safeguard economic, social and cultural rights is progressive in nature and is subject to the availability of financial and operational resources.[8] It is for this reason that the ICESCR ranks subordinate to the ICCPR. As a consequence, States Parties considered that the rights to housing, transportation, employment, cultural life and sport should be addressed only at domestic level. This was the case even though these same States Parties were also signatories to the UDHR of 1948, which does not differentiate between the two sets of rights. In line with the UDHR, all human rights are universal, indivisible, interrelated and interdependent.

Throughout this book, the questions which arise are:

1. What accounts for the dichotomy between these two categories of rights?
2. How do the provisions of the CRPD contribute to the debate?

Proponents of the dichotomy theory rest their arguments upon the following premises. First, they are of the view that economic, social and cultural rights are 'aspirational', as opposed to the 'real' rights which are entrenched in the ICCPR. For instance, the socio-economic right to education is vague and somewhat difficult to define. Hence, the nature and scope for its implementation by states are unclear. Second, it is argued that the implementation of economic, social and cultural rights depends upon positive actions by states whose willingness to uphold such rights is often questionable. States regularly offer the same excuse for failing to adopt measures aimed at implementing economic, social and cultural rights, namely that they are expensive and would require budgetary allocations which are unavailable, given the competing demands upon their purses. Third, there is the principle that the manner and form of implementation of policies must be left to governments' discretion, and their political choices in terms of policies cannot and should not be reviewed by courts. Finally, it is claimed that courts should not adjudicate on economic, social and cultural rights. However, proponents of the dichotomy theory lose sight of the practical effects of discrimination, which fall mostly within the sphere of economic, social and cultural rights; for example, access to the built environment and ICT (Chapter 8), the right to inclusive education (Chapter 9), the right to employment (Chapter 10) or the right to independent living and being included in the community (Chapter 11).

Since 2008, by virtue of its jurisprudence, including Concluding Observations and Recommendations, General Comments and, in particular, its communications under the Optional Protocol, the CRPD Committee has constantly launched and continues to launch assaults on the dichotomy theory of rights. While the CRPD Committee has succeeded in strengthening the efficacy of civil and political rights and in widening its scope of application, it has also effectively closed the traditional status gaps between the two sets of rights.

In common with other international human rights bodies, such as the Committee on the Elimination of Discrimination against Women (CEDAW), the Committee on the Rights of the Child (CRC) and the Committee on the Elimination of Racial Discrimination (CERD), the CRPD Committee explicitly integrates both civil and political rights and economic, social and cultural rights. In the case of the provisions of the CRPD, conservative States Parties could have navigated under the illusion that they would have a greater margin of discretion in the progressive realisation of economic, social and cultural rights as opposed to the civil and political rights of persons with disabilities. However, fortunately this has not been the case. For instance, the right to education has been considered by the CRPD Committee in a General Comment issued on the relevant Article in which the right to education was interpreted as being the right to 'inclusive education'.[9] In another General Comment, the right to independent living and inclusion in the community was considered as both a civil right and a socio-economic right which can be realised only if all economic, civil, social and cultural rights enshrined in this norm are fulfilled.[10] Thus, the rights to education and to independent living and inclusion in the community traditionally understood, defined and classified as socio-economic rights, impose on states obligations which are far more extensive than was initially anticipated. In the following chapters, it will be seen how the CRPD Committee, the youngest of all international UN treaty bodies, has succeeded in laying the concrete foundation for the protection and enhancement of the rights of persons with disabilities. This is very critical for humanity as a whole, at a time when human rights are coming under increasing threat.

This book, which contains 11 chapters, excluding the introduction and the concluding chapter, is divided into three parts: Chapters 1–3 in Part I focus mainly on Article 34 CRPD as well as on the first six articles of the CRPD. Chapters 3–7 deal with civil and political rights in Part II. Chapters 8–11 cover economic, social and cultural rights in Part III. The concluding chapter summarises the main arguments and provides an insight into the way ahead. With the exception of Chapter 1, the remaining chapters are all structured in the same way. We start off by explaining the core elements and normative contents of the different provisions of the Convention. These are illustrated by the use of concrete examples in particular contexts, i.e. how the principles enshrined are applicable to individual cases. At the end of each chapter, we provide the reader with a summary of the Concluding

Observations and Recommendations of the CRPD Committee whilst referring to other authoritative sources to guide the reader in the implementation of the rights at issue.

Chapter 1 is divided into two parts; Part 1 describes and explains how the Convention establishes the Committee, its major international monitoring role and its Rules of Procedure. Part 2 is more technical: it summarises the provisions governing the complaints mechanisms and the procedures under the Optional Protocol to the Convention. It aims to equip persons with or without disabilities with the required knowledge to seek remedies under the Optional Protocols to the CRPD and other international human rights treaty bodies such as the HRC. We explain the criteria of admissibility of complaints or group complaints from a practitioner's point of view.

In Chapter 2, it is argued that: (i) Articles 1–5, together with the Preamble to the Convention, are the major pillars of international disability law and policy; (ii) the framers were right in not formulating a formal definition of disability—the whole world has benefited from the absence of such a definition; and (iii) by sticking to the language of the Convention in line with Paragraph (e) of the Preamble, the Convention has achieved its intended objective. For example, the cross-cutting provision of Article 5 is expanded upon to show its interdependence with other provisions of the Convention. The differences and interrelatedness between the different concepts, including 'equality before the law' and 'equality under the law', 'equal protection of the law' and 'equal benefit of the law' are highlighted and explained. Different types of discrimination are examined and illustrated in the light of the case law. We conclude by showing the contribution of the CRPD in public international law.

Chapter 3 is specifically earmarked for women and children with disabilities in view of the intersectional and aggravated forms of discrimination that they face and experience on a daily basis. General Comment No. 3 on Article 6 on Women and Girls with Disabilities issued by the Committee stresses the importance of the rights of women and girls as enshrined in the Convention.[11] The scope of Article 6 CRPD is chiefly analysed through some specific examples of the case law of the CEDAW Committee which has dealt with women and girls with disabilities. The issues of exploitation, violence and abuse, violence during armed conflicts, and forced sterilisation are also touched upon. These issues demonstrate how negative stereotypes and harmful practices against women and girls with disabilities can be eliminated only through tolerance and acceptance.

Chapter 4 deals with Equal Recognition Before the Law (Article 12 CRPD) and Access to Justice (Article 13 CRPD). The analysis of these two Articles has been merged because the examples of violation of the rights contained therein are inextricably linked. We explain how and why these two Articles fall under the category of civil and political rights and how both Articles are premised on Articles 3, 4 and 5 of the Convention. Concrete examples are given to illustrate the differences between 'reasonable accommodation' within the meaning of Article 5(3) CRPD and 'support' within the ambit of Article 12(3) CRPD. We also explain how 'reasonable accommodation' must meet the criteria of the proportionality test, while 'support' is much wider in its application. In a similar vein, we highlight the differences between 'reasonable accommodation' within the meaning of Article 5(3) CRPD and 'procedural accommodation' within the provision of Article 13(1) CRPD. The case law of the CRPD Committee is extensively referred to in order to show how national courts have misunderstood the two distinct, albeit related provisions and how literal interpretations of de facto discriminatory legislation have led to erroneous decisions in the past.

Chapter 5 focuses on the right to liberty and security of persons with disabilities (Article 14 CRPD) as well as on the right to freedom from torture (Article 15 CRPD). The two Articles have been merged in the same chapter for reasons similar to those of Chapter 4. We deal with the following themes: (i) institutionalisation, without prior conviction of persons with disabilities; (ii) standard protections guaranteed by the ICCPR when persons are arrested, charged and brought to trial; and (iii) interrelatedness between (a) the liberty, security of the person, (b) the right to health and (c) freedom from torture, cruel, inhuman and degrading treatment. As we believe the reader, by then, will have grasped the basic tenets of the arguments presented in the previous chapters, we deliberately cross-analyse the relationship between the civil rights of deprivation of liberty and security of the person (Article 14 CRPD) and the right to protection of physical and mental integrity (Article 17 CRPD) with other economic and social rights such as the right to health (Article 25 CRPD) and the right to rehabilitation (Article 26 CRPD). This chapter seeks to demonstrate the main thrust of the argument throughout the entire book which is closure of the gap between these two sets of rights. The reader is also invited to reflect on the interwovenness of the two categories of rights as part of one single fabric.

Chapter 6 analyses the right to life (Article 10 CRPD) as the supreme right from which all other rights are derived. We look closely at the proposed draft General Comment No. 36 of the HRC on the right to life but apply its principles to the context of disability law and policy discourse.[12] With reference to the recent Concluding Observations of the CRPD Committee, as well as the case law of the HRC, we explore the dynamic nature of the right to life. We dwell upon the inefficacy of other international human rights treaty bodies in analysing disability-based domestic legislation. In so doing, we expose the lacunae in international law reasoning by specifically referring to the death penalty, abortion, euthanasia and enforced disappearance.

In Chapter 7, we elaborate on the guarantees against violations of the right to freedom of expression (Article 21 CRPD) and the right to political and public life (Article 29 CRPD). With regard to persons with psychosocial disabilities who are denied the right to vote and prevented from taking part in elections, it is strongly argued that the exercise of the right to vote imposes on states an obligation to provide support in terms of reasonable accommodations on an equal basis with others. The restriction of the right to vote constitutes a violation of freedom of expression within the meaning of Article 21 CRPD. Through an analysis of the case law of the CRPD Committee and of the HRC, the difficulties faced by States Parties in the implementation of Articles 21 and 29 CRPD are also highlighted. However, we conclude that the lack of political will is the main reason for systematic discrimination in this area of the implementation and monitoring of the CRPD. We also conclude that, without the effective participation of persons with disabilities in public and political life, the whole democratic process can be undermined.

In Chapter 8, we make the bold claim that accessibility is the backbone of the Convention. This is based on recorded attempts by States Parties to place limits on the interpretation of Article 9 CRPD on accessibility. Consequently, the Committee has recently issued a General Comment to clarify the normative contents of Article 9.[13] As demonstrated in the analysis of the case law and the General Comment, 'accessibility' is related to groups, as opposed to 'reasonable accommodation' which is related only to individuals. Therefore, the obligations enshrined in Article 9 CRPD ought to be immediately realised by States Parties. This means that they are under an obligation to provide accessibility before receiving an individual request to enter or use a place or service. Examples of accessibility include the provision of information visually available on all lines of a tram network for the hearing-impaired or the provision and accessibility of banking services by private financial institutions to persons with visual impairment. We also examine the interrelationship between 'accessibility' and 'reasonable accommodation' by analysing how the non-provision of steno-captioning to allow hearing-impaired individuals to perform jury services on an equal basis with others amounts to discrimination. Through the examination of the case law, we therefore highlight the misunderstanding of the wide meaning of accessibility.

Chapter 9 explores the right to education which finds its origin in numerous international treaties. However, the obligations of states under Article 24 CRPD on the right to education are more extensive. It has been interpreted by General Comment No.4 as a right to inclusive education. Since socio-economic rights, such as the right to education, have traditionally been left to the discretion of states, the case law on this subject from international human rights treaty bodies is very scarce. For this very reason, we give domestic examples from several African, European and South American jurisdictions. National courts are increasingly taking into account the normative contents of Article 24, as is elaborated in General Comment No.4. We reflect on the different models of education systems which incorporate exclusion, segregation, integration and inclusion. We show how domestic courts and States Parties have misunderstood the concept of inclusive education and thus point the way forward. We signal to the reader how the right to inclusive education as a socio-economic right is becoming increasingly reviewable by domestic courts.

Chapter 10 focuses on the obligations of States Parties under Article 27 of the Convention. These obligations are wide-ranging and address the barriers which hinder persons with disabilities from full enjoyment of their right to work and employment. We explore the interrelatedness between the right to equality and non-discrimination (Article 5 CRPD) and the right to work and employment of persons with disabilities (Article 27 CRPD). The case law of the CRPD

Committee demonstrates how the failure to provide reasonable accommodation to persons with disabilities in the form of adaptation measures is a violation of their right to employment. The use of quota systems for the inclusion of persons with disabilities in the workforce will also be analysed. States Parties are under an obligation to revise existing legislation which violates the rights of persons with disabilities by excluding them from the labour market. The ambit of the Article in relation to austerity measures is also closely analysed in the context of the CRPD Committee's report on the grave and systematic violations of the right to work and employment of persons with disabilities in the UK.

The main focus of Chapter 11 turns our attention to the advent of General Comment No.5 on Article 19, Living Independently and Being Included in the Community, issued in September 2017. General Comment No.5 makes it clear that Article 19 CRPD contains both civil and socio-economic rights, and thus underlines a hybrid right which is a bridge between the two traditional sets of rights. The right relates to all the other rights enshrined in the Convention. The right to legal capacity is, in that regard, one of the preconditions that must be satisfied in order for persons with disabilities to be included and to participate fully in society. Deinstitutionalisation and the right to adequate housing are the two key issues that have been examined since they are the collective goals of the human rights-based model of disability. It is submitted that the right to independent living and to be included in the community is the most important right if one aims to ensure that all the other rights of persons with disabilities are protected, promoted and respected on an equal footing with others. This is why Article 19 CRPD is regarded as the very soul of the Convention.

The concluding chapter summarises the main thrust of the arguments examined throughout the whole book. We hope that these materials will assist the relevant stakeholders in forming a better understanding of the jurisprudence of the CRPD Committee. The justiciability of economic, social and cultural rights is revisited from an up-to-date perspective, with particular focus on the enormous contribution from international public law. The dynamic nature of economic rights, and civil and political rights means that these will continue to evolve as the traditional gap between the two sets of rights is constantly closing. Its future, however, depends largely upon the implementation of Article 33 CRPD, Article 4(3) CRPD, and the sustainable development agenda 2015–2030 and its goals. We therefore explain in detail the implementation and monitoring mechanisms under Article 33 CRPD, which is a new international obligation that must be fulfilled by States Parties. It is high time that all stakeholders, and in particular disability activists, recharge the battery and secure a commitment from the judiciary to challenge the legality of immoral laws which are structurally or by implication discriminatory.

Notes

1 United Nations General Assembly Resolution (2001) A/RES/56/168.
2 CRPD Committee, Inquiry concerning the United Kingdom of Great Britain and Northern Ireland, 2016, CRPD/C/15/R.2.

3 Equality Act (United Kingdom) 2010, ss 19 and 20.
4 See Status of Ratification of the CRPD and its Optional Protocol at http://indicators. ohchr.org/ accessed 28 January 2018.
5 Article 35 CRPD.
6 Article 36 CRPD.
7 Article 4(3) CRPD.
8 See also Article 4(2) CRPD.
9 Article 24 CRPD; CRPD Committee, General Comment No.4 on Article 24 (Right to Inclusive Education), 2016, CRPD/C/GC/4; See also Chapter 9.
10 CRPD Committee, General Comment No.5 on Article 19 (Living Independently and Being Included in the Community), 2017, CRPD/C/GC/5, para.7.
11 CRPD Committee, General Comment No.3 on Article 6 (Women and Girls with Disabilities), 2016, CRPD/C/GC/3.
12 HRC, Draft General Comment No.36 on Article 6 ICCPR (Right to Life), forthcoming.
13 CRPD Committee, General Comment No.2 on Article 9 (Accessibility), 2014, CRPD/C/GC/2.

PART I
General provisions

1

FUNCTIONS OF THE CRPD COMMITTEE

The establishment of the CRPD Committee

Article 34 of the Convention on the Rights of Persons with Disabilities (CRPD) establishes the Committee on the Rights of Persons with Disabilities. The CRPD Committee comprises 18 independent experts who are elected by ratifying States.[1] In electing experts to the CRPD Committee, the States Parties should be guided by the following considerations set out in Article34(4) CRPD:

> The members of the Committee shall be elected by States Parties, consideration being given to equitable geographical distribution, representation of the different forms of civilization and of the principal legal systems, balanced gender representation and participation of experts with disabilities.

Elections are held in New York during the annual conference of States Parties.[2] The first election was held on 3 November 2008. Details of the rules governing the establishment of the CRPD Committee are set out in Article 34(2)–(13) CRPD. Elected members must be of a high moral standing and, once elected, they sit as experts in their own personal capacity.[3] The rationale is to ensure impartiality and independence on the part of Committee members. Once elected, the members of the Committee serve for a period of four years, and are eligible to seek re-election only once.[4] This limitation of mandate of CRPD Committee members is in contrast with that of the members of other human rights treaty bodies, such as the CEDAW and the HRC, who may seek re-election on two or more occasions. The limited mandate is one of the strengths of the Committee, because it creates an evolving democratic space in which persons with disabilities can continually pursue the advancement of human rights with innovative ideas. It also allows for the accommodation of experts with different types of impairment, and hence it serves to foster diversity. For example, in 2016, Robert George Martin was the first person with a learning disability to be elected to the Committee and Valery Nikitich Rukhledev, who is hearing-impaired, has been provided with a personal assistant to communicate in sign-language.

Article 34(10) CRPD enables the Committee to establish its own Rules of Procedure, and details of the Committee's current 2016 Rules of Procedure are available on the CRPD website.[5] Rule 7 sets out the requirements for accessibility in order to ensure the efficient working of the Committee. These accessibility requirements include access both to the Committee's information and communications, and to the physical environment of Committee meetings. The Committee has set a high standard in this regard in order to encourage other treaty bodies and UN agencies to follow its lead. The strict accessibility requirements of the Rules of Procedure also reflect the first concrete manifestation of the treaty's provisions.

In order to ensure that all Committee members can participate effectively in its work on an equal basis, it is necessary to guarantee that expert members with impairments have access to information in an accessible format, in a timely manner. The Rules of Procedure therefore provide for the use of sign language, Braille and other alternative formats for communication in line with the requirements of Committee members and of others who need access to the Committee's work. The personal assistants of Committee members are allowed access to all the proceedings and to accompany the experts during their deliberations.

The Rules of Procedure guarantee consistency in the Committee's deliberations at all reporting stages by States Parties. Article 35(1) CRPD requires States Parties to submit a comprehensive report on the measures taken to give effect to the provisions of the CRPD and to meet their obligations in conformity with the Convention. This obligation must be fulfilled within two years of ratification. The Committee has already reviewed the initial reports of 69 States Parties in its first 18 sessions. The review of the States Parties' country reports is one of the Committee's major monitoring functions. A State Party must submit an initial country report to the Committee within two years of the coming into force of the Convention, with regard to the particular State Party, and at least every four years thereafter, or as requested by the Committee.[6]

Upon receipt of an initial country report, the Committee prepares a List of Issues (LOI). This consists of a series of questions which allow the members to explore the degree of compliance with the CRPD's provisions. In accordance with Rule 48 of its Rules of Procedure, the Committee limits the number of written questions which are put to the State Party and focus its investigation on priority areas of concern. States Parties are then required to provide brief and precise replies to the LOI. During this process, the Committee holds meetings with civil society, persons with disabilities and Disabled People's Organisations (DPOs) in order for members to check the veracity of the information submitted by States Parties. In conformity with Rules 51 and 52, representatives of national human rights institutions and non-governmental organisations 'may be invited by the Committee to make oral or written statements and provide information or documentation relevant to the Committee's activities under the Convention to meetings of the Committee'.

This is followed by a constructive dialogue between the Committee and the State Party, which is an interactive forum to enable Committee members to put oral questions to the State Party's delegation. These Committee sessions are held in public, and are also broadcast live via webcast.[7] After the constructive dialogue, the Country Rapporteur (who is a Committee member) prepares a report of Concluding Observations and Recommendations to be considered and adopted by the Committee. In its Concluding Observations and Recommendations report, the Committee highlights areas of concern and makes appropriate recommendations to the State Party. Over and above the recommendations highlighted in the report, the Committee usually requests the State Party to implement two measures within a one-year period as a matter of immediate priority. The Committee may also advise the State Party as to how it can seek assistance with capacity-building in specific areas, in order to implement the provisions of the CRPD in a more effective manner.

In September 2013, the Committee has adopted a simplified reporting procedure for the adoption of these periodic States Parties' reports, under which a LOI is prepared by the Committee, the answers to which are deemed to comprise the periodic report for the State Party concerned.[8] Hungary and Tunisia will be the first countries to be examined and reviewed by the Committee.

General comments

General Comments clarify the international human rights standards applicable to the CRPD's provisions.[9] These international norms serve as guidance for the interpretation and application of legislation and policies. General Comments are designed to promote the implementation of the Convention and to assist States Parties in fulfilling their reporting obligations. Courts and tribunals often rely upon General Comments in their deliberations concerning disability-based anti-discrimination legislation. For instance, it may be unclear whether a particular Convention Article is immediately binding upon States Parties, or whether their obligations under that Article may be progressively realised. Moreover, words and phrases in the Convention may be ambiguous or complex, and, when this is the case, General Comments can assist in its interpretation.

To date, the Committee has published six General Comments on the following issues:

- General Comment No.1 on Article 12 Equal Recognition Before the Law;
- General Comment No.2 on Article 9 Accessibility;
- General Comment No.3 on Article 6 Women and Girls with Disabilities;

- General Comment No.4 on Article 24 Right to Inclusive Education;
- General Comment No.5 on Article 19 Right to Independent Living and Being Included in the Community;
- General Comment No.6 on Article 5 Equality and Non-Discrimination.

The Committee is currently working Article 33(3) and Article 4(3) (General Comment No.7).

The salient features of the Convention

The CRPD has two salient features in common with other international human rights treaty bodies. First, it may be described as a supranational, quasi-tribunal because its decisions, at least in theory, ought to take precedence over domestic law and policy. Proponents of legal positivism, such as H.L.A. Hart and John Austin, are very critical of this view as they believe that international law is merely soft law or no law at all since its non-compliance is not the subject of sanctions. In the name of the human rights model of disability, a different view at this premature stage is sufficient to state that, after the Convention against Torture which imposes an obligation upon States Parties to set up a domestic preventative mechanism, the CRPD is the second international human rights treaty body which imposes an obligation on States Parties to monitor the implementation of the Convention at domestic level.[10] In the concluding chapter, we explore the effectiveness of this domestic and international obligation imposed upon States Parties.

The deliberations of the Committee include the following:

- Concluding Observations and Recommendations;
- General Comments;
- The Committee's views on individual and group complaints (case law)[11]; and
- Inquiry reports on States Parties, where it is proved that there are grave or systematic violations of the provisions of the CRPD.[12]

The second salient feature of the Convention is that it may be qualified as a *traité cadre*, or framework treaty, as distinct from a *traité de droit*, or international law treaty. Whereas the provisions of a *traité de droit* are clear and unambiguous, those of a *traité cadre* may be supplemented by secondary sources, including the four categories of the Committee's decisions mentioned above. These secondary sources fill the gaps of the CRPD and, as such, they serve as the cornerstone of its jurisprudence and are the main sources of international law pertaining to persons with disabilities. These decisions are dynamic in character and enable the Committee to respond effectively to societal changes. The Committee's decisions influence socio-economic, political and cultural thinking about how society can best achieve the full inclusion of persons with disabilities. These decisions reflect practice of the highest standards with regard to the implementation of the Convention.

The Optional Protocol to the Convention

The Optional Protocol to the Convention is a side-agreement to the CRPD. One of its aspects is that it establishes an independent complaints mechanism for the Convention. It was adopted on 13 December 2006, and entered into force on 3 May 2008. The Optional Protocol has currently been ratified by 92 countries. In many parts of the world, the fundamental rights and freedoms of persons with disabilities are not respected, promoted nor protected. Persons with disabilities face immense barriers in seeking to access the justice system. Discrimination can be wide-ranging and may take numerous forms, including inaccessible and complex administrative court procedures, substantial delay due to bureaucratic burdens, and/or a failure to provide remedies within domestic legal systems. Persons with disabilities continue to face such barriers irrespective of the fact that their governments have ratified the CRPD and its Optional Protocol. However, the Optional Protocol itself is the primary mechanism for addressing such issues. The CRPD Committee is in essence the tribunal of final instance for assessing whether States Parties have acted in violation of the provisions of the CRPD, or whether they have failed to take necessary measures for the harmonisation of domestic legislation and policy in line with international public law. This is why it is important for human rights activists to continue to advocate for the ratification of the Optional Protocol to the Convention by countries which have not yet done so.

There are numerous pre-conditions which must be satisfied before an individual or group of individuals can refer a case to the CRPD Committee for its views under the Optional Protocol. The individual or group lodging a case before the Committee is referred to as the 'author' of the communication. Before examining the merits of a communication with regard to whether a State Party has violated a substantive provision of the CRPD, the Committee must first determine whether the communication is admissible under the Optional Protocol.[13] The preparation of a communication for submission to the Committee can be complex, time-consuming and costly, and may even require the services of international human rights lawyers. However, this is not a formal requirement for acceptance of a submission.

Admissibility of complaints under the Optional Protocol

It is a general rule that a communication is admissible for consideration by the Committee only if the alleged violation occurred after the Optional Protocol was ratified by the State Party concerned. It is also the case that the author of the communication must have exhausted all available domestic remedies. However, there are several exceptions to these rules. The discussion of the relevant case law which follows seeks to illustrate how international human rights committees operate, and to demonstrate the criteria considered when deciding on questions of admissibility.

Article 2 of the Optional Protocol states that:

The Committee shall consider a communication inadmissible when:

(a) The communication is anonymous;
(b) The communication constitutes an abuse of the right of submission of such communications or is incompatible with the provisions of the Convention;
(c) The same matter has already been examined by the Committee or has been or is being examined under another procedure of international investigation or settlement;
(d) All available domestic remedies have not been exhausted. This shall not be the rule where the application of the remedies is unreasonably prolonged or unlikely to bring effective relief;
(e) It is manifestly ill-founded or not sufficiently substantiated; or when
(f) The facts that are the subject of the communication occurred prior to the entry into force of the present Protocol for the State Party concerned unless those facts continued after that date.

In the case of *X v Tanzania*, one of the questions before the CRPD Committee was whether Mr X had exhausted all domestic remedies before lodging his complaint, as required by Article 2 of the Optional Protocol.[14] On 10 April 2010, Mr X, a person with albinism, was fetching firewood from the bush when two Maasai-Morans came and asked him for tobacco. As he bent down to retrieve some tobacco from his bag, the men hit him on the head with clubs and chopped off his left arm. Mr X's severed arm was never found. The matter was reported to the police, but there was no prosecution. Mr X claimed that, despite his having made a complaint, no investigation was instituted by the competent authorities. A private prosecution is not possible in Tanzania, and no other remedies were available to Mr X under its domestic criminal law.

Before the CRPD Committee, the State of Tanzania argued that Mr X's communication was inadmissible due to the non-exhaustion of all available domestic remedies. It argued that following Mr X's complaint, an investigation was instituted by the police and a suspect was arrested and brought before the District Court on charges of assault causing grievous harm. A trial was commenced at which three witnesses testified, including Mr X. However, during his testimony, Mr X informed the court that the person charged with the offence was not, in fact, one of his attackers. Mr X stated that he could identify his two attackers because they were known to him, and that they were two Maasai men who were his neighbours. As a consequence of Mr X's evidence on identification, the case against the accused persons was withdrawn. The State of Tanzania also argued that the investigation into the attack on Mr X was still ongoing, and that police continued to investigate the matter with a view to arresting the perpetrators. It further submitted that Mr X had not applied for legal aid and hence had not exhausted domestic remedies.

In reply to the State Party's arguments, Mr X submitted that the 'domestic remedies' requirement should never be used as a protective shield by States Parties which have not established a suitable environment for promoting, protecting and preserving the rights of its citizens. He argued that the domestic remedy rule should be applicable only when the following conditions are met. The remedy available must be:

- effective and sufficient; and
- capable of being pursued without impediment.[15]

In the light of this, Mr X submitted that, where the domestic remedies were non-existent, unduly and unreasonably prolonged, or unlikely to bring effective relief, recourse to international measures was required. According to Mr X, Tanzania had failed to conduct an effective investigation and to prosecute his attackers. On the contrary, the State Party had discontinued its investigation into the attack on him before it had identified the perpetrators.

In its ruling on admissibility, the Committee noted that Mr X had not submitted his case to the courts of Tanzania under the Basic Rights and Duties Enforcement Act 1994. However, the Committee rejected Tanzania's argument that Mr X had failed to exhaust his domestic remedies because he could have initiated civil proceedings to obtain compensation for damages and harm, and had failed to do so. The Committee held that the possibility of civil action and/or private prosecution did not constitute an 'effective remedy' in his case. A complaint made to the police by Mr X the day he was attacked remained pending at the date of his petition to the Committee. The Committee further noted that after the abandonment of the initial prosecution, when Mr X had testified that the accused persons were not among his attackers, he was not informed of any new steps which the authorities had taken to investigate the case and to bring the culprits to justice. Under Tanzanian criminal procedures, the examining magistrate may permit the prosecution to be conducted by any person, including the victim. However, it was the Committee's view that in cases of such gravity as Mr X's, the onus to prosecute remained upon the Tanzanian authorities, whose obligations under international law to investigate, prosecute and punish such crimes were non-delegable.

In deciding the question of admissibility, the Committee also took account of the fact that Mr X had brought his case before the Constitutional Court of Tanzania under the Basic Rights and Duties Enforcement Act 1994, together with other victims of similar violent acts, but that at the time of examination of his complaint by the Committee, over eight years later, the matter had still not been heard by the Constitutional Court.[16] It was further noted that the Constitutional Court had experienced difficulties in constituting a bench of three judges to decide the merits of the matter. The Committee therefore concluded that it would not be reasonable to require Mr X to initiate additional proceedings of an unpredictable duration in order to exhaust his domestic remedies.[17]

The Committee recommended the State Party to ensure that the practice of using body parts for witchcraft-related practices is adequately and unambiguously criminalised in domestic legislation, and to develop and implement long-lasting awareness-raising campaigns, and training to address harmful practices and rampant myths affecting the enjoyment of human rights by persons with albinism, and on the scope of the Convention and its Optional Protocol, including on albinism and on the rights of persons with albinism.[18]

As can be seen from Mr X's case, international human rights committees such as the CRPD Committee are required to evaluate the extent to which domestic legislation complies with international human rights norms. When required to make a determination on questions of admissibility, such committees must not only consider the procedural aspects of optional protocols but must also scrutinise substantive domestic law in order to determine whether domestic procedures are unduly prolonged or whether substantive domestic remedies are effective.

The powers of the CRPD Committee are elaborated in its Rule 65 and Rule 75 of its Rules of Procedure.[19] In conformity with Article 5 of the Optional Protocol, the CRPD Committee examines communications in closed session, following which it informs the State Party concerned of its suggestions and recommendations. The State Party must submit a written response to the Committee within six months of receiving the latter's views on a communication.[20] This should include information on any action that has been taken in the light of the suggestions and recommendations of the Committee.

The HRC reached a similar conclusion in a slightly different context in the case of *Yuba Kumari Katwal v Nepal*.[21] The author submitted a communication on behalf of her husband for the violation of his right to life and she argued that she was subject to torture. The State Party (Nepal) argued that the communication was not admissible because the author had not explored all the legal avenues of redress open to her at domestic level, including a petition before the Truth and Reconciliation Commission. Article 5(2)(b) of the Optional Protocol to the International Covenant on Civil and Political Rights (ICCPR) states that the HRC shall not consider any communication from an individual unless it has ascertained that the individual has exhausted all available domestic remedies. This shall not be the rule where the application of the remedies is unreasonably prolonged. The HRC held that:

> it was not necessary to exhaust avenues before non-judicial bodies to fulfil the requirements of article 5 (2 (b)) of the Optional Protocol. With respect to the requirement of the exhaustion of domestic remedies, the Committee noted the author's attempt to obtain a domestic remedy by submitting a writ of habeas corpus to the Supreme Court in 2005 and considered that the State party had provided no concrete information on the First Information Report allegedly lodged by it and thus had not demonstrated that a criminal investigation was being carried out, more than 11 years after Mr. Katwal's arrest, and that it was effective in the light of the serious and grave nature of

the violations alleged by the author. The Committee found that the delay in carrying out an effective investigation had been unreasonably prolonged and concluded that it was not precluded from considering the communication under article 5 (2 (b)) of the Optional Protocol.[22]

Examples of inadmissibility

It is frequently the case that, for technical reasons, international human rights treaty bodies, such as the CRPD Committee, must declare a communication inadmissible, and consequently they cannot examine the merits of the case. For instance, in the case of *D.L. v Sweden*, the author failed to appeal to the court of final instance in Sweden prior to lodging a petition before the CRPD Committee.[23] An appeal would have allowed the Supreme Administrative Court of Sweden to rule on the issue of whether the denial of 'facilitated communication' for persons with autism constituted discrimination. The CRPD Committee declared that the author's communication was inadmissible, reasoning that it would not have constituted 'undue delay' for the Supreme Administrative Court of Sweden to have been allowed one additional year in order to rule on the substantive issue. In appealing to the Supreme Administrative Court, the author would also have fully exhausted his/her domestic remedies. Unfortunately, neither the Supreme Administrative Court of Sweden nor the CRPD Committee was able to examine the merits of the matter; that is, whether the denial of 'facilitated communication' (reasonable accommodation) for persons with autism constituted a violation of the right to education as encompassed in Article 24 CRPD.

The case of *E.C.P. et al v Spain* is authority for the principle that human rights committees cannot exceed their mandates by retrospectively applying international law.[24] In *E.C.P. et al v Spain*, the ICESCR Committee considered the applicability of the Optional Protocol to the ICESCR of 2008 which came into force in Spain on 5 May 2013. However, the facts at issue in the case occurred prior to the enforcement date, and accordingly the CESCR held that, because those facts had not continued after the enforcement date, there were no grounds to conclude that there had been a violation of the ICESCR. The CESCR held that it was precluded *ratione temporis* (by reason of time) from examining the communication and deemed it to be inadmissible under Article 3(2)(b) of the Optional Protocol to the ICESCR.[25]

The ruling in *E.C.P. v Spain* may be contrasted with that of the CRPD Committee case of *Noble v Australia*.[26] In *Noble v Australia*, the violation of the author's rights under Articles 12, 13 and 14 CRPD predated the entry into force of the Optional Protocol to the Convention in Australia (19 September 2009). However, the CRPD Committee held that Mr Noble's communication was admissible as the violation of his right to plead had continued after the coming into force of the Optional Protocol. The author had been denied his right to plead to a criminal charge, on the grounds of his psychosocial and intellectual disability. After the Optional Protocol had come into force in Australia, the State Party had failed to remedy this fundamental defect in its domestic legislation, thereby resulting in an ongoing violation of Mr Noble's plea.[27]

In the case of *D.R. v Australia*, the State Party accepted that some of the grievances complained of by Mr R had occurred prior to 19 September 2009, and that they had continued after the Optional Protocol to the CRPD came into effect.[28] However, Mr R's communication was held to be inadmissible. The State Party submitted that Mr R failed to exhaust all available domestic remedies. Firstly, he had not submitted a complaint to the Queensland Anti-Discrimination Commission, even though disability is included as a ground of discrimination under the Queensland Anti-Discrimination Act 1991. Secondly, at the time when Mr R submitted his communication, the complaints of discrimination which he had submitted to the Australian Human Rights Commission were still under consideration.

The CRPD Committee noted that, whilst it was not necessary to exhaust domestic remedies when their application was unreasonably prolonged or unlikely to bring effective relief, merely doubting the effectiveness of domestic remedies does not absolve the author of a communication from the obligation to exhaust them. The Committee noted that Mr R did not substantiate his arguments, whilst on the other hand, the State Party had referred to a range of successful disability-based discrimination complaints which had been brought under the Disability Discrimination Act. The Committee found, under Article 2(b) of the Optional Protocol, that Mr R's communication was inadmissible in circumstances where it could not be concluded that he had fulfilled his obligation to exhaust domestic remedies.

The mere assertion, without any substantiation, that domestic remedies are ineffective or unreasonably prolonged, does not allow a committee to render a communication admissible. To hold otherwise would be tantamount to asking a Committee to speculate how domestic courts would interpret domestic legislation in the light of international jurisprudence. To embark on such a path would be to usurp the role of the domestic courts.

Interim measures

At the time of lodging a communication, the author may request the CRPD Committee to issue an interim measure, pending its views on the admissibility and the merits of a communication. The CRPD Committee has the discretion to ask a State Party not to pursue a course of conduct; for example, the execution of a prison sentence. Article 4(1) of the Optional Protocol to the CRPD which confers this power upon the Committee provides that:

> At any time after the receipt of a communication and before a determination on the merits has been reached, the Committee may transmit to the State Party concerned for its urgent consideration a request that the State Party take such interim measures as may be necessary to avoid possible irreparable damage to the victim or victims of the alleged violation.

Where the CRPD Committee exercises its discretion under Article 4(1) quoted above, this does not imply a determination on admissibility or on the merits of the communication.

The case of *Vasily Yuzepchuk v Belarus* is instructive with regard to interim measures under the Optional Protocol of human rights treaty bodies.[29] The case was decided by the HRC in 2014. The HRC requested the State Party to await its views, prior to executing Mr Yuzepchuk.[30] Unfortunately, the State Party blatantly ignored the HRC's request. Upon learning of Mr Yuzepchuk's death, the HRC sought urgent clarification from Belarus, drawing its attention to the fact that non-respect of interim measures constitutes a violation by States Parties of their obligations to cooperate in good faith under the Optional Protocol to the ICCPR. As no response was received from Belarus, the Committee finally issued a press release condemning Mr Yuzepchuk's execution.[31]

In the case of *L.M.L v UK*, the CRPD Committee declined Mrs L's request for an interim measure and held that her case was inadmissible because of her failure to substantiate her claim that she was denied access to justice.[32] The State Party argued that Mrs L's complaint should be declared inadmissible, on the ground that it was either manifestly ill-founded or not sufficiently substantiated under Article 2(e) of the Optional Protocol to the CRPD. This was because Mrs L had not provided any evidence in support of her claim that she had been denied access to health care or legal redress on an equal basis with others. Mrs L argued that she had provided reliable evidence that the UK had violated her right to access specialist medical care. The CRPD Committee decided that the allegations raised by Mrs L essentially related to the evaluation of facts and evidence in relation to a medical examination carried out upon her and the treatment provided to her. It was further observed that the CRPD Committee was not competent to re-evaluate findings of fact or the application of domestic legislation, unless it could be ascertained that the proceedings before the domestic court were arbitrary or amounted to a denial of justice. The CRPD Committee therefore decided, for the purposes of admissibility, that Mrs L had failed to substantiate her claim that the conduct of the UK authorities amounted to arbitrariness or a denial of justice.

Inadmissibility of anonymous complaints

The Committee may also deem a communication to be inadmissible where it is anonymous, or where it has not been signed by either the author or his/her designated representative.[33] The Committee must also ascertain that the author is in fact a person with a disability. The case of *Aumeeraudy-Cziffra v Mauritius* is authority for the fact that a non-victim cannot lodge a communication with any international human rights committee.[34]

In the case of *O.O.J. v Sweden*, the author of the communication was a Nigerian national whose son was diagnosed with autism in 2013.[35] The family's application for asylum was rejected by the State Party. Mr O alleged that the deportation of the family from Sweden to Nigeria would amount to a violation of the CRPD. Mr O and his wife were holders of temporary residence permits in Sweden from August 2008 to October 2010. When Mr O applied for a further residence permit on the ground that his son had been diagnosed with autism, his application was rejected by both the Swedish Migration Agency and the Migration Court of Appeal, and a deportation order was issued.

Upon receipt of Mr O's complaint, the CRPD Committee issued an interim measure requesting Sweden not to execute the deportation order pending the CRPD Committee's determination on admissibility. When it examined the issue of admissibility, the CRPD Committee realised that the deportation order had become statute-barred owing to the time lapse between the issuing of the interim order and the consideration of the case on admissibility. It noted that the family of the author had not exhausted their domestic remedies in Sweden, and that it would be possible to institute new proceedings before the immigration authorities. The CRPD Committee decided as follows:

(a) that the communication is inadmissible under Article 2(d) of the Optional Protocol;
(b) that this decision may be reviewed under Rule 71(2) of the Committee's rules of procedure upon receipt of a written request submitted by or on behalf of the victims containing information indicating that the reasons for inadmissibility no longer apply;
(c) that the present decision shall be communicated to the State Party and to the author.[36]

The case law on admissibility illustrates that each communication is assessed on its own particular merits. It should also be noted that, in accordance with Article 6 of the Optional Protocol, the CRPD Committee is empowered to carry out enquiries where there are allegations of grave or systematic violations of the CRPD, an issue which is considered below.

Grave or systematic violations

Article 6 of the Optional Protocol confers on the CRPD Committee the power to carry out inquiries when grave and systematic violations of rights enshrined in the Convention have been alleged. In these circumstances, the CRPD Committee is under an obligation to gather facts and evidence. The CRPD Committee also has a duty to inform the relevant State Party, and to consider the latter's comments. Article 6(1) of the Optional Protocol to the CRPD is self-explanatory and states as follows:

> If the Committee receives reliable information indicating grave or systematic violations by a State Party of rights set forth in the Convention, the Committee shall invite that State Party to cooperate in the examination of the information and to this end submit observations with regard to the information concerned.

The Committee carried out its first inquiry after receiving information that there had been grave and systematic violations of the right to independent living and being included in the community (Article 19 CRPD) and the right to employment (Article 27 CRPD) in the United Kingdom.[37] The Committee concluded that austerity measures which had been implemented in the United Kingdom had had a retrogressive effect upon the enjoyment of rights of persons with disabilities.

Concluding Observations, General Comments and communications are the core elements of the jurisprudence of the CRPD, and frequent reference is accordingly made to them throughout this book. They are analysed in different contexts, depending upon each author's unique circumstances and the pertaining domestic law, and they drive the evolution of International Disability Law, principles and policies.

Notes

1 Article 34(2) CRPD.
2 Article 34(5) CRPD.
3 Article 34(3) CRPD.
4 Article 34(7) CRPD.
5 The latest revised version of the Rules of Procedure of the CRPD are available at: http://tbinternet.ohchr.org/_layouts/treatybodyexternal/Download.aspx?symbolno= CRPD/C/1/Rev.1&Lang=en, accessed 16 March 2018.
6 Article 35(1), (2) CRPD.
7 UN Treaty Body Webcast. Available at: http://www.treatybodywebcast.org/, accessed 16 March 2018.
8 Rules of Procedure, Rule 48 ter.
9 Rules of Procedure, Rule 47:

> 1. The Committee may prepare general comments based on the articles and provisions of the Convention, with a view to promoting its further implementation and assisting States parties in fulfilling their reporting obligations.
> 2. The Committee shall include such general comments in its report to the General Assembly.

10 See Article 33 CRPD.
11 Article 5 Optional Protocol.
12 Article 6 Optional Protocol.
13 Articles 1 and 2 Optional Protocol to the CRPD.
14 *X v Tanzania* (2017) CRPD/C/18/D/22/2014.
15 *X v Tanzania*, para.5.1.
16 *X v Tanzania*, paras 5.6, 7.4.
17 See chapter 5 for the decision on merits.
18 *X v Tanzania*, para.9.
19 Rule 65 deals with the procedure relating to the method of dealing with communications:

> 1. The Committee shall by simple majority and in accordance with the following rules, decide whether the communication is admissible or inadmissible under the Optional Protocol.
> 2. A working group established under rule 63, paragraph 1, of the present rules may declare that a communication is admissible under the Optional Protocol provided that all its members so decide.

3. A working group established under rule 63, paragraph 1, of the present rules may declare a communication inadmissible provided that all the members so agree. The decision will be transmitted to the Committee plenary, which may confirm it without formal discussion. If any Committee member requests a plenary discussion, the plenary will examine the communication and take a decision.

Rule 75 of the Rules of Procedure:

1. Within six months of the Committee's transmittal of its views on a communication, the State party concerned shall submit to the Committee a written response, including any information on any action taken in the light of the views and recommendations of the Committee.
2. Subsequently, the Committee may invite the State party concerned to submit further information about any measures the State party has taken in response to its views or recommendations.
3. The Committee may request the State party to include information on any action taken in response to its views or recommendations in its reports under Article 35 of the Convention.
4. The Committee shall designate for follow-up on views adopted under Article 5 of the Optional Protocol a Special Rapporteur or working group to ascertain the measures to be taken by States Parties to give effect to the Committee's views.
5. The Special Rapporteur or working group may make such contacts and take such action as is appropriate for the due performance of their assigned functions and shall make such recommendations for further action by the Committee as may be necessary.
6. The Special Rapporteur or working group in charge of the follow-up mandate may, with the approval of the Committee and the State party itself, make any necessary visits to the State party concerned.
7. The Special Rapporteur or working group shall regularly report to the Committee on follow-up activities.
8. The Committee shall include information on follow-up activities in its report under Article 39 of the Convention.

20 Rule 75(1) of the Rules of Procedure.
21 *Yuba Kumari Katwal v Nepal* (2015) CCPR/C/113/D/2000/2010.
22 Ibid, para.6.3.
23 *D.L. v Sweden* (2017) CRPD/C/17/D/31/2015.
24 *E.C.P. et al v Spain* (2016) E/C.12/58/D/13/2016.
25 Article 3(2)(b) of the Optional Protocol to the ICESCR states that the Committee shall declare a communication inadmissible when the 'facts that are the subject of the communication occurred prior to the entry into force of the present Protocol for the State Party concerned unless those facts continued after that date'.
26 *James Marlon Noble v* Australia (2016) CRPD/C/16/7/2012.
27 See summary of facts and discussion on merits in Chapter 4 and Chapter 5.
28 *D.R. v Australia* (2017) CRPD/C/17/D/14/2013.
29 *Vasily Yuzepchuk v Belarus* (2014) CCPR/C/112/D/1906/2009.
30 Rule 92, Rules of Procedure of the HRC 2012.
31 Human Rights Committee, 99th Session, HR/CT/726 on 26 March 2010 http://www.un.org/press/en/2010/hrct726.doc.htm Accessed 16 March 2018.
32 *L.M.L. v UK* (2017) CRPD/C/17/D/27/2015.
33 Article 2 Optional Protocol CRPD.
34 *Aumeeraudy-Cziffra v Mauritius* (1981) CCPR/C/12/D/35/1978.
35 *O.O.J. v Sweden* (2017) CRPD/C/18/D/28/2015.

36 Rule 71 (2) of the Rules of Procedure states:

A decision of the Committee declaring a communication inadmissible under Article 2(d) of the Optional Protocol may be reviewed at a later date by the Committee upon receipt of a written request submitted by or on behalf of the individual concerned containing information indicating that the reasons for inadmissibility referred to in Article 2 (d) no longer apply.

37 CRPD Committee, Inquiry concerning the United Kingdom of Great Britain and Northern Ireland, 2016, CRPD/C/15/R.2.

2

PILLARS OF THE CRPD

Introduction

Ten years after the world adopted the CRPD, it remains the principal authority of international human rights law for persons with disabilities. The guiding principles enshrined in the Preamble and Articles 1–5 are the pillars of the Convention which endorse international moral norms. Article 1 of the UDHR provides that '[a]ll human beings are born free and equal in dignity and rights', a principle enshrined in Article 1 of the CRPD and expanded upon throughout the Convention. Articles 1–5 of the CRPD set out the universal standards that are demanded from States Parties to secure the full realisation of the rights enshrined in the Convention. The normative contents of the Preamble and Articles 1–5 are based on the principles of the international rule of law. These principles are powerful tools for the interpretation of the Convention and have greatly contributed to the evolution of the jurisprudence of the CRPD Committee, in particular its case law.

With the consultation and participation of persons with disabilities and their representative organisations, States Parties have a duty under the Convention to devise and implement legislative, administrative and policy changes in conformity with the rule of law. Disability inclusion as a cross-cutting human rights, broad-based theme is meant to be understood as entrenched within legal systems, policies and programmes. This is with a view to eliminating those socio-economic and political barriers which society has placed in the way of persons with disabilities.

The international rule of law as enshrined in all international law instruments guides States Parties in implementing the Convention. It ranks above the considerations of both government and citizens, and we are all subject to its binding principles. Persons with disabilities are therefore equal before and under the law. However, equality is an ideal which can be achieved only through the equalisation of opportunities, or even through positive discrimination (affirmative measures).

This is why States Parties have the discretion to fulfil their obligations progressively with regard to certain areas of internationally binding law; for example, in the field of economic, social and cultural rights. However, the actions and inactions of States Parties should never sacrifice the principles underpinning Articles 1–5 of the CRPD.

Another exigency of the rule of law requires that those who are more vulnerable to prejudice and discrimination be afforded more protection. This principle applies to everyone in relation to all human rights and fundamental freedoms, and prohibits discrimination on the basis of a list of non-exhaustive categories such as 'race, colour, sex, language, religion, political or other opinion, national, ethnic, indigenous or social origin, property, birth, age or other status'.[1]

The rule of law would be an empty concept if there were no independent or impartial tribunal or court to uphold its content and spirit. Constitutional courts and tribunals must therefore be vested with the necessary jurisdiction to nullify laws, administrative decisions and policies whenever these instruments transgress the provisions of internationally-binding Conventions. When the fundamental rights and freedoms of persons with disabilities are infringed, there must ultimately be recourse to an independent judiciary, as required by the doctrine of separation of powers. The rule of law can be a reality only if the legislature and the executive are subject to the power of an independent judiciary. Such factors ultimately determine the extent to which all peoples have the right of self-determination, in line with Article 1 ICCPR. The rule of law is the central measure by which international treaty bodies assess the extent to which States Parties respect, promote and protect the human rights of citizens.

The Preamble and Article 1 CRPD

Article 1 provides that the purpose of the Convention is to promote and protect the human rights of all persons with disabilities and 'to promote respect for their inherent dignity'. The interpretation of 'all persons with disabilities' must be read in light of paragraph (e) of the Preamble. This provides a non-exhaustive list of categories of impairment, thereby leaving it to the CRPD Committee to apply the relevant principles to new situations. The categories of impairment are never closed and their evolution may be traced within the jurisprudence of the CRPD Committee. Paragraph (e) of the Preamble stipulates that disability is an evolving concept and that it results from the interactions between persons with impairments and attitudinal and environmental barriers that hinder their full and effective participation in society on an equal basis with others.

The case of *X v Tanzania* illustrates how the CRPD Committee applied the reasoned principle enshrined in paragraph (e) of the Preamble to address the question of whether albinism was a disability. The Committee held as follows:

> [A]lbinism is a relatively rare, non-contagious, genetically inherited condition that affects people worldwide regardless of ethnicity or gender. It results

from a significant deficit in the production of melanin and is characterized by the partial or complete absence of pigment in the skin, hair and eyes [. . .] A human rights-based model of disability requires the diversity of persons with disabilities to be taken into account (preamble, para (i)) together with the interaction between individuals with impairments and attitudinal and environmental barriers (preamble, para (e)).[2]

The CRPD Committee concluded that albinism falls within the meaning of disability as enshrined in Article 1 of the Convention. Article 1 CRPD, together with paragraph (e) of the Preamble, indicates clearly that persons with disabilities are right-holders and that those rights are indivisible and inalienable. It is notable that the second paragraph of Article 1 does not provide a definition of 'persons with disabilities' but only states that they include 'those who have long-term physical, mental, intellectual or sensory impairments which in interaction with various barriers may hinder their full and effective participation in society on an equal basis with others'.

The framers of the CRPD deliberately avoided stipulating a definition of disability, or of persons with disabilities. To embark on such a path was unnecessary, and could have yielded unintended consequences, such as fostering the medical model of disability. At the same time, such an open-ended definition does not facilitate an analysis or enumeration of the core elements of the experience of impairment as a human rights-based concept. Nor does it necessarily facilitate a full understanding of how discrimination manifests itself at the interface between life experiences and social and environmental barriers. During the negotiation of the Convention, the International Disability Caucus (IDC) opposed any attempt to formulate a definition of disability. In the event, the linkage of impairment to disability was a sensible compromise.

Paragraph (h) of the Preamble to the CRPD recognises that 'discrimination on the basis of disability is a violation of human dignity and worth of the human person', whilst paragraph (i) holds that the 'diversity of persons with disabilities' must be recognised. The aim here was to allow the principles to evolve and to be applied to novel situations, as was the case in *X v Tanzania*. The Committee's jurisprudence, including its Concluding Observations of 69 countries, is testimony to the framers' success in seeking to facilitate an evolving understanding of the concept of disability. The Concluding Observations demonstrate how the rule of law is frequently misunderstood in the context of the rights and dignity of persons with disabilities. This is especially the case when States Parties are called upon to implement the Convention in line with fundamental principles. The scope of approaches which States Parties may adopt in seeking to implement the Convention is wide. States Parties may adopt a caring or paternalistic approach towards the protection of persons with disabilities. Alternatively, persons with disabilities may be perceived as tragic or helpless. Some States Parties adopt a more functionalist perspective, focusing on the extent to which persons with disabilities are able to work. Others may seek to 'fix' or cure persons with disabilities, to make them as 'normal' as possible.[3]

Article 1 of the Convention has also been interpreted in Concluding Observations as a way to exclude policies aimed at the 'prevention of disability'. Such preventative policies are reflective of the medical model of disability, and are beyond the scope of the CRPD. The notion of 'prevention of disability' assumes that there is something medically wrong with persons with disabilities which needs to be modified or fixed. It has become increasingly necessary for the CRPD Committee to urge States Parties to amend legislation and policies aimed at preventing disability. Furthermore, the use of terms such as 'invalidity pension', 'crippled' and 'dumb', which violate the principle of the inherent dignity of the person, also falls within the ambit of Article 1 CRPD and is contrary to the rule of law principle, as contained in both Article 1 and the Preamble. In the course of Concluding Observations, States Parties have been reminded of the need to refrain from derogatory language and of the need to convey a positive image of persons with disabilities. For instance, the CRPD Committee noted that the legislation of the State of Lithuania makes frequent use of derogatory language such as 'deaf-mute' and 'disorder', when referring to persons with disabilities.[4] The CRPD Committee also noted that the State of Ethiopia perpetuates negative perceptions of persons with disabilities with legislation and policies that employ derogatory terms such as 'insane' and 'infirm' to refer to persons with disabilities.[5]

Article 2—Definitions

Article 2 CRPD defines many of the key concepts upon which the Convention is based, such as 'communication', 'discrimination', 'reasonable accommodation', and 'universal design'. The definitions allow for a pragmatic approach to the enhancement of human rights standards, which has its roots in these imaginative concepts. Article 2 seeks to address the real issues affecting the daily living conditions of persons with disabilities. As will be seen in the ensuing discussion on Article 5, Equality and Non-Discrimination—on the particular terms 'discrimination' and 'reasonable accommodation'—there is a sense that the definitions are legitimately owned by persons with disabilities and their representative organisations. This sense of ownership may well reflect the close collaboration of persons with disabilities and their representative organisations in the drafting of the Convention. The practical value of the concepts defined in Article 2 CRPD is that they can serve as yardsticks to measure the degree to which States Parties are complying with the Convention. The analysis below shows how these definitions, along with the definition of discrimination, have evolved since 2008. The principles of discrimination law have been applied in order to widen the scope of civil and political rights. Discriminatory practices in relation to economic, social and cultural rights in numerous areas have also become increasingly justiciable.

Article 3—General principles

Article 3 CRPD enunciates the general principles underpinning the Convention as follows:

(1) Respect for inherent dignity, individual autonomy including the freedom to make one's own choices, and independence of persons;
(2) Non-discrimination;
(3) Full and effective participation and inclusion in society;
(4) Respect for difference and acceptance of persons with disabilities as part of human diversity and humanity;
(5) Equality of opportunity;
(6) Accessibility;
(7) Equality between men and women;
(8) Respect for the evolving capacities of children with disabilities and respect for the right of children with disabilities to preserve their identities.

The provisions enshrined in Article 3 CRPD are inspirational, reflecting our rich heritage of international moral values. Article 3 sets out the international human rights norms which are necessary for the promotion and protection of inalienable rights. It upholds the values enshrined in several international bills of rights, including the UDHR, ICCPR and CESCR. For instance, Article 1 UDHR provides that:

All human beings are born free and equal in dignity and rights. They are endowed with reason and conscience and should act towards one another in a spirit of brotherhood.

Article 4—General obligations

Article 4 (1) CRPD sets out the general obligations of States Parties to the Convention in the following terms:

1. States Parties undertake to ensure and promote the full realization of all human rights and fundamental freedoms for all persons with disabilities without discrimination of any kind on the basis of disability. To this end, States Parties undertake:

   (a) To adopt all appropriate legislative, administrative and other measures for the implementation of the rights recognized in the present Convention;
   (b) To take all appropriate measures, including legislation, to modify or abolish existing laws, regulations, customs and practices that constitute discrimination against persons with disabilities;
   (c) To take into account the protection and promotion of the human rights of persons with disabilities in all policies and programmes [...]

Article 4(1) CRPD imposes an absolute and immediate obligation upon States Parties to incorporate the Convention into their own domestic legal systems. The increase in ratification of the CRPD signals the beginning of the end of an era of apartheid against persons with disabilities. One might even expect States Parties to amend their constitutions so as to recognise persons with disabilities as a class which is the subject of perpetual discrimination.

However, the initial reports of States Parties so far reviewed in the Concluding Observations of the CRPD Committee have proved to be as deceptive as they are perplexing. One plausible explanation would be that Article 4(2) CRPD is being used as a powerful defence. It states that:

> With regard to economic, social and cultural rights, each State Party undertakes to take measures to the maximum of its available resources and, where needed, within the framework of international cooperation, with a view to achieving progressively the full realization of these rights, without prejudice to those obligations contained in the present Convention that are immediately applicable according to international law.

As mentioned above, Article 4(2) CRPD restricts States Parties' obligations to the 'progressive realisation' of economic, social and political rights. It should be noted, however, that the CRPD Committee has been proactive in providing further clarification on the issue, in order to avoid a wide interpretation of the provisions of Article 4(2). The CRPD Committee observed that

> The duty of progressive realization entails a presumption against retrogressive measures in the enjoyment of economic, social and cultural rights. When retrogressive measures are adopted, States parties should demonstrate that they have been introduced after careful consideration of all alternatives and they are duly justified by reference to the totality of the rights provided for in the Convention, in the context of the use of the maximum available resources of the State party.[6]

The CRPD Committee referred to the criteria adopted by the CESCR which state that

> the prohibition of retrogression in the realization of economic, social and cultural rights, States parties should demonstrate that:
>
> (a) There was reasonable justification for the action;
> (b) Alternatives were comprehensively examined;
> (c) There was genuine participation of affected groups in examining proposed measures and alternatives;
> (d) The measures were not directly or indirectly discriminatory;
> (e) The measures will not have a direct impact on the realization of the rights set out in the Convention; or an unreasonable impact on acquired

rights or whether an individual or group will be deprived of access to the minimum level of social security;

(f) Whether there was an independent review of the measures at the national level.[7]

Poor policy-making and gaps in legislative frameworks and their implementation are often the consequence of the non-participation of persons with disabilities and their representative organisations in the decision-making processes of states. The obligations of States Parties under Article 4(3) CRPD are explicit. It provides that:

> In the development and implementation of legislation and policies to implement the present Convention, and in other decision-making processes concerning issues relating to persons with disabilities, States Parties shall closely consult with and actively involve persons with disabilities, including children with disabilities, through their representative organizations.

None of the 69 countries which have been reviewed thus far under the CRPD Committee's Country Report procedures has succeeded in complying with its obligations under Article 4(3) to the satisfaction of the CRPD Committee. During the Committee's recent Review of the UK, the State Party conceded that there were serious gaps in its implementation of the CRPD which had arisen from the lack of meaningful participation of Disabled Persons Organisations (DPOs) in policy formation.[8]

Article 4(4) CRPD states that 'nothing in the present Convention shall affect any provisions which are more conducive to the realization of the rights of persons with disabilities and which may be contained in the law of a State Party or international law in force for that State'. There should be no restriction upon or derogation from any of the human rights and fundamental freedoms recognised or existing in any State Party to the CRPD pursuant to law, Conventions, regulation or custom under the excuse that the Convention does not recognise such rights or freedoms or that it recognises them to a lesser extent.

Article 5—Equality and non-discrimination

Article 5 CRPD provides that:

1. States Parties recognize that all persons are equal before and under the law and are entitled without any discrimination to the equal protection and equal benefit of the law.
2. States Parties shall prohibit all discrimination on the basis of disability and guarantee to persons with disabilities equal and effective legal protection against discrimination on all grounds.

3. In order to promote equality and eliminate discrimination, States Parties shall take all appropriate steps to ensure that reasonable accommodation is provided.
4. Specific measures which are necessary to accelerate or achieve de facto equality of persons with disabilities shall not be considered discrimination under the terms of the present Convention.

In August 2017, the CRPD Committee held a one-day discussion on the proposed contents of General Comment No.6 on Article 5 on equality and non-discrimination.[9] The purpose of the discussion was to examine the scope of the normative contents of the Article and to consider proposals from civil society as to how the CRPD Committee can best guide States Parties in implementing the Convention. Submissions were received from civil society organisations, disabled persons and DPOs. During the discussion, the Chair of the CRPD Committee, Professor Theresia Dugener, described Article 5 as the 'golden thread' running through the Convention.[10] This golden thread is evident in much of the jurisprudence of the CRPD Committee as discrimination is connected with other provisions of the CRPD.

While the inclusion of terms such as 'substantive' or 'inclusive' equality within proposed General Comment No.6 can be meritorious, it may be wise from a practical point of view to focus more closely on the actual language of the Convention and to elaborate upon the interpretation of its basic concepts, such as 'equality before the law', 'equality under the law', 'equal benefit of the law' and 'equal protection of the law'. A stronger understanding of these concepts would assist in achieving de facto equality (i.e., equality in practice) for persons with disabilities. It is by focusing upon the language of the Convention that one may continually bridge the gap between the attainment of civil and political rights on the one hand, and economic, social and cultural rights on the other. At any rate, the obligations upon States Parties to promote equality and non-discrimination in accordance with Article 5 CRPD is absolute and non-delegable, and must be realised in conformity with other internationally-binding sources of law, such as Article 7 of the Universal Declaration of Human Rights (UDHR). Article 7 UDHR states that '[a]ll are equal before the law and are entitled without any discrimination to equal protection of the law'. Since the adoption of the UDHR in 1948, its principles have been echoed in all subsequent human rights Conventions. However, whilst Article 5 CRPD cannot claim to create new rights, its scope is much wider than that of its predecessors.

Since the ratification of the CRPD, some States Parties have introduced anti-discrimination legislation which explicitly includes the prohibition of disability-based discrimination. These provisions have been embedded within the constitutional frameworks of states. For instance, the Republic of Moldova has recently adopted Law No.121 of 25 May 2012 on equality and Law No.60 of 30 March 2012 on the social inclusion of persons with disabilities.[11] Similarly, the State of Montenegro has adopted the Prohibition of Discrimination against Persons with Disabilities Act in 2011.[12] These legislative measures have broadened the protection of the rights of persons with disabilities. However, anti-discrimination legislation and national monitoring frameworks have failed to maintain the standards of protection which are required for conformity with Article 5 CRPD. The best of laws have been erroneously interpreted by domestic courts to such an extent that the Committee has had to remind States Parties regularly of the need to train members of the judiciary, legal professionals and prison officers in the principles of the CRPD. For instance, the Committee, in its Concluding Observations on Luxembourg, recalled that the State Party should '[p]rovide mandatory and ongoing capacity-building programmes, including training, on the provisions of the Convention for law enforcement personnel, members of the judiciary, and members of the legal profession'.[13]

Recently, the United Nations High Commissioner for Human Rights confirmed the serious nature of the discrimination which is experienced by persons with disabilities.[14] The report noted that national laws and policies tend to perpetuate 'exclusion, isolation, discrimination and violence against persons with disabilities', regardless of international human rights law standards. It further stated that:

Factors such as deprivation of legal capacity, forced institutionalization, exclusion from general education, pervasive negative stereotypes, prejudices, and lack of access to employment prevent persons with disabilities from enjoying their rights fully, on an equal basis with others. In particular, women and girls with disabilities face considerable restrictions on the exercise of their rights relative to men and other women and girls, due to, for instance violence, abuse or neglect, and have fewer opportunities in terms of education and employment.[15]

The scope of Article 5(1) CRPD was evident in the communication *Jungelin v Sweden*, in which the CRPD Committee observed that:

> Article 5, paragraphs 1 and 2, imposes on the State Party the general obligations to recognize that all persons are equal before and under the law and are entitled without any discrimination to the equal protection and equal benefit of the law, and to prohibit all discrimination on the basis of disability and guarantee to persons with disabilities equal and effective legal protection against discrimination on all grounds.[16]

Article 5(1) CRPD makes no specific reference to persons with disabilities. The principles of equality and non-discrimination are applicable to individual groups and across the entire jurisdiction of a state. Particular reference must be made to Article 4(5) CRPD, which provides that 'the provisions of the present Convention shall extend to all parts of federal states without any limitations or exceptions'. It is in these simple, yet powerful, terms that Article 4(5) CRPD restores de facto equality to persons with disabilities.

Equality before the law

The constitutions of many states include the principle of 'equality before the law'. These constitutional provisions are often firmly embedded and they afford essential protection against all forms of discrimination. At its simplest, the principle of equality before the law means that the law is blind to the personal characteristics or attributes of individuals or groups of individuals. At least in theory, the law should guarantee equal treatment for all persons appearing before the judiciary.

The capacities of the individual or group of individuals concerned should be immaterial. Capacity varies from person to person, regardless of whether she/he is an accused person, a witness, a lawyer, a prosecutor or an usher. The express recognition that all persons with disabilities are equal before the law imposes an obligation upon States Parties to ensure that law enforcement agencies and public and private administrative bodies do not discriminate against any person on the ground of actual or perceived disability. The duty upon States Parties to guarantee such protection to all persons is non-delegable.

Equality under the law

The provision in Article 5(1) CRPD recognises that the judiciary, law enforcement agencies and all citizens are equal under the law. It is an important feature of the international rule of law which requires governments to be governed by law. The law must guide the actions of those who are entrusted with political power. A further aspect of equality under the law requires the law itself to be in conformity with international moral norms. According to Lon L. Fuller, a system of rules should satisfy certain criteria. The rules must be: expressed in general terms; publicly promulgated; prospective in effect; expressed in understandable terms; consistent with one another; not require conduct beyond the powers of the affected parties; not be changed so frequently that the subject cannot rely on them; and be administered in a manner consistent with their wording.[17]

The principle that all persons with disabilities are equal under the law means that there should be no law that allows for the specific denial, restriction or limitation of the rights of persons with disabilities. It also requires that disability should be mainstreamed in all legislation and policies.

Equal protection and equal benefit of the law

The dual principles of 'equal protection' and 'equal benefit' of the law are well established within public international law. For example, Article 7 UDHR provides that

> All are equal before the law and are entitled without any discrimination to equal protection of the law. All are entitled to equal protection against any discrimination in violation of this Declaration and against any incitement to such discrimination.

These principles require States Parties to refrain from any discrimination against persons with disabilities, when enacting laws and formulating policies. For instance, affirmative measures may include the repeal of legislation which does not allow a deaf person to be accompanied by her personal assistant in order to discharge her public duty, as was the case in *Gemma Beasley v Australia*.[18] The State Party's refusal to amend the law in order to allow Mrs Beasley to serve as a jury member assumed her incapacity. In order to grant Mrs Beasley equal protection and equal benefit of the law, she needed to be treated differently, but on an equal basis with others.

A further example of the principles of equal protection and equal benefit of the law arose in the case of *Nyusti and Takács v Hungary*.[19] This communication concerned the retrofitting of ATM machines and other banking services for persons with visual and other types of impairment. The dissenting judgment by the lower Hungarian court was endorsed by the CRPD Committee. The lower court held that relevant provisions of the legislation pertaining to discrimination in Hungary 'extended the scope of its application to all civil relations, irrespective of whether the parties thereto were public or civil sector operators, where services were provided to numerous clients'.[20] It is arguable whether the plaintiffs who were visually impaired would have neither the equal protection nor the equal benefit of the law if they were treated in the same way as their non-disabled counterparts insofar as access to ATMs and other banking services was concerned.

The requirement for the 'reasonable accommodation' of persons with disabilities is an obligation which falls upon states. However, it also binds private sector bodies.[21] Under a private contract, persons with disabilities ought to be treated differently from their non-disabled counterparts in order to have equal benefit of the law. It is a long-established principle under the common law system and in other jurisdictions that if like cases must be treated alike, different cases must be treated differently. Lord Hoffmann famously stated that '[. . .] treating like cases alike and unlike cases differently is a general axiom of rational behaviour'.[22] He went on to say that 'persons should be uniformly treated, unless there is some valid reason to treat them differently'.[23] Persons with disabilities should not be an exception to the application of this analogous principle.

Discrimination

Article 5(2) CRPD provides that 'States parties shall prohibit all discrimination on the basis of disability and guarantee to persons with disabilities equal and effective legal protection against discrimination on all grounds'. The obligation under Article 5(2) is very strict and has two limbs:

- Equality and non-discrimination must be justiciable concepts in all spheres of life, including economic, social and cultural life;
- Courts must be vested with the power to nullify laws which fall below the standards required by the Convention.

It follows that persons with disabilities must be provided with civil remedies, including civil actions for damages and criminal prosecutions, for failure by States

Parties to respect the right to equality and non-discrimination. Discrimination takes different forms, including direct discrimination, indirect discrimination, discrimination by association, structural discrimination, harassment, and intersectional and multiple discrimination.

Direct discrimination takes place when persons with disabilities are treated differently, in a manner less favourable than others, or when they are simply excluded in a situation where a non-disabled counterpart would receive a benefit. Direct discrimination may also occur where there is a deliberate detrimental act or omission on the basis of disability in a situation where no non-disabled comparator exists. For example, failure to provide assistance to an intellectually disabled person when giving a statement to the police could result in a false confession. This might result in a criminal charge in relation to an offence which had not been committed. Direct discrimination occurs in numerous guises. However, common examples might include a child being refused school admission on the ground of disability; a person being denied an employment opportunity on the ground of disability; or a person being denied entry to a public amenity on the ground of disability.

Indirect discrimination concerns laws, policies or practices which are of a neutral nature, but which have a negative impact on persons with disabilities. In *H.M. v Sweden*, the State Party argued that the Swedish Constitution respected the principle that all persons are equal before and under the law, a premise which was reflected in Swedish legislation, including the Planning and Building Act 2010, the relevant Act in the case.[24] The State Party argued that the 2010 Act was applied in the same manner to everyone, whether or not they had a disability. It was also argued that H.M.'s application for a building permit had been rejected in line with a policy which applied equally to everyone. The CRPD Committee held that a law which is applied in a neutral manner may have a discriminatory effect, when the particular circumstances of the individuals to whom it is applied are not taken into consideration. According to the CRPD Committee, 'the right not to be discriminated against in the enjoyment of the rights guaranteed under the Convention can be violated when States, without objective and reasonable justification, fail to treat differently persons whose situations are significantly different'.[25] It can be argued, therefore, that a law may not constitute indirect discrimination if the legitimate aim being pursued is reasonably and objectively justifiable, and the means required for achieving that aim are proportionate and necessary.

Discrimination by association occurs when persons without disabilities are rendered incapable, or are disabled, by virtue of their association with a person with disabilities. In *Coleman v Attridge Law*, the mother of a child with disabilities was discriminated against by her employer, who was concerned that she would be less productive and less available because of her association with the child.[26] The court held that the principle of equal treatment extended to all disability-based discrimination and was not limited to the protection of those who are themselves disabled.

Structural or systemic discrimination occurs when societal systems include patterns of discriminatory practices. Such practices may be either open or hidden. Sometimes, discrimination is embedded in a country's constitution. Discrimination may become institutionalised within cultural traditions and social norms. In these cases, the system itself is discriminatory and it serves to legitimise harmful and negative stereotypes of persons with disabilities. For example, the belief that persons with albinism are superhumans who should be subjected to witchcraft and experimentation leads to discriminatory practices that become culturally rooted.[27]

Harassment is yet another form of discrimination which may affect people, disabled or otherwise. It consists of systematic unwanted conduct or actions resulting in intimidation and the violation of a person's dignity. Harassment may also create an environment which is conducive to further harassing behaviour. Examples of harassment include teasing and abusive mockery directed at persons with disabilities. Cyber-bullying and online hate crimes are more recent discriminatory phenomena which are particularly vicious and harmful.

Multiple or intersectional discrimination occurs when an individual is affected by two or more forms of discrimination at the same time. An individual may suffer from either direct or indirect discrimination, while also being denied reasonable accommodation and suffering harassment. Persons with disabilities are more likely to be discriminated against on multiple grounds. 'Multiple discrimination' has been defined by the CRPD Committee as 'a situation where a person can experience discrimination on two or several grounds, in the sense that discrimination is compounded or aggravated', while 'intersectional discrimination' has been described as 'a situation where several grounds operate and interact with each other at the same time in such a way that they are inseparable'.[28]

The case of Sarah Reed, who died in prison in 2016 whilst awaiting assessment regarding her fitness to plead to a criminal charge, is an example.[29] Ms Reed's case aptly illustrates the concepts of both multiple and intersectional discrimination. Ms Reed arguably suffered multiple discrimination on the grounds of race, disability and gender. As a remand prisoner, she also faced discrimination at an institutional level within the criminal justice system, which served as a locus for other forms of discrimination to coalesce, thereby giving rise to intersectional discrimination. It is also worth noting the United Kingdom Mental Health Units (Use of Force) Bill 2017–19 in this regard. The Bill was recently presented to Parliament by Steve Reed MP, following the death in 2010 of Mr Olaseni Lewis (Seni) in Bethlem Royal hospital, which he had voluntarily attended to receive mental health care.[30]

Reasonable accommodation

Article 5(3) CRPD states that '[i]n order to promote equality and eliminate discrimination, States Parties shall take all appropriate steps to ensure that reasonable accommodation is provided'. The denial of reasonable accommodation is another form of discrimination and the CRPD jurisprudence reaffirms that the right to reasonable accommodation must be fulfilled upon ratification of the Convention. It should be noted that the principle of reasonable accommodation applies to individuals rather than groups. Another distinguishing feature of the reasonable accommodation principle is that its test contains a justification element. This justification element differs from that of the tests for either direct or indirect discrimination, both of which concepts may be applied either to individuals or to groups. Article 5(3) CRPD places the burden upon States Parties to take all appropriate steps to ensure necessary modifications and adjustment, except where to do so would impose a disproportionate or undue burden on the state. Reasonable accommodation may include making existing facilities more accessible to persons with disabilities and adapting learning materials and school curricula to children with psychosocial disabilities.

Regrettably, the defence of 'disproportionate or undue burden' has been very broadly interpreted by States Parties with resultant negative consequences for the rights of persons with disabilities. This has been the case notwithstanding the repeated reminders from the CRPD Committee to States Parties that the adoption of retrogressive measures which result in a failure to provide reasonable accommodation constitutes an unambiguous violation of Article 5(3) CRPD. In *H.M. v Sweden,* the CRPD Committee held that

> [T]he author's health condition is critical and access to a hydrotherapy pool at home is essential and an effective – in this case the only effective – means to meet her health needs. Appropriate modification and adjustments would thus require a departure from the development plan, in order to allow the building of a hydrotherapy pool . . . the Planning and Building Act allows for departure from the development plan, and that it can thus accommodate, when necessary in a particular case, an application for reasonable accommodation aimed at ensuring to persons with disabilities the enjoyment or exercise of all human rights on an equal basis with others and without any discrimination.[31]

Given the interplay between Article 5 and the other provisions of the Convention, it is no coincidence that most of the jurisprudence of the CRPD to date has been shaped by its provisions.

Conclusion

In 2018, the CRPD Committee will celebrate the tenth anniversary of its establishment. The fundamental principles in Articles 1–5 of the Convention have been instrumental in defining the direction of the Committee's work. These principles, along with those of diversity, inherent dignity and inalienable rights contained in the Preamble to the Convention have inspired the formulation of the Committee's Concluding Observations since its inception. Complaints received under the Optional Protocol have been rigorously analysed in accordance with the fundamental principles and the result has marked the beginning of an era of change for persons with disabilities. The jurisprudence of the CRPD Committee has contributed to shaping the way in which society thinks of disability-based discrimination and associated legislation and policy. Article 5 of the Convention, its 'golden thread', has made a unique contribution to advancing its application to novel situations, most notably those concerning situations of multiple or intersectional discrimination. In the following chapters, it will be further explained how the fundamental principles of the CRPD have impacted upon the development of legal reasoning in the ten years since the establishment of the Committee.

Summary of Concluding Observations and Recommendations

In its Concluding Observations on proposed General Comment No.6 on Article 5 Equality and non-discrimination, the CRPD Committee expressed concern that the medical model continues to dominate the definition of disability, and associated criteria for needs assessment, especially with regard to access to services for persons with disabilities. The CRPD Committee noted that persons with psychosocial and intellectual impairments were particularly hard hit by the persistent use of the model to define disability. The needs of such persons were more likely to be rendered invisible by the application of policies underpinned by the medical model.

The CRPD Committee expressed its disappointment that the eloquent words contained in countries' action plans were frequently not implemented. The lack of participation of persons with disabilities or the representative organisations in the formulation, implementation and monitoring of disability legislation and policy remains problematic. States Parties' use of derogatory language regarding persons with disabilities in both legislation and practice continues to be a source of concern for the Committee.

With regard to Article 5 CRPD, the Committee noted that there is no definition of 'disability-based discrimination' within the Convention, and furthermore, that its definition of 'discrimination' does not consistently include all types of discrimination which are covered by the Convention; in particular, the denial of reasonable accommodation. For example, failure to provide reasonable accommodation is not routinely considered in the process of monitoring access to education or employment. There are also widespread constitutional and legislative weaknesses in the enforcement provisions concerning the right to equality and non-discrimination. Remedies for failing to provide reasonable accommodation are inadequate, and in some cases non-existent. At times, the availability of a remedy depends upon the goodwill of public officials or the availability of resources. There is a lack of effective complaint mechanisms, including recourse to suitably empowered Ombudspersons, National Human Rights Commissions, or equivalent tribunals for the speedy investigation and resolution of complaints. Difficulties in the areas of monitoring, enforcement, remedies and delay are compounded by the failure to allocate sufficient resources to the implementation of the rights of persons with disabilities, as enshrined in the Convention.

The absence of suitably robust measures to protect victims of discrimination and harassment against reprisal was a further point of concern for the Committee. Implementation of Convention rights was further impeded by the widespread lack of understanding amongst stakeholders of the concepts of both multiple and inter-sectional discrimination. The Committee noted that the formulation of policy was not being sufficiently guided by research into the cumulative effect of discrimina-tion, in particular disability gender-based discrimination. Finally, the Commit-tee's own failure to adopt disaggregated data collection policy, with regard to the complaints received by it, was highlighted. This is an area in which it is hoped the Committee will take urgent remedial action, given its regular criticism of States Parties for similar failings.

In view of the above problems, the Committee has made a series of recom-mendations to States Parties which are contained in its proposed General Com-ment No.6. The Committee recommends that States Parties should investigate the extent to which national legislation is in harmony with the Convention. They should also examine efficacy of their legislative repeal processes, when faced with discriminatory laws and regulations which are inconsistent with the Conven-tion. States Parties should also investigate whether there is a need to change or to abolish customs and practices which discriminate against persons with disabilities. The Committee urged States Parties to explicitly include disability as a prohibited ground for discrimination within anti-discrimination legislation, and to ensure that they enacted disability-inclusive anti-discrimination legislation which was broad in scope, and which provided effective legal remedies.

Such legislation should extend to both the public and private sector, and it should encompass education, employment and access to goods and services. It should also address disability-specific forms of discrimination such as segregated education, institutionalisation and the denial or restriction of legal capacity. The denial of access to sign language (interpretation), Braille and other alternative modes of communication should also be prohibited. Persons with disabilities should be afforded the same standard of protection from discrimination as that which applies to other social groups. According to the Committee, all forms of discrimination against persons with disabilities should be prohibited, including direct and indirect discrimination, harassment, the denial of reasonable discrimination and intersec-tional discrimination.

The Committee also recommended that there should be a programme of capacity-building, to include training for public authorities, to ensure that there is a proper awareness of obligations arising from the Convention. Clear guide-lines should be developed to ensure that States Parties respect their obligations regarding accessibility, reasonable accommodation, and compliance with universal design standards. They must also establish accessible and effective redress mecha-nisms for victims of disability-based discrimination and ensure that they have access to justice, on an equal basis with others. Where complaints of discrimination are made by persons with disabilities, national anti-discrimination legislation should protect them against reprisals, including adverse treatment or adverse consequences as a result of making a complaint or of taking proceedings to enforce compliance with equality provisions.

States Parties should develop and implement equality policies which are inclusive of all persons with disabilities. They should do this by working in close consultation with persons with disabilities, DPOs, national human rights institutions and other relevant stakeholders. States Parties should also seek to raise awareness in society about the scope, content and practical consequences of the rights of persons with disabilities. Such awareness-raising programmes should include state officials from all branches of government and also from within the private sector. Appropriate measures should be put in place to ensure the monitoring of inclusive equality procedures. These measures should include the collection and analysis of disaggregated data concerning persons with disabilities. Where necessary, such data collection systems should be improved to ensure that they are fit for monitoring and evaluation purposes. The Committee also recommended that States Parties should ensure that they have in place national implementation and monitoring mechanisms, in accordance with the provisions of Article 33 CRPD. Such mechanisms must be adequately resourced in order to address disability-based discrimination, and also multiple and intersectional discrimination, against persons with disabilities in the course of their work. Finally, States Parties should adopt specific measures to achieve inclusive equality, in particular for persons with disabilities experiencing intersectional discrimination, including women, children, elderly, indigenous and persons from the Lesbian, Gay, Bisexual, Transgender and Intersex (LGBTI) communities.

Notes

1 Para. (p), Preamble, CRPD.
2 *X v Tanzania* (2017) CRPD/C/18/D/22/2014, para.7.6.
3 CRPD Committee, General Comment No.6 on Article 5 (Equality and Non-Discrimination), was adopted on 9 March 2018.
4 CRPD Committee, Concluding Observations on the Initial Report of Lithuania, 20 April 2016, CRPD/C/LTU/CO/1.
5 CRPD Committee, Concluding Observations on the Initial Report of Ethiopia, 31 August 2016, CRPD/C/ETH/CO/1.
6 CRPD Committee, Inquiry concerning the United Kingdom of Great Britain and Northern Ireland, 2016, CRPD/C/15/R.2, para.46.
7 Ibid.
8 Committee on the Rights of Persons with Disabilities reviews report of the United Kingdom, 24 August 2017, available at http://www.ohchr.org/EN/NewsEvents/Pages/DisplayNews.aspx?NewsID=21993&LangID=E Accessed 19 March 2018.
9 See Day of General Discussion (DGD) on Article 5-Equality and Non-discrimination, 18th Session, 27 August 2017 at http://www.ohchr.org/EN/HRBodies/CRPD/Pages/EqualityAndNon-discrimination.aspx, accessed 19 March 2018.
10 Ibid.
11 CRPD Committee, Concluding Observations on the Initial Report of the Republic of Moldova, 18 May 2017, CRPD/C/MDA/CO/1.

12 CRPD Committee, Concluding Observations on the Initial Report of Montenegro, 22 September 2017, CRPD/C/MNE/CO/1.

13 CRPD Committee, Concluding Observations on the Initial Report of Luxembourg, 29 August 2017, CRPD/C/LUX/1, para.27 (b).

14 OHCHR, Equality and Non-Discrimination under Article 5 of the Convention on the Rights of Persons with Disabilities, 9 December 2016, A/HRC/34/26, para.6.

15 Ibid, para.6.

16 *Marie-Louise Jungelin v Sweden* (2014) CRPD/C/12/D/5/2011, para.10.4.

17 Lon L. Fuller, *The Morality of the Law*, Yale University Press, 1964.

18 *Gemma Beasley v Australia* (2016) CRPD/C/15/D/11/2013.

19 *Nyusti and Takács v Hungary* (2013) CRPD/C/9/D/1/2010.

20 Ibid, para.2.9.

21 Article 4(1)(e) CRPD.

22 *Matadeen v Pointu* [1999] 1 AC 98, para.109.

23 Ibid.

24 *H.M. v Sweden* (2012) CRPD/C/7/D/3/2011.

25 Ibid, para.8.3.

26 *Coleman v Attridge Law* (C-303/06, CJEU).

27 See *X v Tanzania*.

28 CRPD Committee, General Comment No.3 on Article 6 (Women and Girls with Disabilities), 2016, CRPD/C/GC/3, para.4.

29 Nigel Newcomen (UK Prisons and Probation Ombudsman) January 2017, Independent investigation into the death of Ms Sarah Reed a prisoner at HMP Holloway on 11 January 2016, available at http://www.ppo.gov.uk/app/uploads/2017/07/L250-16-Death-of-Ms-Sarah-Reed-Holloway-11-01-2016-SID-31–40.pdf accessed 19 March 2018.

30 Mental Health Units (Use of Force) Bill 2017–19, available at https://services.parliament.uk/bills/2017-19/mentalhealthunitsuseofforce.html accessed 19 March 2018.

31 *H.M. v Sweden*, para.8.5.

3

WOMEN AND GIRLS WITH DISABILITIES

Introduction

Throughout history, women and girls with disabilities have been the subject of violence, abuse and exploitation. Rape, sexual assaults, victimisation and discrimination have all contributed to their marginalisation in society. In 2013, Human Rights Watch reported that women and girls with disabilities in India were forced into mental hospitals and other institutions, where they faced unsanitary conditions, the risk of physical and sexual violence, and experienced involuntary treatment, including the use of electro convulsive therapy.[1] Such inhumane and degrading treatment, which is replicated in many states, creates a vicious circle of poverty and deprivation.

The fate of women and girls with psychosocial and intellectual impairments is even worse. Their neglect, abandonment, ill-treatment and ostracism in society are overwhelming. Ritual witchcraft practices such as the use of virginity testing, supposedly with a view to 'curing' HIV Aids, is yet another form of cruel treatment to which disabled women and girls are subjected. Women with disabilities are routinely abused and ostracised under the pretext of cultural myths.[2] Forced abortion and sterilisation are also commonplace practices today, often occurring in the most liberal and democratic societies. The European Disability Forum has expressed concern that in twenty-first-century Europe, women and girls with disabilities 'continue to be deprived of many of their human rights, including being sterilised against their consent or knowledge, depriving them from their dignity and power over their sexual and reproductive rights'.[3]

Other forms of discrimination to which women and girls with disabilities may be subjected deny them autonomy over their own sexual and reproductive lives. Laws and policies often have the effect of depriving women with disabilities of their legal capacity to open bank accounts, to inherit or manage property, or even to marry the person of their choice. For instance, in Ireland, it has been argued that the effect of the Lunacy Regulation (Ireland) Act 1871 has been to disbar persons with intellectual disabilities from acquiring real property.[4] Section 2 of the aforementioned 1871 Act defines a lunatic as 'any person found by inquisition idiot, lunatic or of unsound mind, and incapable of managing himself or his affairs'. However, the Assisted Decision-Making (Capacity) Act 2015, when fully implemented, will fortunately replace the archaic regime under the 1871 Act with a co-decision regime based upon a functional approach to the issue of mental capacity.

Male dominance of the legislative, executive and judicial branches of governments is the norm in many states, with the result that decision-making and policy remain the exclusive province of men. In its Concluding Observations on the initial report of Latvia, the CRPD Committee expressed its concern at the continuing low level of participation by women with disabilities in political and public life.[5] In relation to the Islamic Republic of Iran, the CRPD Committee was concerned about the multiple and intersectional discrimination faced by women and girls with disabilities, including various forms of gender-based violence, and lack of public policies to ensure their development, advancement and empowerment.[6] With regard to Ethiopia, the CRPD Committee urged the State Party to strengthen protection for persons with disabilities against violence, exploitation and abuse, and in particular for women and girls.[7] It further noted the lack of data on effective measures to prevent violence against women with disabilities in Bosnia and Herzegovina.[8]

In light of the Committee's widespread concerns about women and girls with disabilities, human rights activists, in particular feminists and academics, have been proactive in calling upon society to respond appropriately. Activists have argued that society must rethink itself if the situation of women and girls with disabilities is to be fully understood. However, the rethinking process has been slow and gradual, even at the level of the UN.

The protection of the rights of women under international law

In 1909, Dicey, a fervent advocate of the rule of law, published a paper entitled 'Women's Suffrage', which sought to deny women the right to vote. At the heart of this thinking was the grim reality that women were not considered equal to men. It was only in the aftermath of the Second World War that a number of states came together to declare a series of inalienable fundamental rights of the human person, including women. The preamble to the UDHR specifically reaffirmed the equal rights of men and women. Article 3 ICCPR subsequently stipulated that States Parties should ensure the equal rights of men and women in the exercise of all civil and political rights. Article 3 ICESCR, on the other hand, extended the right to equality to include the enjoyment of all economic, social and cultural rights. However, these provisions were insufficient to redefine the place of women and girls in many societies or to guarantee them the full enjoyment of all their rights on an equal basis with men.

The revival of interest in feminism in the decades following the Second World War provided a rational, intellectual premise for the eventual adoption in 1979 of a Convention aimed at eliminating all forms of discrimination against women (CEDAW). However, CEDAW omitted to provide for respect and protection for the rights of women and girls with disabilities. Moreover, at the time of CEDAW's adoption, the concept of multiple or intersectional discrimination was not yet understood by the international community. The world had to wait for CEDAW's General Recommendation No.18 of 1991 where express reference was made to women with disabilities, and even then, women and girls with disabilities continued to lack a coherent and binding international covenant to affirm their rights.[9] Nor was there an authoritative international forum in which women and girls with disabilities would take the lead on matters pertaining to their daily living conditions. Whilst the inclusion of Article 6 in the CRPD was bitterly opposed during the drafting of the Convention, it finally filled the lacuna in international human rights law regarding the rights of women and girls with disabilities.

The scope of Article 6 CRPD

Both Article 6 CRPD and General Comment No.3 on Women and Girls with Disabilities address the issue of multiple or aggravated forms of discrimination.[10] General Comment No.3 offers an analysis of the situation of women and girls with disabilities and also examines the interplay between the different elements of society:

> Ensuring the human rights of women requires, first and foremost, a comprehensive understanding of the social structures and power relations that frame laws and policies, as well as of economic and social dynamics, family and community life, and cultural beliefs. Gender stereotypes can limit women's capacity to develop their own abilities, pursue professional careers and make choices about their lives and life plans. Both hostile/negative and seemingly benign stereotypes can be harmful. Harmful gender stereotypes need to be recognized and addressed in order to promote gender equality. The Convention enshrines an obligation to combat stereotypes, prejudices and harmful practices relating to persons with disabilities, including those based on sex and age, in all areas of life.[11]

Article 6 (2) CRPD requires affirmative action by States Parties to initiate measures based upon positive discrimination to ensure that women and girls with disabilities can develop to their full potential in order to participate fully in society. However, social change is needed to guarantee their fundamental rights and freedoms. Article 6 CRPD requires States Parties not merely to refrain from taking discriminatory actions regarding women; it requires them actually to recognise women with disabilities as distinct right-holders whose voices must be heard. Women with disabilities must be empowered to participate actively in decision-making in all areas which affect their lives.[12] Article 6(2) CRPD requires States Parties to act in conformity with all their obligations under the Convention 'to ensure the full development, advancement and empowerment' of women with disabilities.

Article 6 CRPD guarantees protection to women and girls with disabilities in the enjoyment of both their civil and economic rights. Paragraph (s) of the Preamble to the Convention emphasises 'the need to incorporate a gender perspective in all efforts to promote the full enjoyment of human rights and fundamental freedoms by persons with disabilities'. Similarly, Article 16 CRPD on the right to freedom from exploitation, violence and abuse, Article 23 CRPD on the respect for family life, Article 25 CRPD on the right to health, and Article 28 CRPD on adequate standards of living and social protection are the main provisions which specifically target states' obligations towards women and girls with disabilities. To date, there have been no communications under the Optional Protocol to the CRPD which deal directly with discrimination experienced by women and girls with disabilities. Consequently, an analysis of CEDAW and domestic case law will be necessary to explore the impact of the provisions of Article 6 CRPD and General Comment No.3 on the lives of women and girls with disabilities.

Multiple and/or intersectional discrimination

Women with disabilities continue to face multiple or aggravated forms of discrimination, on the one hand by virtue of being women and on the other hand by virtue of being persons with disabilities. The CRPD Committee has defined 'multiple discrimination' as 'a situation in which a person experiences discrimination on two or more grounds, leading to discrimination that is compounded or aggravated' while 'intersectional discrimination' has been defined as 'a situation where several grounds interact with each other at the same time in such a way as to be inseparable'.[13] Discrimination on the basis of both gender and disability may be intermingled with one another and also with other types of identity, such as age, religion, politics or sexual orientation or on the basis of one's ethnic, indigenous, national or social origin. Refugee, migrant or asylum seeker status may also be factors upon which discrimination is based.

In *S.V.P. v Bulgaria*, Ms SVP claimed that her daughter had been diagnosed as mentally retarded with an affective disorder as a result of an act of severe sexual violence which had occurred in 2004 when she was just seven years old.[14] The child had encountered the perpetrator near her home and she was raped in his nearby apartment. Two years following the offence, the accused was charged with the lesser offence of sexual molestation and in June 2006, the court approved a plea negotiation in respect of the lesser offence.

According to Ms SVP, this outcome was detrimental to her daughter as the accused, having admitted the lesser offence of sexual molestation, had received only a three-year suspended sentence when in fact his sentence should have been much longer for the offence of rape. She further argued that the State Party had failed to adopt adequate legislative and policy measures to guarantee her daughter's rights against the risk of further violence from the perpetrator who continued to live in the neighbouring apartment block. Ms SVP further submitted that the State Party had not ensured that adequate legislative and policy measures were in place for her protection from sexual violence and its consequences, nor had it established a reliable system for the effective compensation of victims which ought to have included compensation in respect of moral damages.

Furthermore, the execution procedure for civil court judgments did not provide guarantees of real compensation, nor did the Legal Aid Act 2006 allow for legal aid in respect of the execution procedure, even for victims who were disabled as a result of the sexual violence. Ms SVP argued that the state of Bulgaria had failed to protect her daughter from the effects of the negative stereotypes surrounding women with disabilities who had experienced sexual violence. She further submitted that the effect of Bulgarian law and the plea-bargaining process which took place was to legitimise the sexual violence her daughter had experienced.

The CEDAW Committee found that the State of Bulgaria had failed to take positive measures to enact adequate criminal law provisions to effectively punish acts of rape and other forms of sexual violence, in accordance with its obligations under Article 2(b) CEDAW.[15] The state had also failed to enact legislation to put in place adequate support and protection for victims of sexual violence. The CEDAW Committee concluded that the state of Bulgaria had failed to establish appropriate policies, including health-care protocols and hospital procedures which were necessary in light of the sexual violence the victim had experienced. For these reasons, the Committee found that the State of Bulgaria had violated the rights of Ms SVP's daughter under Article 12 CEDAW.[16]

Whilst the CEDAW Committee noted that as a result of the sexual violence inflicted upon Ms SVP's daughter where the latter had consequently been diagnosed as a person with a disability, it failed to consider the issue of multiple or intersectional discrimination in her case, and in particular whether the provisions of the CRPD had been breached. However, in the subsequent case of *R.P.B. v The Philippines*, the CEDAW Committee adopted a different approach to disability and gender-based discrimination (i.e., multiple discrimination).

In *R.P.B. v the Philippines*, Ms RPB, a deaf-mute woman, was raped by her neighbour in 2006 when she was 17 years old.[17] The matter was reported to the police on the same day but for five years the case made little or no progress at the level of the Regional Trial Court, and in 2011 the defendant was eventually acquitted. In considering the case, the CEDAW Committee examined whether negative stereotypes and myths about rape amounted to both gender- and disability-based discrimination. The CEDAW Committee noted that reasonable accommodation in the form of a sign-language interpreter had not been provided to Ms RPB, a failure which had effectively denied her the opportunity to testify. The CEDAW Committee proceeded to analyse the intersectionality between gender, age and disability.

The CEDAW Committee noted the use by the trial court of gender-based myths and stereotypes about rape and rape victims during the trial which had resulted in the defendant's acquittal. There had also been a failure on the court's part to consider Ms RVP's particular vulnerability as a deaf girl, nor had it conducted the proceedings without undue delay. Ms RPB's argument to the effect that the Philippines had failed to protect her from gender-based discrimination—in particular by failing to provide her as a woman with a disability with accessibility to the court on an equal basis with other victims—was also noted. The CEDAW Committee recalled its General Recommendation No.18 in which it had observed that 'disabled women are considered as a vulnerable group [. . .] who suffer from a double discrimination linked to their special living conditions'.[18] The CEDAW Committee reasoned that it was crucial to ensure 'that women with disabilities enjoy effective protection against sex and gender-based discrimination by States Parties and that they have access to effective remedies'.[19] It thus held that negative stereotypes within the judicial system affected the right of women to a fair and just trial:

> [T]he judiciary must take caution not to create inflexible standards of what women or girls should be or what they should have done when confronted with a situation of rape based merely on preconceived notions of what defines a rape victim. In the particular case, the compliance of the State party's obligation to banish gender stereotypes on the grounds of article 2 (f) needs to be assessed in the light of the level of gender, age and disability sensitivity applied in the judicial handling of the author's case.[20]

The cases of Ms SVP and Ms RBP both predated the adoption of General Comment No.3 and also post-dated the adoption of the CRPD. The CEDAW Committee's recommendations in both cases were quite general in nature and did not sufficiently explore the compounded nature of gender and disability-based discrimination in the light of the CRPD. In Ms SVP's case, it simply recalled Bulgaria's obligations under Article 12 CEDAW concerning the right to health, and in so doing, the CEDAW Committee left the impression that disability is a medical condition. It was an opportunity for the CEDAW Committee to mainstream disability issues from a fresh, non-discrimination perspective in line with Article 1 CEDAW. Equally, the application of the corresponding CRPD provision concerning the right to non-discrimination (Article 5 CRPD) would arguably have shed more light on the issue of aggravated forms of discrimination experienced by women and girls with disabilities. Bulgarian legislation and policy do not guarantee the protection of rape victims with disabilities in the course of criminal investigations or trials, nor does it guarantee such protection for victims who avail themselves of rehabilitation services (Articles 5, 13 and 26 CRPD). In Ms SVP's case, the Bulgarian criminal justice system effectively endorsed the view that sexual violence against women and girls with disabilities was a mild form of violence.

The Preamble to the CRPD recognises that women with disabilities may suffer from multiple or aggravated forms of discrimination, as was the case in *S.V.P. v Bulgaria*.[21] However, in neither of the above cases did the CEDAW Committee expressly refer to its General Recommendation No.25, which stipulates that certain groups of women who, 'in addition to suffering from discrimination directed against them as women, may also suffer from multiple forms of discrimination based on additional grounds such as race, ethnic or religious identity, disability, age, class, caste or other factors'.[22]

It appears that in Ms SVP's case, the CEDAW Committee missed an opportunity to remind the State Party that a lack of legislative and policy measures guaranteeing non-discrimination with regard to access to the justice system for direct participants in proceedings was a violation of Articles 5(3), 13 and 26 CRPD. In both the above cases, the States Parties were obliged to provide Ms RPB and Ms SVP with procedural accommodation or age-appropriate accommodation. Access to justice is a civil right, and in view of the violence to which the victims were exposed, the obligations of the States Parties were non-delegable. As such, in line with *X v Tanzania*, States Parties are required to investigate the alleged offence and to prosecute offenders in order to provide remedies against the discrimination experienced by rape victims.[23]

General Comment No.3 sets out State Parties' obligations regarding the implementation of non-discriminatory measures concerning multiple or intersectional discrimination and it also offers them guidance in that regard.[24] It states that women with disabilities may be subject to multiple discrimination, not only in the public realm, but also in the private sphere; for example, within the family when interacting with private social service providers. International human rights law has long acknowledged States Parties' responsibility for discrimination perpetrated by private, non-state actors. In order to ensure that complaints involving more than one type of discrimination are fully considered with regard to both liability and remedies, States Parties must adopt legal provisions and procedures that explicitly recognise the possibility of multiple discrimination.

In the above cases, a clear message ought to have been sent to the States Parties concerned that they cannot evade liability simply because the perpetrators of the sexual violence in both cases were non-state actors. It is a long-established principle in international public law that omission to introduce legislation to combat oppression and discrimination will de facto render states liable. Article 5(2) CRPD refers to States Parties' obligations to prohibit discrimination, not only on the basis of disability, but also on other grounds. The rationale behind Article 5(2) CRPD is that the concept of multiple discrimination recognises that individuals do not experience discrimination as members of a homogeneous group but, rather, as individuals with multidimensional layers of identities, statuses and life circumstances.[25]

Freedom from exploitation, violence and abuse

Violence against women may be described as 'any act of gender-based violence that results in, or is likely to result in, physical, sexual or psychological harm or suffering to women, including threats of such acts, coercion or arbitrary deprivation of liberty, whether occurring in public or in private life'.[26] In its General

Recommendation No.19, the CEDAW Committee has defined gender-based violence as 'a form of discrimination that seriously inhibits women's ability to enjoy rights and freedoms on a basis of equality with men'.[27]

Whereas Article 16 CRPD containing the right to freedom from exploitation, violence and abuse applies to all persons with disabilities, it offers an additional layer of protection for women and children with disabilities. Article 16 CRPD can be used as an effective tool in combatting gender and disability-based violence and other forms of exploitation against women and girls with disabilities. It requires that States Parties take both pre-emptive and corollary measures in relation to violence against women and children. It also confers a positive obligation upon States Parties to legislate and to take other appropriate measures regarding domestic violence perpetrated against women and children with disabilities behind the closed doors of homes and institutions which may otherwise go unpunished. The CRPD Committee has observed in General Comment No.3 that

> Violations relating to deprivation of liberty disproportionately affect women with intellectual or psychosocial disabilities and those in institutional settings. Those deprived of their liberty in places such as psychiatric institutions, on the basis of actual or perceived impairment, are subject to higher levels of violence, as well as to cruel, inhuman or degrading treatment or punishment and are segregated and exposed to the risk of sexual violence and trafficking within care and special education institutions. Violence against women with disabilities in institutions includes: involuntary undressing by male staff against the will of the woman concerned; forced administration of psychiatric medication; and overmedication, which can reduce the ability to describe and/or remember sexual violence.[28]

Unfortunately, in Ms SVP's case, the CEDAW Committee did not directly engage with the systemic discrimination which is often experienced by women with disabilities. On the contrary, the CEDAW Committee appeared to suggest that Ms SVP's disability was a matter for her individual concern rather than being a factor of relevance to the Bulgarian court. Nor did the CEDAW Committee recognise that social conditions which serve to perpetuate violence against women and girls with disabilities arise due to barriers which are deeply embedded in society. The CEDAW Committee chose instead to focus on the vulnerability of women and girls with disabilities as 'impaired' individuals. It is suggested that, if faced with a similar case of multiple or intersectional discrimination, the CRPD Committee would have taken into account the interplay between gender and disability in the wider social context.

Women and girls with disabilities undoubtedly face a greater risk of exploitation than their non-disabled counterparts as a direct result of their disabilities.[29] However, stigmatising them as 'vulnerable' has the effect of burdening them even further, when the focus should instead be upon the need to change stereotypical attitudes which prevail in society. Offenders are often of the view that women and girls with disabilities are easy prey and that they are vulnerable because they lack the mental and/or physical ability to defend themselves. Because of their impairment, they often cannot fully assess the risks to which they may be exposed, nor can they find an escape route or adequately defend themselves if threatened. In its General Comment No.3, the CRPD Committee noted that

> Perpetrators may act with impunity because they perceive little risk of discovery or punishment given that access to judicial remedies is severely restricted, and women with disabilities subjected to such violence are unlikely to be able to access helplines or other forms of support to report such violations.[30]

Violence and armed conflict

During armed conflicts, the use of violence against women and girls with disabilities may include the intentional infliction of physical harm as a means of repression and alienation. Repressive violence occurs when women and girls with disabilities are denied their basic socio-economic, civil and political rights, whilst alienating violence refers to oppressive practices which undermine their development—for example, as a result of sexism. The CEDAW Committee has noted that specific groups of women and girls are at particular risk of violence during armed conflicts.[31] It has recently condemned the displacement and devastation experienced by women in Gaza and it also highlighted the particularly serious risks faced by women and girls with disabilities in the course of the Gaza conflict.[32]

Globally, Disabled Persons Organisations (DPOs) have been instrumental in the fight for women's rights. For instance, the CEDAW Committee has made reference to a submission it has received from Women Enabled International (WEI) and Nigeria Partners highlighting the multiple layers of discrimination which women and girls with disabilities may face in Nigeria, including gender and disability-based discrimination.[33] As a result of negative stereotypes surrounding both gender and disability, and also multiple discrimination, women and girls with disabilities in Nigeria are frequently given less priority within families, have less access to education, and are considered less eligible for marriage or capable of founding families. They are also subjected to violence, especially sexual violence, more frequently than their non-disabled counterparts.

Women and girls with disabilities are often abandoned by their families with little or no access to essential services when the latter flee their communities due to the outbreak of violence. They also often find it impossible to access sexual and reproductive health information and services, including those aimed at the prevention and treatment of HIV, because there is a pervasive stereotypical belief that women with disabilities do not have sex and are incapable of becoming parents.[34] Instead of providing support for women and girls with disabilities who seek to combat sexual violence, many governments have responded to the issue by subjecting them to forced sterilisation; a form of 'reproductive' discrimination which adds yet another layer of discrimination to their already heavy encumbrance.

Forced sterilisation

In the 1927 case of *Buck v Bell*, the US Supreme Court held that that legislation catering for the permissible sterilisation of women with intellectual disabilities was not unconstitutional.[35] The decision effectively legitimised the sterilisation of women with intellectual disabilities deemed to be 'feebleminded'. In the twentieth century alone, more than 70,000 women with disabilities in the US have been sterilised without their consent.[36]

In the UK, the House of Lords adopted a similar position, albeit 60 years later, in the case of *Re F (Mental Patient: Sterilisation)*.[37] The House of Lords had to determine whether a pregnant woman with a serious mental disability was incapable of consenting to sterilisation. It held that medical treatment can be justified without consent when it is in the best interests of the patient. In other words, where a woman does not have the mental capacity to appreciate the nature and effect of the sterilisation procedure, she will be deemed to lack the legal capacity to decide for herself.

In the case of *Secretary of the Department of Health and Community Services v JWB and SMB* (Marion's Case), the High Court of Australia had to decide whether it was for the court or for the parents of a 13-year-old girl with an intellectual disability to consent to her sterilisation.[38] The High Court held that where the child was not legally competent, it was for the Family Court to make an order for the sterilisation. The High Court was of the view that the risk of parents or medical practitioners making a wrong decision in such a situation was much more significant than the risk of a court doing so. The Family Court was best placed to arrive at an objective decision based on the best interests of the child.

These cases illustrate how the forced sterilisation of women and girls with disabilities has become culturally engrained as a non-discriminatory practice in many parts of the world. There are many reasons for this normalisation of the violation of the human rights of women with disabilities, including eugenics, menstrual management and pregnancy prevention.[39] The Special Rapporteur on the Rights of Persons with Disabilities has rightly stressed the importance of gathering evidence regarding the extent of forced sterilisation. She has further addressed the 'medicalisation' of the reproductive health challenges faced by women and girls with disabilities. Institutionalised women with intellectual and psychosocial disabilities are at a significantly higher risk than others of being subjected to forced sterilisation.

The Special Rapporteur has cited judgments from the Constitutional Courts of both Colombia and Spain to the effect that forced sterilisation is often performed on a precautionary basis due to the vulnerability of women and girls with disabilities to sexual abuse.[40] Such judgments reflect the fallacy that sterilisation will enable women and girls with disabilities who are considered to be 'unfit for parenthood' to improve their quality of life without having to cope with the 'burden of pregnancy'. However, it is not apparent from these judgments how sterilisation can protect women and girls with disabilities from sexual abuse. It may be argued that sterilisation may serve to actually increase their risk of sexual abuse. The Director of the Action Program for Equality and Social Inclusion (Columbia) has commented on the 2014 ruling of the Constitutional Court of Columbia as follows:

> Sterilization does not protect anybody from sexual violence and in fact it is a risk factor. With this decision the Court disregarded its obligations under the Convention on the Rights of People with Disabilities, ratified by Colombia. The Convention requires that States recognize people with disabilities' full legal capacity to make their own decisions and that they provide the necessary supports to do so.[41]

The CEDAW Committee has also criticised the State of Columbia for failing to guarantee that sterilisation will not take place without the free and informed consent of women with disabilities.[42] In the same vein, the Special Rapporteur has maintained that forced sterilisation is a deplorable practice which may have adverse consequences on the mental and physical integrity of women and girls with disabilities. For this reason, it is incumbent upon States Parties to criminalise and eradicate the practice of forced sterilisation as it constitutes a direct violation of Article 17 CRPD (right to physical and mental integrity).

Discrimination at the crossroads

The view that women and girls with disabilities may suffer from multiple and aggravated forms of discrimination has been gaining currency in international public law debates. As the above case law has illustrated, women and girls with disabilities are a group which face discrimination on many levels, both systemic and structural. Whilst they face discrimination as women and also as persons with disabilities, it is often the case that their social and economic conditions may compound the barriers they face. This multiple discrimination may be further aggravated by the intersection of ethnicity, race and other factors. This phenomenon of multiple or intersectional discrimination is most apparent in developing countries.

It is regrettable that international human rights treaty bodies, especially the CEDAW Committee, have not yet adopted a holistic approach to the problem of multiple and intersectional discrimination. For example, in the case of *A.S. v Hungary*, the CEDAW Committee recognised that the sterilisation of Ms AS—a Hungarian woman from the Roma community—violated several provisions of the CEDAW.[43] However, the CEDAW Committee failed to directly address the issue of intersectional discrimination in the case. Ms AS had required a caesarean section after going into labour and was asked by her treating doctor to sign some consent forms which, unbeknown to Ms AS, included a consent form for a sterilisation operation. It was only after having been sterilised that Ms AS came to understand the full implications of the procedure which had been carried out. The CEDAW Committee found that several of Ms AS's rights had been violated in the circumstances, including: the right to be provided with information and advice on family planning; the right to non-discrimination in relation to medical procedures and the right to freely decide on the number of children she wished to bear (Articles 10(h), 12 and 16(1)(e) CEDAW).

However, the CEDAW Committee did not take into account the fact that Ms AS might have been discriminated against on grounds of her ethnic and religious affiliations. Article 12(1) CEDAW provides that 'States Parties shall take all appropriate measures to eliminate discrimination against women in the field of health care in order to ensure, on a basis of equality of men and women, access to health care services, including those related to family planning'. The adoption of a purposive approach on the CEDAW Committee's part to the interpretation of Article 12(1) CEDAW may have prompted it to examine the intersectional discrimination that Ms AS faced in accessing healthcare services and to explore whether the discrimination she faced as a woman was compounded by a failure to be given special attention to 'the health needs and rights of women belonging to vulnerable and disadvantaged groups'.[44] According to Ms AS,

> She would never have agreed to the sterilization as she has strict Catholic religious beliefs that prohibit contraception of any kind, including sterilization. Furthermore, she and her partner live in accordance with traditional Roma customs—where having children is said to be a central element of the value system of Roma families.[45]

Instead, there was an assumption on the part of the CEDAW Committee that all women suffer from a unique form of discrimination. The reality is that women are not a homogeneous group and Ms AS's forced sterilisation did not arise solely on the basis of her gender. It arose due to her experience of other forms of discrimination, including her attachment to the minority Roma community in Hungary. It is also regrettable that the CEDAW Committee missed the opportunity in its analysis of Ms AS's case to refer to other international human rights treaties and their jurisprudence. For instance, the CEDAW Committee could have considered the General Recommendations of the Committee on the Elimination of Racial Discrimination (CERD) regarding gender-related racial discrimination and also on discrimination against Roma people.[46]

It has been noted above that the CEDAW Committee could also have taken a different approach to its analysis of discrimination in the case of *R.P.B. v Philippines*. It could have chosen to integrate the jurisprudence of other human rights treaty bodies into its analysis, for instance, the General Comment of the CRC Committee on the Rights of Children with Disabilities or General Comment No.3 of the CRPD Committee on the Rights of Women and Girls with Disabilities.[47] These sources could have been valuable interpretative tools for examining the intersection of gender, age and disability in Ms RPB's case. An intersectional approach to discrimination requires international human rights bodies to use new analytical tools and remedies through specific measures that may go beyond those typically provided in cases of discrimination on the basis of a single ground.

The CEDAW Committee's General Recommendation No.35 on gender-based violence (updating General Recommendation No.19) has considered the challenges faced by women and girls with disabilities and, in particular, the issues they face in the context of gender-based violence.[48] For instance, the CEDAW Committee has classified medical procedures which are performed on women with disabilities without their informed consent as a form of gender-based violence and has called upon States Parties to repeal legislation that permits such violence. The CEDAW Committee has further called on States Parties to repeal laws that deter women from reporting gender-based violence, including 'guardianship laws that deprive women of legal capacity or restrict the ability of women with disabilities to testify in court'.[49] It has also recommended that States Parties should establish accessible protection mechanisms to prevent violence against women and girls with disabilities. These include removing communication barriers which victims with disabilities may face, and the development and dissemination of accessible information, including to persons with disabilities.

Conclusion

Multiple and aggravated forms of discrimination continue to be experienced by women and girls with disabilities, a situation which calls for ongoing concerted efforts on the part of the international community in order to address this continuing threat to human rights. Whilst the CRPD has advanced the debate on the elimination of all forms of discrimination, other human rights treaty bodies must follow its lead if multiple and aggravated forms of discrimination against women and girls with disabilities are to be combated. Consistency in promoting the human rights model of disability is needed to eradicate all forms of violence, abuse and exploitation. This requires an understanding of the social context which serves to reproduce the marginalisation of women and girls in society.

The above case law illustrates how States Parties have been slow to respond to the challenges and how patriarchal societies remain resistant to change. The Special Rapporteur's recent report on sexual and reproductive health and rights of girls and young women with disabilities has highlighted the magnitude of the problem. Whilst governments may bring positive changes through the adoption of new policies and legislation in line with the CRPD, it may take longer to truly change the hearts and souls of men. In 2016, the UN General Assembly adopted a resolution addressing the impact of multiple and intersecting forms of discrimination and violence in the context of racism, racial discrimination, xenophobia and related forms of intolerance on the full enjoyment of all human rights by women and girls.[50] In 2017, the UN adopted a further resolution on the Implementation of the Convention on the Rights of Persons with Disabilities and the Optional Protocol thereto on the situation of women and girls with disabilities.[51] These are important steps at the international level. However, change at national, community and family level is also needed if discrimination against women and girls with disabilities is to end, once and for all.

Summary of Concluding Observations and Recommendations

The recommendations of General Comment No.3 concerning women and girls with disabilities by the CRPD Committee offer a blueprint for States Parties seeking to address the problem of multiple discrimination and to make the development, advancement and empowerment of women and girls with disabilities a reality.

In accordance with paragraph 63 of the recommendations of General Comment No.3 concerning multiple discrimination, States Parties should ensure that they repeal all discriminatory laws, and end policies and practices that prevent women with disabilities from asserting their rights in accordance with the CRPD. They must ensure that gender- and disability-based discrimination and associated intersectional forms of discrimination are prohibited, and that sexual violence against women and girls with disabilities is prohibited by law, with appropriate penalties to deter the commission of such offences. All forms of forced gender- or disability-based medical procedures must also be prohibited by law, including forced sterilisation, forced abortion and the imposition of non-consensual birth control on persons with disabilities. States Parties must also ensure that the rights of women with disabilities are respected in policies, especially those relating to women and to persons with disabilities.

There is a need for States Parties to address all barriers which may impact upon the participation of women with disabilities in decision-making, policy and legislative measures which affect their quality of life. The voices of women and girls with disabilities, as well as those of their representative organisations, must be heard by States Parties, and their views must be taken into account in designing, implementing and monitoring programmes affecting them. Furthermore, in order to ensure the effective implementation of Article 6 CRPD, and the elimination of all forms of discrimination, in particular multiple and intersectional discrimination, women with disabilities and their representative organisations must be consulted regarding the collection and analysis of data in all areas of life concerning them. Such data collection systems must be fit for the purpose of effectively monitoring and evaluating the efficacy of relevant legislation and policy. Finally, States Parties must ensure that their international cooperation programmes are disability- and gender-sensitive and fully inclusive of the needs of women with disabilities. The implementation by States Parties of the UN 2030 Agenda on Sustainable Development, including national programmes for the attainment of the Sustainable Development Goals and all other international cooperation programmes, must be disability- and gender-sensitive. Such programmes must reflect accurately the needs of women with disabilities, in line with the aforementioned data analysis.

In accordance with paragraph 64 of General Comment No.3 concerning the development, advancement and empowerment of women with disabilities, States Parties should repeal legislation and amend policies which prevent women with disabilities from fully and effectively participating in political and public life on an equal basis with others. They must ensure that women with disabilities can take full advantage of their right to form organisations and networks, and that they have access to organisations and networks promoting women's rights in general, on an equal basis with others.

Affirmative action measures must be adopted by States Parties to ensure the empowerment of women with disabilities and such measures must be agreed following consultation with them and their representative organisations, with a view to combating inequality and ensuring equality of opportunities. These affirmative action measures should include: access to justice; the elimination of violence; respect for home and family life; sexual health and reproductive rights; health; education; employment and social protection. In accordance with Article 9 CRPD and General Comment No.2 (2014), States Parties must ensure that both public and private services and facilities are fully accessible to women with disabilities. Training and education programmes should be established for both public and private service providers to ensure that the services they supply comply with relevant human rights norms, and that service providers can combat prevailing discriminatory values. In conformity with General Comment No.1 (2014), States Parties must adopt effective measures to support women with disabilities in exercising their legal capacity, so that they may either give or withhold their free and informed consent and make decisions concerning their own lives. Women with disabilities should be supported and encouraged to assume leadership roles within public decision-making bodies and States Parties should support and promote the establishment of organisations and networks of women with disabilities.

States Parties must promote research into issues of concern to women with disabilities, with particular attention being paid to barriers which may exist to their development, advancement and empowerment. In order to ensure that women with disabilities and their needs are fully accounted for in data collection systems relating to women and to persons with disabilities, States Parties must ensure that they, and their representative organisations, fully participate in the design, implementation, evaluation and monitoring of such data collection systems. In order to attain improved public policies and practices, States Parties must also establish effective consultation mechanisms, to better understand 'the diverse lived experiences of women with disabilities'.

Finally, in seeking to eliminate legal, procedural and social barriers to the development, advancement and empowerment of women with disabilities, States Parties must support and promote cooperation and assistance at national, regional, international and global levels. They must also ensure that women with disabilities are included in the design, implementation and monitoring of international cooperation projects and programmes affecting their lives.

Notes

1 Human Rights Watch, 'Treated Worse than Animals, Abuses against Women and Girls with Psychosocial or Intellectual Disabilities in Institutions in India', 3 December 2014. Available at https://www.hrw.org/report/2014/12/03/treated-worse-animals/abuses-against-women-and-girls-psychosocial-or-intellectual, accessed 19 March 2018.

2 See for instance Angie Stone-MacDonald, 'Cultural Beliefs and Attitudes about Disability in East Africa', *Review of Disability Studies: An International Journal 8:1 2014*, available at http://www.rdsjournal.org/index.php/journal/article/download/110/367 Accessed 19 March 2018.

3 European Disability Forum and European Parliament, 'Hearing on Ending the Forced Sterilisation of Women and Girls with Disabilities', 5 December 2017, http://www.edf-feph.org/newsroom/news/ending-forced-sterilisation-women-and-girls-disabilities accessed 19 March 2018.

4 See Aine Hynes (2017) 'Assisted Decision-Making (Capacity) Act 2015 - Update on Implementation' *Irish Mental Health Lawyers Association Annual Conference 2017*, available at: https://www.ucc.ie/academic/law/docs/mentalhealth/conferences/2017/11.05-A. Hynes-08Apr2017.pdf accessed 19 March 2018.

5 CRPD Committee, Concluding Observations on the Initial Report Latvia, 10 October 2017, CRPD/C/LVA/CO/1, para.10 (a).

6 CRPD Committee, Concluding Observations on the Initial Report of Iran, 10 May 2017, CRPD/C/IRN/CO/1, para.14.

7 CRPD Committee, Concluding Observations on the Initial Report of Ethiopia, 4 November 2016, CRPD/C/ETH/CO/1.

8 CRPD Committee, Concluding Observations on the Initial Report of Bosnia and Herzegovina, 2 May 2017, CRPD/C/BIH/CO/1.

9 CEDAW Committee, General recommendation No.18 (Disabled Women), 1991, INT_CEDAW_GEC_4729_E.

10 CRPD Committee, General Comment No.3 on Article 6 (Women and Girls with Disabilities), 26 August 2016, CRPD/C/GC/3.

11 General Comment No.3, para.8.

12 General Comment No.3, para.7.

13 General Comment No.3, para.4.

14 *S. V.P. v Bulgaria* (2012) CEDAW/C/53/D/31/2011.

15 Article 2(b) CEDAW provides that States should 'adopt appropriate legislative and other measures, including sanctions where appropriate, prohibiting all discrimination against women'.

16 Article 12(1) CEDAW provides that' States Parties shall take all appropriate measures to eliminate discrimination against women in the field of health care in order to ensure, on a basis of equality of men and women, access to health care services, including those related to family planning.'

17 *R.P.B. v the Philippines* (2014) CEDAW/C/57/D/34/2011.

18 CEDAW Committee, General Recommendation No.18.

19 *R.P.B. v the Philippines*, para.8.3.

20 *R.P.B. v the Philippines*, para.8.8.

21 Preamble, para.(p) CRPD 2007.

22 CEDAW Committee, General Recommendation No.25 on Article 4(1) (Temporary Special Measures), 2004, para.12.

23 See *X v Tanzania* in Chapter 5.

24 General Comment No.3, para.18.

25 General Comment No.3, para.16.

26 United Nations General Assembly, 'Declaration on the Elimination of Violence Against Women', December 1993, A/RES/48/104, Article 1.

27 CEDAW Committee, General Recommendation No. 19 (Violence against Women), 1992.

28 General Comment No.3, para.53.

29 Catalina Devandas Aguilar (Special Rapporteur on the Rights of Persons with Disabilities), Sexual and Reproductive Health and Rights of Girls and Young Women with Disabilities, 14 July 2017, A/72/133.

30 General Comment No.3 para.53.

31 CEDAW Committee, General Recommendation No. 30 (Women in Conflict Prevention, Conflict and Post-Conflict Situations), 2013.

32 CEDAW Committee, Statement on the Situation in Gaza, July 2014.

33 NGO Submission to the CEDAW Committee Pre-Sessional Working Group for Nigeria October 2016 available at https://womenenabled.org/pdfs/WEI%20and%20Nigeria%20Partners%20CEDAW%20Review%20Submission%20June%2012%202017.pdf accessed 19 March 2018.

34 See Catalina Devandas Aguilar, Sexual and Reproductive Health and Rights of Girls and Young Women with Disabilities.

35 *Buck v. Bell*, 274 U.S. 200 (1927).

36 See Adam Cohen, *Imbeciles: The Supreme Court, American Eugenics, and the Sterilization of Carrie Buck*, Penguin 2016; Roberta Capko, 'Involuntary Sterilisation of Mentally Disabled Women', *Berkley Women's Law Journal* (2013) 8 (1).

37 *Re F (Mental Patient: Sterilisation)* [1990] 2 AC 1.

38 *Secretary of the Department of Health and Community Services v JWB and SMB* (1992) 175 CLR 218.

39 Catalina Devandas Aguilar, Sexual and Reproductive Health and Rights of Girls and Young Women with Disabilities, para.29.

40 Constitutional Court of Colombia, Decision C-133/14 of 11 March 2014; Decision C-182 of 13 April 2016; Constitutional Court of Spain, Decision 215/1994 of 14 July 1994.

41 Andrea Parra, Director of the Action Program for Equality and Social Inclusion (PAIIS) of the Universidad de los Andes in Colombia, cited in Center for Reproductive Rights, Organizations in several countries reject decision of the Colombian Constitutional Court allowing for sterilization of minors with disabilities without their consent, 18 March 2014. Available at https://www.reproductiverights.org/press-room/Organizations-in-several-countries-reject-decision-of-the-Colombian-Constitutional-Court, accessed 19 March 2018.

42 CEDAW Committee, Concluding Observations on the Combined Seventh and Eighth Periodic Reports of Colombia, 29 October 2013, CEDAW/C/COL/CO/7–8, para.30(e).

43 *A.S. v Hungary* (2006) CEDAW/C/36/D/4/2004.

44 CEDAW Committee, General Recommendation No. 24, Article 12 CEDAW (Women and Health), 1999, para.6.

45 *A.S. v Hungary*, para.2.4.

46 CERD Committee, General Recommendation No.25 (Gender Related Dimensions of Racial Discrimination), 20 March 2000; CERD Committee, General Recommendation No.27 (Discrimination against Roma), 2000.

47 CRC Committee, General Comment No.9 (The Rights of Children with Disabilities), 27 February 2007, CRC/C/GC/9.

48 CEDAW Committee, General Recommendation No. 35 (Gender-Based Violence against Women), 26 July 2017, CEDAW/C/GC/35.

49 Ibid, para.29.

50 UN General Assembly, Draft Resolution addressing the impact of multiple and intersecting forms of discrimination and violence in the context of racism, racial discrimination, xenophobia and related intolerance on the full enjoyment of all human rights by women and girls, 28 June 2016, A/HRC/32/L.25.

51 UN General Assembly, Implementation of the Convention on the Rights of Persons with Disabilities and the Optional Protocol thereto: Situation of Women and Girls with Disabilities, 13 November 2017, A/C.3/72/L.18/Rev.1.

PART II
Civil and political rights

4

LEGAL CAPACITY AND ACCESS TO JUSTICE

Introduction

Article 12 equal recognition before the law is primarily referred to as 'legal capacity'. It bestows on persons with disabilities the capacity to have control over their own lives on an equal basis with others. It also refines and polishes the concept of the inalienable right to self-determination, as enshrined in Article 1 ICCPR by virtue of which all persons can freely determine their political status and pursue their economic, social and cultural development. The obligations of States Parties are exemplified by, but are not limited to, Article 12(5) CRPD which stipulates that

> States Parties shall take all appropriate and effective measures to ensure the equal rights of persons with disabilities to own or inherit property, to control their own financial affairs and to have equal access to bank loans, mortgages and other forms of financial credit. States should also ensure that persons with disabilities are not arbitrarily deprived of their property.

The positive realisation of the right to legal capacity must comply with Article 12(1)–(5) and with the other provisions of the Convention.

There is a thin, but important, demarcation line between 'equality before the law' within the meaning of Article 5 CRPD and 'equal recognition before the law' within the ambit of Article 12(3) CRPD. One fundamental difference relates to the provision of reasonable accommodation. Reasonable accommodation has been defined in Article 2 CRPD as 'necessary and appropriate modification and adjustments not imposing a disproportionate or undue burden, where needed in a particular case, to ensure to persons with disabilities the enjoyment or exercise on an equal basis with others of all human rights and fundamental freedoms'. Article 12(3) CRPD places States Parties under an obligation to take appropriate measures to provide access to the support persons with disabilities may require in the exercise of their legal capacity.

While 'reasonable accommodation' within the meaning of Article 5 CRPD is subject to an undue burden and the proportionality test, 'support' within the meaning of Article 12(3) CRPD is not subject to any such limit. Under Article 12(3) CRPD, States Parties are peremptorily required to provide support to persons with disabilities to ensure the fulfilment of all their rights in order to ascertain their equal recognition before and under the law. States Parties cannot progressively realise the right to equal recognition before the law as civil and political rights do not fall under the purview of Article 4(2) CRPD. In its first General Comment, the CRPD Committee declared that the right to equality before the law as encompassed in Article 12 is deeply rooted in the ICPPR and indeed falls within the category of civil and political rights.[1] Civil and political rights are an immutable category of rights which are 'assigned at the moment of ratification and States parties are required to take steps to immediately realise those rights'.[2] It follows from the General Comment that States Parties are under an obligation to immediately begin taking steps towards the realisation of the rights enshrined in Article 12 upon ratification of the CRPD. As the CRPD Committee has put forward, these steps must be deliberate, well planned and include consultation with, and the meaningful participation of, persons with disabilities and their representative organisations.

It should further be highlighted that Article 4(1)(b) CRPD places obligations on States Parties to 'take all appropriate measures, including legislation, to modify or abolish existing laws, regulations, customs and practices that constitute discrimination against persons with disabilities'. The substituted decision-making and guardianship regimes of States Parties which make it possible to restrict and even deny the legal capacity of persons with disabilities are still a reality today. For instance, in its Concluding Observations on the initial report of Qatar, the CRPD Committee noted with concern that that the legislative framework of the State Party was not in conformity with Article 12 CRPD.[3] Article 305 of the Qatari Criminal Code, Article 34 of the Guardianship (Assets of Minors) Act No.40 of 2004, and Article 127 of the Civil Code restricted, inter alia, the exercise of the rights of persons with disabilities to vote, to marry, to have a family, to give and/or withdraw free and informed consent, to choose where and with whom to live, as well as the right to access the justice system.

Access to justice does not only refer to physical accessibility to courts or other administrative buildings. The scope and contents of Article 13 CRPD are broad insofar as States Parties are under an obligation to provide legal safeguards in order to

> ensure the right to a fair trial, due process and the safe and full participation of persons with disabilities, especially persons with psychosocial and/or intellectual disabilities, in all judicial proceedings, including through the provision of procedural and gender- and age-appropriate accommodation, in particular sign language interpretation for persons with hearing impairment and accessible formats of legal and judicial information and communication for persons with visual impairment.[4]

The right to legal capacity is, on that account, a prerequisite to effectively access the justice system. Since persons with physical as well as psychosocial, intellectual, or any other form of impairment possess the legal personality required in the exercise of their legal capacity, they have the right and the legitimate expectation to be recognised as persons before the law with equal standing in courts and tribunals. States Parties are therefore under an obligation to ensure that persons with disabilities have access to legal representation on an equal basis with others. Legal capacity and access to justice are inextricably linked, even though they are fundamentally different legal concepts. For example, the denial of legal capacity to a person with a psychosocial or intellectual disability which has the effect of preventing him/her to benefit from a will would constitute a violation of his right to equal recognition before the law under Article 12 of the Convention. The aggrieved person could also invoke a violation of his/her right to effectively access the justice system under Article 13 CRPD if he/she was not provided with procedural accommodation to enable him/her to challenge his/ her presumed legal incapacity.

The international rule of law requires that Articles 12 and 13 are premised upon the general principles which are embedded in Articles 3–5 of the Convention. These Articles respectively set out the general principles underpinning the Convention, the general obligations of States Parties in accordance with it, and its provisions relating to equality and non-discrimination. The wide and purposive application of Articles 12 and 13 to the provisions contained in Articles 3–5 was not originally envisaged by the framers of the Convention. In fact, there was a lot of pessimism with regard to the practical effect of the Convention during the time of its negotiation. It was feared that the requirement for 'support' within Article 12(3) and for 'procedural and age-appropriate accommodations' within Article 13(1) would be narrowly construed. It was also assumed that the proportionality and undue burden test which is applicable to 'reasonable accommodation' would further restrict the enjoyment of fundamental rights and freedoms of persons with disabilities as enshrined in Articles 12 and 13 of the Convention. It was also believed that States Parties would be allowed an uncontrolled margin of discretion with regard to the implementation of the rights to legal capacity and access to justice in line with Article 4(2) of the Convention.

In fact, as the jurisprudence illustrates, there have been attempts by States Parties to limit those rights which are deeply entrenched in Articles 12 and 13 and they have not fully appreciated that equal recognition before the law is a threshold right on which other rights are intertwined and interdependent. Their acts and omissions have led to serious miscarriage of justice.

Miscarriage of justice

In *James Marlon Noble v Australia*, the author, who had a psychosocial impairment, claimed that Australia had violated his rights under Articles 5(1), 12 and 13 of the Convention.[5] He had been charged with several counts of sexual assault. However, even though Mr Noble was never given the opportunity to plead to the charges, nor was he ever found guilty by a court of law, he nevertheless spent more than ten years in jail. The alleged victim in the case later withdrew all charges made against him. Mr Noble contended that the way in which the courts dealt with his disability in declaring him 'unfit to plead' constituted a violation of his right under Article 12(3) to exercise his legal capacity on an equal basis with others. He submitted that he had not been provided with the required support to enable him to plead to the charges. He also averred that he had been denied access to justice as embedded in Article 13(1).

Mr Noble was first arrested in 2002 and was remanded in custody at a correctional centre rather than being released on bail. The prosecution in the case filed an expert report which indicated that Mr Noble was unfit to plead to the charges. Given that the expert report was not conclusive, both the defence and the prosecution requested a further psychiatric assessment, in conformity with the Criminal Law (Mentally Impaired Defendant) Act 1996. At another hearing, the prosecutor advised the court that Mr Noble had been assessed by a psychiatrist, but that he had received only a preliminary report. The matter was adjourned once more. On 24 January 2003, the reports of three psychiatrists were finally presented to the court, two of which concluded that Mr Noble was unfit to plead while the other recommended that a further assessment be carried out. The latter report noted that Mr Noble 'appeared to understand the nature of the charges against him', and that he had expressed his intention to plead not guilty. Whilst the prosecution and the defence did not formally agree that the defendant was unfit to plead, both sides advised the court that, in the circumstances, such a finding was possible and also desirable. The court reserved its decision, and in the meantime, Mr Noble was once again remanded in custody.

Mr Noble appeared again before the District Court on 7 March 2003, whereupon it was held that he was unfit to plead. Mr Noble was made the subject of a custody order pursuant to the Mentally Impaired Defendant Act 1996. In line with the 1996 Act, the Mentally Impaired Accused Review Board was responsible for the control of Mr Noble's custody order and the Board determined that he should be detained in custody at a correctional centre, alongside convicted criminals. Mr Noble remained there for almost nine more years, during which time his case was periodically reviewed by the Board. In 2010, a forensic psychologist performed an assessment of Mr Noble's intellectual functioning and concluded that he was capable of standing trial, conditional upon the provision of assistance to him throughout the legal process.

Following the psychological assessment, Mr Noble's legal representative immediately applied for a court order to allow him to plead not guilty to the original charges or, in the alternative, to pray for a discontinuance in respect of the offences with which he was initially charged. On 20 September 2010, it was determined that there would be no further prosecution. The Director of Public Prosecutions (Western Australia) advanced two reasons for the discontinuance of the prosecution. Firstly, there was the substantial period of time which Mr Noble had already spent in custody, which far exceeded any reasonable term of imprisonment he might have served had he actually been convicted on all charges. Secondly, it was conceded that there was a very limited prospect of securing a conviction in the matter given the poor quality of the available evidence. Mr Noble's legal representative applied for an order that his client was fit to plead. However, on 5 November 2010, the court determined that it did not have jurisdiction to deal with such an application. Furthermore, Mr Noble was prevented from bringing his case before any other court, having exhausted all available domestic remedies. In the circumstances, the immediate and unconditional release of Mr Noble would have been expected. However, he continued to be held in custody and had to wait for the CRPD Committee to express its dismay regarding his detention before he was finally released.

The CRPD Committee recalled that under Article 12(2) of the Convention, States Parties have the obligation to recognise that persons with disabilities enjoy legal capacity on an equal basis with others in all aspects of life. It further recalled that under Article 12(3), States Parties have an obligation to provide access to the support which persons with disabilities may require in order to exercise their legal capacity. In accordance with Article 13(1), States Parties should ensure effective access to justice for persons with disabilities on an equal basis with others, including through the provision of procedural and age-appropriate accommodations.

In preventing Mr Noble from pleading not guilty, the State Party prevented him from testing the evidence presented to him. Adequate support was not provided by the authorities of the State Party to enable Mr Noble to stand trial and plead not guilty. In the circumstances, Mr Noble could never clear his name against the charges he faced. He was treated as a sexual offender and was presumed to be guilty. The CRPD Committee concluded that there was a breach of Mr Noble's rights under Articles 12, 13 and 14 of the Convention. It held that the decision to detain or release Mr Noble was based upon his intellectual disability. In the absence of any criminal conviction against him, this had the effect of converting his disability into the core cause of his detention.

The scope of the right to legal capacity

In *Fijalkowska v Poland*, the HRC had to examine whether the involuntary commitment of the author to a psychiatric institution—in particular, the fact that she was committed without legal representation and without receiving a copy of a committal order until more than four months after the order was issued and after the expiry of the deadline to file an appeal—amounted to a violation of her rights under Articles 9 and 14 ICCPR.[6] Although the HRC came to the right conclusion in *Fijalkowska v Poland*, it would appear that its legal reasoning was flawed.[7] The HRC was of the view that 'confinement of an individual to a psychiatric institution amounts to an acknowledgement of that individual's diminished capacity, legal and otherwise'.[8] It made no distinction between the concepts of legal capacity and mental capacity.

It should be highlighted here that in *Noble v Australia*, once the author's intellectual disability was invoked and certified, he was presumed to have a cognitive impairment and, as a result, he was deemed to be unable to plead. The CRPD Committee has made it clear that 'unsoundness of mind' and other discriminatory labels are not legitimate reasons for the denial of legal capacity in the form of both legal standing and legal agency.[9] Under Article 12 of the Convention, actual or perceived deficits in mental capacity must not be used to justify the denial of legal capacity.

Legal capacity is composed of two elements: legal standing and legal agency. Legal standing concerns the substantive rights of persons with disabilities and the recognition of their legal personality. Legal agency refers to the means to act upon those substantive rights and to ensure that such actions are upheld in law. These two elements of legal capacity are inextricably linked and both are essential in order to ensure the right to equal recognition before the law. According to the CRPD Committee, mental capacity is not 'an objective, scientific and naturally occurring phenomenon' because it is dependent upon the political and social contexts in which it evolves.[10]

According to the CRPD Committee, in the majority of the State Party reports which it has examined to date, States Parties have shown a lack of awareness regarding mental and legal capacity:

> [T]he concepts of mental and legal capacity have been conflated so that where a person is considered to have impaired decision-making skills, often because of a cognitive or psychosocial disability, his or her legal capacity to make a particular decision is consequently removed. This is decided simply on the basis of the diagnosis of an impairment (status approach), or where a person makes a decision that is considered to have negative consequences (outcome approach), or where a person's decision-making skills are considered to be deficient (functional approach). The functional approach attempts to assess mental capacity and deny legal capacity accordingly. It is often based on whether a person can understand the nature and consequences of a decision and/or whether he or she can use or weigh the relevant information. This approach is flawed for two key reasons: (a) it is discriminatorily applied to people with disabilities; and (b) it presumes to be able to accurately assess the inner-workings of the human mind and, when the person does not pass the assessment, it then denies him or her a core human right—the right to equal recognition before the law. In all of those approaches, a person's disability and/or decision-making skills are taken as legitimate grounds for denying his or her legal capacity and lowering his or her status as a person before the law. Article 12 does not permit such discriminatory denial of legal capacity, but, rather, requires that support be provided in the exercise of legal capacity.[11]

The discussion which follows elaborates on the scope of the basic principles enshrined in Article 12, in light of the serious miscarriage of justice which Mr Noble suffered. According to Article 12(1), States Parties 'reaffirm that persons with disabilities have the right to recognition everywhere as persons before the law'. The CRPD Committee took the view that Article 12(1) guarantees that every human being shall be respected as a person possessing legal personality, and that this is a prerequisite for the recognition of one's legal capacity.[12]

Article 12(2) provides that States Parties 'shall recognise that persons with disabilities enjoy legal capacity on an equal basis with others in all aspects of life'. The CRPD Committee opined that legal capacity consists of the ability to be a rights-holder and also an actor under the law.[13] To be a rights-holder entitles a person with disabilities to the full protection of his or her rights within the legal system. To be deemed an 'actor' under the law empowers a disabled person to engage in transactions and to create, modify or terminate legal relationships, such as the right to marry, to divorce, to procreate or to adopt children.

The meaning of 'support' under Article 12(3)

Article 12(3) states that States Parties 'shall take appropriate measures to provide access by persons with disabilities to the support they may require in exercising their legal capacity'. The CRPD Committee elaborates on the requirement for 'support':

> Support in the exercise of legal capacity must respect the rights, will and preferences of persons with disabilities and should never amount to substitute decision-making. Article 12, paragraph 3, does not specify what form the support should take. 'Support' is a broad term that encompasses both informal and formal support arrangements, of varying types and intensity. For many persons with disabilities, the ability to plan in advance is an important form of support, whereby they can state their will and preferences which should be followed at a time when they may not be in a position to communicate their wishes to others. All persons with disabilities have the right to engage in advance planning and should be given the opportunity to do so on an equal basis with others. States parties can provide various forms of advance planning mechanisms to accommodate various preferences, but all the options should be non-discriminatory.[14]

The Committee further notes that support is a relative concept which may vary significantly in accordance with the diverse needs of persons with disabilities.[15]

In the case of *Bujdoso et al v Hungary*, intellectually disabled persons under guardianship were deprived of their right to vote.[16] The State Party failed in its duty to take the measures which were necessary to guarantee that persons with disabilities could exercise their right to legal capacity pursuant to Article 12(3) of the Convention. The authors of the complaint in *Bujdoso et al v Hungary* were denied appropriate support measures—based upon their actual or perceived disabilities—to enable them to participate in elections. In the circumstances, the CRPD Committee concluded that the domestic courts and legislature had completely misunderstood the obligations of States Parties under Article 12(3).

In *Makarov v Lithuania*, the author Mr Makarov submitted a communication on behalf of his wife, Mrs Makarova, who was the victim of a road accident and had consequently died of the injuries she sustained in the accident.[17] Mrs Makarova was not provided with a copy of the court's verdict in her case. Furthermore, she was denied the right to file an appeal in the matter, and was also denied any form of legal assistance. The prosecutor in her case failed to file a civil lawsuit on her behalf, and during the court proceedings her confidential health information was disclosed in public. The court failed to include an award of compensation for Mrs Makarova in its verdict and she was generally denied justice by the authorities of the State Party. Mrs Makarova was not provided with any form of reasonable accommodation which would have enabled her to have her position explained to the court during the proceedings. She was unable to attend the court hearings as a consequence of her injuries and her resultant disability. In the circumstances, support for Mrs Makarova was required in the form of legal representation at both first instance and on appeal. However, the State Party failed to provide her with such support.

The CRPD Committee had to decide whether the decisions of the State Party in the case of the author's wife had violated both her rights to equal recognition before the law and access to justice. Recalling its earlier jurisprudence in *Noble v Australia*, the CRPD Committee emphasised that even if States Parties had a margin of discretion to determine the procedural accommodation that would enable Mrs Makarova to exercise her legal capacity, her relevant rights must at any rate be respected. She was also not provided with any form of reasonable accommodation to enable her to attend the hearings. She was denied support, presumably under Article 12(3), since the State Party did not provide her with legal representation in first instance and for the appeal. According to the CRPD Committee, failure to provide reasonable accommodation for the author's wife to take part to the court hearings and the subsequent appeal procedure related to her case thus amounted to a violation of her rights under both Articles 12(3) and 13(1) of the Convention.

Article 12(4)

Article 12(4) provides that:

> States Parties shall ensure that all measures that relate to the exercise of legal capacity provide for appropriate and effective safeguards to prevent abuse in accordance with international human rights law. Such safeguards shall ensure that measures relating to the exercise of legal capacity respect the rights, will and preferences of the person, are free of conflict of interest and undue influence, are proportional and tailored to the person's circumstances, apply for the shortest time possible and are subject to regular review by a competent,

independent and impartial authority or judicial body. The safeguards shall be proportional to the degree to which such measures affect the person's rights and interests.

The safeguards set out in Article 12(4) must be sufficient to afford protection from abuse for persons with disabilities on an equal basis with others. The 'best interests' principle which has traditionally been applied to protect the rights of persons with disabilities is insufficient for that purpose, in accordance with the requirements of Article 12 of the Convention. According to the CRPD Committee, the determination of what constitutes the best interests of a person with disabilities should be replaced by a determination of the 'best interpretation of the person's will and preferences'.[18]

Neither Mr Noble nor Mrs Makarova benefited from the application of the above cardinal principles. As a consequence, they did not have access to their respective justice systems on an equal basis with others. In *Noble v Australia*, the legislative framework in the form of the Mentally Impaired Defendant Act 1996 was structurally discriminatory, the effect of which was to deprive Mr Noble of his legal capacity to plead. In Mrs Makarova's case, she suffered from discrimination because of the judge's failure in both the interpretation and application of the relevant law. Both Mr Noble and Mrs Makarova were denied a remedy because of judicial failings to understand the provisions of Articles 12(3) and 13 of the Convention. Sadly, Mrs Makarova died without ever having had a sense that justice had been done.

Effective access to the justice system

In accordance with Article 13 of the CRPD, independent and impartial courts must afford protection to persons with disabilities in their capacity as either direct or indirect consumers of legal services. The voices of persons with disabilities must be heard and discriminatory legislation must be challenged so that decision-makers can be held accountable. The provisions of Article 13(1) impose a new set of criteria upon courts which are in line with the international rule of law. The article enumerates the conditions which must be satisfied in order for persons with disabilities to effectively access the justice system, that is to say, to enable them to have a meaningful day in court and to benefit from due process on an equal basis with others.

The first requirement of Article 13(1) is that States Parties are under an obligation to ensure effective access to justice for persons with disabilities on an equal basis with others. In this context, 'effective access to justice' requires States Parties to repeal procedural and substantive legislative constraints which prohibit access to justice for persons with disabilities. Article 13(1) heralds a new culture of legal interpretation which reflects an understanding of the requirements of persons with disabilities. The court environment must be more conducive to, and tolerant of, human diversity and members of the judiciary must lose their arrogance and come down from their ivory towers. Article 13(1) also identifies the preconditions which must be met in order to ensure effective access to the justice system for persons with disabilities. These include the obligation of States Parties 'to provide procedural and age-appropriate accommodation'.

Reasonable accommodation and procedural accommodation

In *Gemma Beasley v Australia*, the author had a hearing impairment and communicated using Australian sign language (Auslan).[19] She was summoned to serve as a juror before the Supreme Court of New South Wales. Upon been made aware of Mrs Beasley's hearing impairment, the court requested her to send a medical certificate so that she could be excused from jury service. Mrs Beasley made numerous attempts to convince the court of her ability to serve as a juror. However, her request to perform jury service was turned down.

According to Mrs Beasley, the State Party's denial of her request to perform jury service implied that deaf persons were unsuitable or incapable of effectively serving as jurors. It further implied that the provision of Auslan interpretation to a hearing-impaired juror did not constitute 'reasonable accommodation', because a deaf person using Auslan is unable to sufficiently comprehend courtroom communications. The denial of Mrs Beasley's request also indicated that jury deliberations which included both a hearing-impaired person and her interpreter were liable to compromise the right of the accused to a fair trial. This is because the presence of a thirteenth person in the jury room in the form of the interpreter would violate the common law rule which requires that jury deliberations must remain confidential between the 12 jurors. There was a further implication that the presence of an Auslan interpreter in the jury room would unreasonably impede the effective and efficient administration of justice.

The State Party argued that Mrs Beasley's claim was beyond the purview of Article 13 of the Convention because the requirement for effective access to justice contained therein is limited to the right of persons with disabilities to gain access to justice. According to the State Party, the right to access to justice for persons with disabilities did not extend to a right for them to participate in the different components of the justice system. In this regard, the State Party relied upon the *travaux préparatoires* of the Convention to argue that 'direct and indirect participations' extend only to the parties or witnesses in a case. It was the State Party's contention that jurors are not included within the meaning of Article 13(1). The State Party further stated that recourse to Auslan interpreters would be too costly and would result in unreasonable delay of trials.

Mrs Beasley declared that she could not agree with the reasoning of the State Party and contended that her right to effective access to justice included the provision of procedural accommodation. She also argued that the provision of reasonable accommodation in the form of an Auslan interpreter was in line with the State Party's obligations under Article 5(3) of the Convention. The rights of persons with disabilities to procedural accommodation and reasonable accommodation are fundamentally different. On the one hand, the provision of procedural accommodation in Mrs Beasley's case would require the State Party to either repeal or amend its law so that an oath could be sworn by an Auslan interpreter whose presence was necessary in the jury room to enable a hearing-impaired person to participate in the jury process. Such an oath would have had the effect of excluding an Auslan interpreter from being classed as a thirteenth juror. On the other hand, the provision of reasonable accommodation simply requires that an Auslan interpreter be made available to a hearing-impaired juror. In Mrs Beasley's case, the provision of such an adjustment would have been neither unduly burdensome nor disproportionate. It is, however, important to highlight that 'procedural and age-appropriate accommodation' as encompassed in Article 13 imposes a strict obligation upon states and is not subject to the undue burden and proportionality test, contra 'reasonable accommodation' enshrined in Article 5 CRPD. The obligation under Article 13 is one which states must immediately realise given that the right to access the justice system is a civil and political right.

The CRPD Committee rejected the State Party's argument and concurred with Mrs Beasley's submissions. It was held that 'effective access to justice' refers to accessibility to the justice system in general, and that the terms 'direct and indirect participants' contained in Article 13(1) cannot be interpreted in such a way as to exclude jurors. The State Party had a duty to ensure that its citizens with disabilities were provided with effective access to justice on an equal basis with others to facilitate their effective role as 'direct and indirect participants in all phases of legal proceedings'.[20] This duty included a requirement to provide procedural and age-appropriate accommodation. Given that the performance of jury duty is an integral element of the Australian judicial landscape, such activity amounts to 'participation' in judicial proceedings. The CRPD Committee therefore held that the State Party did not take the measures which were necessary in Mrs Beasley's case to allow her to perform her jury duty, namely the provision of an Auslan interpreter. It therefore recommended that the State Party should make amendments to its laws, regulations, policies and programmes, in close consultation with persons with disabilities and their representative organisations, to ensure access to justice on an equal basis with others for persons with hearing impairments. The CRPD Committee also ordered the State Party to provide Mrs Beasley with an appropriate remedy, including adequate compensation.

The provision of procedural accommodation is a cornerstone of the justice system which is indispensable to guaranteeing fairness to persons with disabilities, irrespective of their capacity or status, as direct or indirect participants in the justice system. Procedural accommodation is a core value of Article 13 which enhances the spirit of the rule of law. The barrier which prevented Mrs Beasley from serving as a juror was the failure to provide her with procedural accommodation. Australian law had the effect of marginalising her and making her vulnerable to discrimination. The legal system also failed to provide her with a remedy for the discrimination and humiliation which she suffered.

In *Makarov v Lithuania*, the CRPD Committee considered the precedent for the provision of procedural accommodation which was established in *Gemma Beasley v Australia*. The CRPD Committee reaffirmed that, whilst States Parties have a margin of discretion to determine the procedural accommodations which are necessary to enable persons with disabilities to exercise their legal capacity, the relevant rights of the person concerned must first and foremost be respected. That did not happen in Mrs Makarova's case. As the direct victim of the accident in question, she was clearly a 'direct participant' in the relevant legal proceedings but was nonetheless denied access to the justice system in clear violation of her rights under Article 13(1) of the Convention.

Conclusion

The case law which has been considered above demonstrates that the normative contents of the Convention have not yet been effectively harmonised within domestic legal systems. Whilst judges are often criticised for their judicial activism, they nevertheless continue to construe legal instruments very narrowly in the field of disability law. Given its independent and impartial role, the judiciary has not been proactive in declaring legislation such as the Australian Jury Act 1977 of New South Wales to be discriminatory, or in declaring it to be either unconstitutional, or null and void, on the basis that it is contrary to the spirit of the Convention. This is a matter of serious concern given the civil nature of the rights which are enshrined in Articles 12 and 13 of the Convention. Instead, judges have deliberately chosen to uphold laws which are, by their very nature, structurally discriminatory, per *Bujdoso et al v Hungary*. It for this reason that the framers of the Convention required that there should be appropriate training for those working in the field of administration of justice, including the police and prison staff, regarding the requirements of Article 13(2) of the Convention. Such training is needed to ensure effective access to justice for persons with disabilities.

Summary of Concluding Observations and Recommendations

In its General Comment No.1 on Article 12 (Equal recognition before the law), the CRPD Committee has made a series of recommendations on how States Parties and other relevant stakeholders can implement Articles 12 and 13.

Article 12

The Committee called upon States Parties to ensure that persons with disabilities have access to legal representation on an equal basis with others. This is necessary to ensure equal opportunity before the law and equal standing before courts and tribunals for persons with disabilities. The Committee stressed that the right to legal capacity of persons with disabilities should not be the subject of interference, and where such interference does occur, persons with disabilities must be permitted to challenge it, either in their own right or with the benefit of legal representation, to defend their rights, where necessary, through the courts. Persons with disabilities should not be excluded from performing legal or judicial roles. Nor should they be precluded from performing civic duties, such as participating as jurors or as witnesses in trials.

The Committee also recommended that appropriate training must be given to police officers, social workers and other first responders to ensure that they recognise the full legal capacity of persons with disabilities, and that they respect their right to be treated as equal before the law. This requires that the same weight be attributed to their statements and complaints as is afforded to those of non-disabled persons. Full recognition of the legal capacity of persons with disabilities requires that they have the opportunity to testify in a tribunal or court of law on an equal basis with others. It is important that the judiciary receive training so that they fully understand their obligations regarding the legal capacity of persons with disabilities, such obligations to include upholding their rights to both legal agency and legal standing. Where necessary, States Parties must also ensure that suitable training is provided to other stakeholders, including legal decision-makers and service providers, to ensure that persons with disabilities are treated as equal before the law.

The Committee also recommended reform of the national legislation of States Parties which premises disability upon the application of status, functional or outcome-based models of disability. Such models must be replaced with those which are based upon supported decision-making, and they must be adequately resourced, so that persons with disabilities can properly navigate the legal system. This is in accordance with their rights which are enshrined in the general principles of Article 3 of the Convention and the key provisions of General Comment No.1. It includes the requirement to provide support for persons with disabilities in line with their rights, will and preferences, rather than providing support for them in accordance with what others perceive as being in their best interests. States Parties must abolish substituted decision-making in all spheres of life, and to this end it is necessary for them to review their legislation and to repeal or amend where it is not in line with the Convention. Where necessary, States Parties must initiate new policies in the areas of mental capacity and mental health law. They must make greater efforts to ensure that they have robust systems in place for data collection and research programmes in order to establish supported decision-making regimes which meet their national requirements. Finally, States Parties must ensure that asylum seekers and refugees within their jurisdictions can fully exercise their rights as enshrined in the Convention.

Article 13

The Committee has also made a series of recommendations concerning Article 13 of the CRPD (Access to Justice). Firstly, it recommended that there is a need to develop and implement capacity-building programmes concerning the rights of persons with disabilities for key stakeholders in the legal system, including the judiciary, prosecutors, police officers and prison staff. There is also a need to design and implement a decision-making regime for persons with intellectual or psychosocial disabilities who are taking part in court proceedings. Sufficient resources should be allocated by States Parties for these purposes. Where necessary, persons with disabilities should have recourse to legal aid, to ensure they have proper access to all areas of the law. It is also necessary to remove fees which are currently charged to access courts and employment tribunals, and which impede access to justice for persons with disabilities. States Parties must also ensure that there is adequate procedural accommodation for persons with disabilities who are participating in the legal system, such measures to include the provision of sign language interpreters for persons with hearing impediments, so that they can participate as jurors, on an equal basis with others. Persons with disabilities should also be empowered to work in the justice system, and States Parties should provide them with all necessary support to enable them to do so.

States Parties should recognise the diversity of both the disability community and the individual requirements of persons with disabilities. This recognition is necessary to ensure that persons with disabilities can fully access the justice system on an equal basis with others. States Parties must respect the autonomy of persons with disabilities and recognise the principle of legal capacity for all. They must also ensure that they have effective systems for communicating with persons with disabilities, to facilitate their full participation in all aspects of life. States Parties must recognise the complex nature of intersectional discrimination and its particular impact upon persons with disabilities. Intersectional discrimination includes discrimination based upon cultural practices, religion and other forms of social identification. To conclude, States Parties must also ensure that people are not identified purely upon the basis or otherwise of disability.

Notes

1 CRPD Committee, General Comment No. 1 on Article 12 (Equal Recognition Before the Law), 11 April 2014, CRPD/C/GC/1, para.30.
2 Ibid.
3 CRPD Committee, Concluding Observations on the Initial Report of Qatar, 2 October 2015, CRPD/C/QAT/CO/1, para.23.
4 CRPD Committee, Concluding Observations on the Initial Report of Armenia, 8 May 2017, CRPD/C/ARM/CO/1, para.21.
5 *James Marlon Noble v Australia* (2016) CRPD/C/16/7/2012.
6 *Fijalkowska v Poland* (2006) CCPR/C/84/D/1061/2002.
7 See discussion on *Fijalkowska v Poland* in Chapter 5.
8 *Fijalkowska v Poland*, para.8.3.
9 General Comment No.1, para.13.
10 Ibid, para.14.
11 Ibid, para.15.
12 Ibid, para.11.
13 Ibid, para.12.
14 Ibid, para.17.

15 Ibid, para.18.
16 *Bujdoso et al v Hungary* (2013) CRPD/C/10/D/4/2011.
17 *Makarov v Lithuania* (forthcoming) CRPD/C/18/D/30/2015.
18 General Comment No.1, para.21.
19 *Gemma Beasley v Australia* (2016) CRPD/C/15/D/11/2013.
20 Ibid, para.8.9.

5

SECURITY OF THE PERSON

Introduction

The right to liberty of the person is narrowly defined as freedom from confinement of the body.[1] On the other hand, the right to security of the person refers to the protection of individuals against deliberate infliction of mental or bodily injury, regardless of whether or not the victim is detained.[2] These practices may also amount to torture, cruel, inhuman or degrading treatment as defined by Article 1(1) CAT, Article 7 ICCPR and Article 15 CRPD. The restraint of the liberty of persons with disabilities can take numerous forms solely on the basis of actual or perceived impairment. Examples include detention of persons with disabilities in institutions, either with or without their informed consent, or through the use of substituted decision-making regimes. In its Concluding Observations on the initial report of Peru, the CRPD Committee expressed concern on the use of continuous forcible medication, including neuroleptics, and poor material conditions in psychiatric institutions where some persons have been institutionalised for more than ten years without appropriate rehabilitation services.[3] It is more problematic when persons with psychosocial impairments are charged with criminal offences. In many cases, confessions are extracted from them by illegal or unfair means.

This is why Article 9 ICCPR and Articles 14 and 15 CRPD provide the essential safeguards prior to a person's arrest, and also during interrogation, questioning, detention and trial. States Parties must be reminded of their other international obligations under both Articles 14 and 16 ICCPR when enacting legislation. Article 14 ICCPR reinforces the recognition of the right to access to justice systems by specifying that 'everyone shall be entitled to a fair and public hearing by a competent, independent and impartial tribunal established by law'. Article 16 ICCPR expressly endorses the right to be recognised everywhere as a person before the law. The failure of States Parties to harmonise their legislative frameworks in conformity with the standards of international public law cannot be excused as this omission may result in serious miscarriages of justice.

Persons with disabilities may also be deprived of their liberty and personal security through forced institutionalisation amounting to mental and/or physical torture. As we discussed in the previous chapter, this is an artefact of the medical model of disability whereby the will, autonomy, and preferences of persons with disabilities are simply ignored. When persons with psychosocial disabilities are confined in hospitals without their consent, the domestic legislation of States Parties often do not comply with the provisions of Articles 14 and 15 of the CRPD. This is so as many States Parties still have mental health legislation which is discriminatory either by its very nature or in its application. For example, the CRPD Committee observed that the applicable domestic legislation on mental health in Denmark allowed for compulsory, non-consensual hospitalisation or treatment of persons with mental or psychosocial impairment in medical institutions if the person is considered to be a danger to himself or to others.[4] Under Article 14 CRPD, this approximates to a deprivation of liberty and/or security on the basis of disability. The free and informed consent of a person with psychosocial or intellectual disabilities should be required before treatment in, or committal to, a mental health institution. This can be achieved only when substituted decision-making regimes are replaced with those which are premised upon supported decision-making. It is necessary to further ensure the physical and mental integrity of persons with psychosocial impairments in line with Article 17 CRPD.

In this chapter, the safeguards against the arbitrary deprivation of liberty, the protection of the security of the person and freedom from torture in accordance with Articles 14 and 15 of the Convention will be examined. Their interplay with other provisions of the Convention, such as the rights to health, to habilitation and rehabilitation, and accessibility will be explored (Articles 25, 26 and 9 CRPD respectively). The rights to health, rehabilitation and accessibility are categorised as being of an economic and social nature.[5] Traditionally, such rights were considered to be non-justiciable, because their implementation depends upon the financial resources which are available to a State Party.[6] The question that arises is to what extent States Parties have a margin of discretion in upholding the rights to health, habilitation and rehabilitation in circumstances where persons with disabilities are detained, imprisoned and tortured.

Liberty, detention and imprisonment

The claims of the author in *James Marlon Noble v Australia* under Articles 5, 12 and 13 CRPD have already been examined in the previous chapter.[7] Mr Noble also claimed that his rights under Article 14(1)(b) of the Convention were violated. Article 14(1)(b) provides that persons with disabilities should not be deprived of their liberty unlawfully or arbitrarily. It also requires that any deprivation of liberty should be in conformity with the law and that the existence of a disability shall in no case justify a deprivation of liberty. Mr Noble submitted that he was deprived of his liberty pursuant to discriminatory legislation in the form of the Criminal Law Mentally Impaired Defendants Act (MIDA) 1996, in breach of Article 14(1)(b) of the Convention. Had this not been the case, it was unlikely that Mr Noble would have been convicted of the offences with which he was charged. In the event that he had pleaded guilty and been convicted, he would probably have been released from prison within three years. Instead, Mr Noble, an innocent person, was imprisoned for more than ten years. He alleged that, whilst in prison, he was at significant risk of harm from other prisoners and that he was subjected to unjustifiable restrictions of his liberty.

Following his release from prison, Mr Noble was subject to ten civil detention conditions which were oppressive in nature. He was obliged to engage in programmes at the direction of a supervising officer. He was forbidden from possessing or using any illicit substance, including cannabis, nor was he permitted to consume alcohol. At the direction of his supervising officer, Mr Noble was required to undergo regular random testing for all forms of illicit substances and alcohol. He was forbidden from having any contact with his alleged victims and also from having contact with any female children under the age of 16 years, unless supervised by an adult who had been previously approved by his supervising officer. Mr Noble was not allowed to stay away from his primary residence overnight unless he was staying at a place which was pre-approved by the Mentally Impaired Defendants Review Board. Nor was he allowed to change his address without the Board's prior approval. Mr Noble was not even permitted to enter licensed premises and he was also required to submit to breath-testing as requested by the police.[8]

The CRPD Committee was of the opinion that

> Following the decision of the District Court of Western Australia of March 2003 according to which the author was declared unfit to plead, he was detained in prison without having been convicted of any offence, and after all the charges against him were quashed in application of the Mentally Impaired Defendants Act.[9]

The decision to detain Mr Noble in the absence of a criminal conviction was based upon the assessment of the State Party's authorities of his intellectual disability. This had the effect of converting Mr Noble's disability into the core cause of his detention. This was a violation of Article 14(1)(b) of the Convention which expressly provides that 'the existence of a disability shall in no case justify a deprivation of liberty'.

It is clear that many important safeguards which are contained in international human rights treaties were not complied with in Mr Noble's case. The ICCPR, which comprises the right to liberty and security of the person in its Article 9, had been ratified by Australia along with its Optional Protocol. However, the ICCPR was presumed to be inoperative and, as such, inapplicable in Mr Noble's case. The first principle enshrined in Article 9 ICCPR is that no one should be subjected to arbitrary arrest or detention or deprived of his liberty, except on such grounds and in accordance with such procedure as are established by law. In Mr Noble's case, it is highly doubtful whether the police carried out a fair enquiry based on reasonable suspicion or upon prima facie evidence.[10] A second requirement of Article 9 ICCPR is that, at the time of arrest, a person shall be promptly informed of the reason for his arrest and of the charges against him.[11] In Mr Noble's case, it was only at the time when a determination of his cognitive impairment was made that it was revealed to the court that he could not take a plea. This determination was not made at the time of his arrest, detention or interrogation, and it is unclear as to how the police officers communicated with Mr Noble during this period, bearing in mind that he was suspected of serious sexual offences.

The final requirement of Article 9 ICCPR is that, upon arrest and being detained on a criminal charge, the accused person must be brought without delay before a judge who will exercise judicial power over him.[12] In Mr Noble's case, it is not disputed that he was brought before the court. However, he did not receive a fair trial within a reasonable time as he did not have an opportunity to plead to the charges. It was only following Mr Noble's mental health assessment in 2012 that he was finally entitled to take proceedings before a court, almost a decade after his initial detention. This clearly constituted an unreasonable delay in being able to challenge the unlawfulness of his detention, even more so because he had to wait for the CRPD Committee to have his civil detention conditions set aside. Moreover, notwithstanding the injustice which Mr Noble had suffered, the issue of compensation was only raised for the first time before the CRPD Committee.

A similar situation to that of Mr Noble's had previously arisen before the HRC in the case of *Fardon v Australia*.[13] Mr Fardon was sentenced to 14 years' imprisonment for rape, sodomy and unlawful assault on a female. His prison sentence expired on 30 June 2003. However, in June 2003, the Queensland Dangerous Prisoners (Sexual Offenders) Act (DPSOA) 2003 came into force. The Attorney-General of Queensland filed an application under the DPSOA 2003 for an order that the author be detained for an indefinite period. The Supreme Court of Queensland held that the provisions in the DPSOA 2003 were constitutional. Since the author was alleged to be a serious danger to the community, he had to be indefinitely detained. The High Court of Australia dismissed the author's appeal contesting the constitutional validity of the provisions authorising Queensland courts to detain persons under the DPSOA 2003.

The HRC had to determine whether the sections of the DPSOA 2003 which provided for the lawful detention of Mr Fardon after the end of his 14-year term of imprisonment were arbitrary in nature. It held that there had been a violation of Mr Fardon's right to liberty and security under Article 9(1) of the ICCPR for the following reasons:

(1) the author had already served his 14-year term of imprisonment and yet he continued, in actual fact, to be subjected to imprisonment in pursuance of a law which characterises his continued incarceration under the same prison regime as detention. This purported detention amounted,

in substance, to a fresh term of imprisonment which, unlike detention proper, is not permissible in the absence of a conviction for which
imprisonment is a sentence prescribed by law.

(2)   Imprisonment is penal in character. It can only be imposed on conviction for an offence in the same proceedings in which the offence is
tried. The author's further term of imprisonment was the result of Court
orders made, some 14 years after his conviction and sentence, in respect
of predicted future criminal conduct which had its basis in the very
offence for which he had already served his sentence. This new sentence
was the result of fresh proceedings, though nominally characterised as
'civil proceedings', and fall within the prohibition of Article 15 paragraph 1 of the Covenant. In this regard, the Committee further observes
that, since the DPSOA was enacted in 2003 shortly before the expiry of
the author's sentence for an offence for which he had been convicted in
1989 and which became an essential element in the Court orders for his
continued incarceration, the DPSOA was being retroactively applied to
the author. This also falls within the prohibition of Article 15 paragraph 1
of the Covenant, in that he has been subjected to a heavier penalty
'than was applicable at the time when the criminal offence was committed'. The Committee therefore considers that detention pursuant to
proceedings incompatible with article 15 is necessarily arbitrary within
the meaning of article 9, paragraph 1, of the Covenant.

(3)   The DPSOA prescribed a particular procedure to obtain the relevant
Court orders. This particular procedure, as the State Party conceded,
was designed to be civil in character. It did not, therefore, meet the due
process guarantees required under Article 14 of the Covenant for a fair
trial in which a penal sentence is imposed.

(4)   The 'detention' of the author as a 'prisoner' under the DPSOA was
ordered because it was feared that he might be a danger to the community in the future and for purposes of his rehabilitation. The concept
of feared or predicted dangerousness to the community applicable in the
case of past offenders is inherently problematic. It is essentially based on
opinion as distinct from factual evidence, even if that evidence consists
in the opinion of psychiatric experts. But psychiatry is not an exact science. The DPSOA, on the one hand, requires the Court to have regard
to the opinion of psychiatric experts on future dangerousness but, on
the other hand, requires the Court to make a finding of fact of dangerousness. While Courts are free to accept or reject expert opinion and
are required to consider all other available relevant evidence, the reality
is that the Courts must make a finding of fact on the suspected future
behaviour of a past offender which may or may not materialise. To avoid
arbitrariness, in these circumstances, the State Party should have demonstrated that the author's rehabilitation could not have been achieved
by means less intrusive than continued imprisonment or even detention,
particularly as the State Party had a continuing obligation under Article
10 paragraph 3 of the Covenant to adopt meaningful measures for the

reformation, if indeed it was needed, of the author throughout the 14 years during which he was in prison.[14]

In *Noble v Australia*, the CRPD Committee did not analyse the case in the light of the provisions of Article 9(1) ICCPR as applied by the HRC in *Fardon v Australia*. Nor did the CRPD Committee directly rely on the provisions of Article 15(1) ICCPR when coming to its final decision.[15] Mr Noble was found guilty of an act which did not constitute a criminal offence at the time at which he was charged with the offence and, worse still, a heavier penalty was imposed upon him than would otherwise have been the case. It would appear that the HRC's jurisprudence on Articles 9(1) and 15(1) of the ICCPR, with its careful analysis of the normative contents of these Articles, was insufficiently considered by the CRPD Committee in Mr Noble's case. This may be illustrated by reference to the ten civil conditions which were imposed upon Mr Noble after his release from jail. The CRPD Committee did not consider the claim of the Mr Noble under Article 14(2) CRPD insofar as he failed to exhaust domestic remedies that could have resulted in an alteration of the conditions to which he objected. Article 14(2) CRPD states that:

> States Parties shall ensure that if persons with disabilities are deprived of their liberty through any process, they are, on an equal basis with others, entitled to guarantees in accordance with international human rights law and shall be treated in compliance with the objectives and principles of this Convention, including by provision of reasonable accommodation.

The CRPD Committee should have instead been guided by the provisions of Article 15(1) ICCPR. Article 14(2) CRPD equally embraces the principles enshrined in Article 15(1) ICCPR. Whilst being guided by the precedential value set out by the HRC in *Fardon v Australia*, the CRPD Committee could have found the claim of Mr Noble under Article 14(2) CRPD to be admissible.

Freedom from torture or cruel, inhuman or degrading treatment or punishment

It should be recalled that in *Noble v Australia*, the CRPD Committee also held that the indefinite detention of the author for more than 13 years constituted inhuman or degrading treatment. The irreparable psychological effects that indefinite detention may have on the detained person and the repeated acts of violence to which he was subjected during his detention amounted to a violation of Article 15 CRPD. Article 15 CRPD states that:

1. No one shall be subjected to torture or to cruel, inhuman or degrading treatment or punishment. In particular, no one shall be subjected without out his or her free consent to medical or scientific experimentation.

2. States Parties shall take all effective legislative, administrative, judicial or other measures to prevent persons with disabilities, on an equal basis with others, from being subjected to torture or cruel, inhuman or degrading treatment or punishment.

Article 15(1) CRPD has adopted the definition contained in Article 1(1) of the Convention against Torture and Other Cruel, Inhuman or Degrading Treatment or Punishment (CAT). In *X v Tanzania*, the CRPD Committee demonstrated its willingness to be consistent with the international law definition of its sister treaty body, i.e. CAT.[16] The core elements of torture include: (i) severe pain or suffering; (ii) intent; (iii) purpose; and (iv) state involvement. Adducing evidence in support of the four elements may prove to be very difficult and may cause injustice to litigants both before domestic and international forums. The questions that arise are whether Article 15 CRPD can be invoked:

- when the state avails itself of the defence of good faith which negates the element of intention or purpose, or where the state argues that its intention is to protect a person with disability from more pain;
- where torture is alleged and the author claims that the state was only negligent, i.e. that it falls below the standard of intent and/or purpose; and
- where the state has completely failed to act, with this resulting in torture.

It is submitted that—as is the case in many jurisdictions—once an allegation of torture is made, the burden of disproving it should shift to the state. The standard of proof should be beyond reasonable doubt. The other issue which calls for consideration is on the situation of the victim where the state has completely failed to act to prevent torture or where the act of torture is inflicted by a non-state actor.

Torture by omission

In *X v Tanzania*, Mr X's left arm was chopped off and was never found. Yet, his attackers were never arrested nor prosecuted. The CRPD Committee upheld the definition of torture as is enshrined in Article 1(1) of CAT which provides that:

the term 'torture' means any act by which severe pain or suffering, whether physical or mental, is intentionally inflicted on a person for such purposes as obtaining from him or a third person information or a confession, punishing him for an act he or a third person has committed or is suspected of having committed, or intimidating or coercing him or a third person, or for any reason based on discrimination of any kind, *when such pain or suffering is inflicted by or at the instigation of or with the consent or acquiescence of a public official or other person acting in an official capacity* [. . .][17]

The CRPD Committee recalled that the obligation on States Parties to prevent torture and inhuman and degrading treatment violations applies to acts committed by both state and non-state actors.[18] The CRPD Committee took the view that expedition and effectiveness in the arrest and prosecution are particularly important in the adjudication of torture cases. The suffering experienced by Mr X owing to the lack of action (i.e. omission) by the State Party that would allow the effective prosecution of the suspected perpetrators of the crime thus became a cause of re-victimisation and amounted to psychological torture and/or ill-treatment. For these reasons, the CRPD Committee established that the State of Tanzania had violated Article 15 of the Convention.

As previously mentioned, in the field of civil rights, including the right to liberty and security and the right to freedom from torture, States Parties' obligations are onerous and strict. They are obligations which are non-delegable, meaning that they cannot be outsourced to non-state actors. Even if States Parties delegate the responsibility of arrest, prosecution and detention to private companies, they will still be liable for the acts and omissions of these non-state actors. This is why it is crucial for States Parties to legislate in a manner consistent with international norms which do not expose their citizens to material acts or omissions which may constitute torture. They also have a duty to harmonise their legislation so that persons with disabilities are not exposed to unbearable pressures which are distressing in the extreme.

Medical or scientific experimentation

The second premise of Article 15(1) CRPD stipulates that '[i]n particular, no one shall be subjected without his or her free consent to medical or scientific experimentation'. Strict adherence to the requirement of intent or purpose in situations where persons with disabilities are unable to consent freely to medical or scientific experimentation may be problematic. Some examples are the administration of psychotropic drugs or other forced psychiatric treatment to persons with disabilities in institutions.[19] In its Concluding Observations on the initial report of Costa Rica, the CRPD Committee was appalled at the adoption of Bill No.17777 on Biomedical Research which authorised the guardians of persons declared legally incapable to make decisions concerning their participation in scientific experimentation and research without their free and informed consent.[20]

Intent cannot and should not be interpreted as meaning the aim, plan or purpose of the state, but rather it can be inferred from its surrounding circumstances, including the person's impairment, age, family background, and other circumstances which led the person to be in institutional care. Nowak argued that

> [T]he requirement of intent in article 1 of the Convention against Torture can be effectively implied where a person has been discriminated against on the basis of disability. This is particularly relevant in the context of medical treatment of persons with disabilities, where serious violations and discrimination against persons with disabilities may be masked as 'good intentions' on the part of health professionals. Purely negligent conduct

lacks the intent required under article 1, and may constitute ill-treatment if it leads to severe pain and suffering.[21]

This analysis sheds light on the overall understanding of the entire scope of Article 15 CRPD, when read in conjunction with Article 1(1) CAT, as particular and express reference is made to any reason based on discrimination of any kind. The latter includes disability-based discrimination as exemplified by both *Noble v Australia* and *X v Tanzania*.

The CRPD has always been mindful of examining Articles 14(2) and 15 CRPD in the light of other provisions of the CRPD, including Articles 9, 25 and 26, which relate to accessibility, health and rehabilitation respectively. While this approach is highly commendable, it is also important for international treaty bodies to guarantee consistency, certainty and predictability in international public law.

Liberty, detention and accessibility

In the case of *X v Argentina*, the author claimed that he was deprived of his liberty following the failure by the State of Argentina to provide him with appropriate measures on an equal basis with others whilst in detention.[22] Mr X is an Argentine national who was held in pre-trial detention at the Marco Paz Federal Prison Complex II (MPFPC). On 27 January 2010, while still in detention, he underwent spinal surgery to replace a cervical disc. However, the following day, Mr X suffered a stroke which left him with multiple disabilities, including a sensory balance disorder, a cognitive disorder and impaired visuospatial orientation. With the permission of the Federal Criminal Court, Mr X was subsequently transferred to the FLENI Institute, a rehabilitation centre in Escobar. Whilst at the FLENI Institute, Mr X's condition stabilised and he commenced rehabilitation.

On 7 April 2010, the FLENI Institute informed the Federal Criminal Court that Mr X's recovery was such that he could continue his rehabilitation as a day patient. On the same day, he applied to have his pre-trial detention converted to house arrest, on the ground that this was the most appropriate form of detention which was compatible with his best treatment. Detention in the form of house arrest would have enabled Mr X to avail himself of the services of a carer and of disability-friendly facilities. House arrest would have allowed Mr X easy access to the FLENI Institute. However, the Federal Court rejected Mr X's application for house arrest on 6 August 2010 and instead ordered his transfer to the central prison hospital of the Buenos Aires Federal Penitentiary Complex (BAFPC). The Court maintained that Mr X's pre-trial detention did not prevent him from undergoing appropriate rehabilitation therapy.

On 15 August 2011, the Federal Criminal Court once again rejected Mr X's request for house arrest on the grounds that his physical and mental condition did not preclude him from receiving the appropriate treatment and care necessary for his recovery in prison. This decision was the subject of an appeal to the Federal Chamber of the Criminal Court of Cassation. On 18 November 2011, it was upheld and the proceedings were referred back to the Federal Criminal Court. However, on 29 December 2011, the Federal Criminal Court rejected Mr X's application for house arrest once again on the basis that the risks inherent in his travelling to and from the rehabilitation centre were the same, regardless of whether he was in custody or under house arrest. A further appeal against this decision was lodged with the Federal Chamber of the Criminal Court of Cassation on 5 January 2012. It was on the basis of these facts that Mr X claimed a violation of his rights under Article 14(2) of the Convention.

Mr X submitted that in considering whether he was unfit for prison, the court ought to have taken into consideration several factors, including the facilities at the prison hospital, his state of health, the nature of the prison infrastructure and the extent to which incarceration might adversely affect his health. Mr X argued that the lack of appropriate infrastructure at the prison hospital for a person with his disability and the second-rate conditions of health-care and detention there constituted an affront to his dignity. Mr X also complained that during the first eight months of his incarceration, he had been placed in a first-floor cell where he had no access to fresh air or natural light, contrary to Article 14(2) of the CRPD.

The reasoning of the CRPD Committee in Mr X's case was based upon Article 14(2) CRPD and also upon application of the accessibility principles which are enshrined in Article 9 CRPD. In line with Article 3 CRPD, accessibility is a general principle of the Convention. It follows that it applies to situations in which persons with disabilities are deprived of their liberty. Article 14(2) CRPD unequivocally enunciates that States Parties are under an obligation to ensure that the deprivation of liberty of persons with disabilities should be treated 'in compliance with the objectives and principles of this Convention'. In Mr X's case, the State Party had a duty to ensure that it respected the right to accessibility of persons with disabilities who are held in custody. States Parties must take all necessary measures, including the identification and removal of obstacles to access, as well as to ensure that persons with disabilities in prison may live independently and fully participate in all aspects of daily prison life on an equal basis with others.

Liberty and institutionalisation

Given that Article 14(2) CRPD embraces the principles enshrined in Article 9 ICCPR, it is interesting to note how the HRC applied those principles in a case concerning a person with disabilities which was considered by the HRC prior to the adoption of the CRPD.[23] The decision in *Fijalkowska v Poland* is also instructive with regard to the procedural safeguards which are necessary to ensure that the institutionalisation of a person with disabilities conforms to the standards set down in Article 9 ICCPR. The HRC's reasoning reflects the fact that the institutionalisation of persons with disabilities is repugnant to their fundamental right to liberty and security. The latter is a right from which States Parties cannot derogate.

Ms Fijalkowska had been suffering from schizophrenic paranoia since 1986. On 12 February 1998, she was committed to a psychiatric institution following a court order. Ms Fijalkowska left the institution on 29 April 1998 and continued treatment as an outpatient until 22 July 1998, whereupon her treatment was completed. On 1 June 1998, Ms Fijalkowska requested copies of the transcript of the court hearing and committal order of February 1998. She received a copy of the court's decision on 18 June 1998 and lodged an appeal against it six days later. Ms Fijalkowski's appeal was dismissed on the ground that she had missed the statutory deadline for lodging such an appeal. However, she was instructed on how to lodge an appeal to the Supreme Court. Ms Fijalkowska was assigned a legal aid lawyer to prepare her Supreme Court appeal which was nevertheless later rejected. Ms Fijalkowska's subsequent claim, in which she sought a judicial review of the Polish Law on Psychiatric Health Protection, the legislation which provided for her confinement, was also rejected by the Supreme Court.

Ms Fijalkowska contended that she had been committed to a psychiatric institution against her will. She argued that the Law on Psychiatric Health Protection, which formed the basis of the decision to confine her, was incompatible with the provisions of Article 7 ICCPR, which prohibits torture, and also of Article 9 ICCPR, on deprivation of liberty. She further argued that she had been confined to a mental institution without legal representation and that she had not received a copy of the committal order until 18 June 1998, by which time it was too late to lodge an appeal against it.

The HRC held that the failure to provide Ms Fijalkowska with legal representation or with a copy of the committal order at the time of her committal amounted to arbitrary detention within the meaning of Article 9 of the ICCPR. The HRC was also of the view that a State Party had a particular obligation to protect vulnerable individuals within its jurisdiction, including the mentally impaired. The HRC acknowledged that where an individual's mental health is so impaired, the issuance of a committal order may be unavoidable in order to prevent harm to the individual or others.[24] However, in the present case, no such special circumstances were advanced. For these reasons, the HRC found that Ms Fijalkowska's committal order was arbitrary and constituted a breach of Article 9(1) ICCPR.

The HRC recommended that the State of Poland should provide Ms Fijalkowska with an adequate remedy, including compensation, and that it should make the necessary legislative changes to ensure that similar violations do not occur in future. Persons with disabilities are more frequently exposed to discriminatory practices as a result of mental health legislation and policy choices. The HRC indicated that States Parties should abolish legal provisions which legitimise the involuntary committal of persons with disabilities to mental health facilities where such confinement is based upon actual or perceived impairments. This mirrors the subsequent position of the CRPD Committee regarding the prohibition upon involuntary committal based purely upon actual or perceived impairment, for instance, in the case of *James Marlon Noble v Australia*.

Regrettably, the legislative frameworks of many States Parties still discriminate against persons with disabilities and permit their non-consensual and involuntary treatment. As a result, the institutionalisation of persons with disabilities remains a global problem. However, the advent of the CRPD has brought about changes. Since its establishment, the CRPD Committee has pressed States Parties to review the legal basis of the committal of persons with psychosocial impairments to mental health institutions. For example, in relation to the Republic of Korea, the CRPD Committee recommended that 'until the law is amended, all cases of deprivation of liberty of persons with disabilities in hospitals and specialized institutions [should] be reviewed and that the review [should] include a possibility of appeal'.[25]

In situations where States Parties do not have legislation in place providing for a total ban on the deprivation of liberty, the possibility of legislative review allows persons with psychosocial or intellectual disabilities to challenge their arbitrary, but otherwise lawful detention. The HRC made such a recommendation to the Russian Federation in light of the State Party's denial of legal capacity to persons with mental disabilities. In its Concluding Observations on the Russian Federation, the HRC noted that persons with disabilities who are denied legal capacity 'have no legal recourse to challenge other violations of their rights, including ill-treatment or abuse by guardians and/or staff of institutions they are confined to, which is aggravated by the lack of an independent inspection mechanism regarding mental health institutions'.[26]

The use of forced institutionalisation is a clear infringement of the right to personal liberty and security of persons with disabilities, in accordance with Article 14 CRPD. States Parties are under an obligation to abolish legislative and policy measures which either permit or continue to uphold involuntary commitment, especially when such commitment is imposed by threat. The UN Special Rapporteur on Torture and Other Cruel, Inhuman or Degrading Treatment or Punishment has also called for the repeal of legislation which allows for the institutionalisation of persons with psychosocial impairments on the basis of their disability, without their prior consent.[27]

The CRPD Committee has continually pushed for States Parties to initiate a process of de-institutionalisation, in line with the provisions of Article 19 CRPD concerning the right to independent living and to be included in the community.[28] Persons with disabilities who are deprived of their liberty are often exposed to forced treatment in circumstances where their living conditions may be such as to cause irreversible damage to their mental and physical integrity. The human rights model of disability requires that persons with intellectual or psychosocial impairments are free from bodily confinement. It also requires that the security of the person must be recognised as freedom 'from injury to the body and the mind, or bodily and mental integrity'.[29]

Liberty, security and integrity

Article 17 CRPD provides for the protection of the physical and mental integrity of persons with disabilities in the context of involuntary treatment. It will be recalled that in *X v Argentina*, Mr X alleged that the delay in providing medical treatment amounted to a violation of his physical and mental integrity. In a reasoned decision, the CRPD Committee opined that the State Party was under an obligation to ensure that

> the conditions of detention in which persons with disabilities are held do not become more onerous or cause greater physical and psychological suffering of an extent that would constitute cruel, inhuman or degrading treatment or that would *undermine their physical and mental integrity*.[30]

In its first General Comment, the CRPD Committee shed further light on the issue of mental and physical integrity:

> As has been stated by the Committee in several concluding observations, forced treatment by psychiatric and other health and medical professionals is a violation of the right to equal recognition before the law and an infringement of the rights to personal integrity (art. 17); freedom from torture (art. 15); and freedom from violence, exploitation and abuse (art. 16). This practice denies the legal capacity of a person to choose medical treatment and is therefore a violation of article 12 of the Convention. States parties must, instead, respect the legal capacity of persons with disabilities to make decisions at all times, including in crisis situations; must ensure that accurate and accessible information is provided about service options and that non-medical approaches are made available; and must provide access to independent support. States parties have an obligation to provide access to support for decisions regarding psychiatric and other medical treatment.[31]

Forced treatment is particularly problematic for persons with cognitive disabilities and legislation which provides for it should be abolished. Domestic policies which promote such practices should be also abandoned. Despite empirical evidence of the lack of efficacy of forced treatment and also the testimony of mental health systems users who have experienced deep pain and trauma as a result, States Parties persist with such archaic mental health care regimes.[32] The CRPD Committee therefore recommended that States Parties ensure that decisions which concern a person's mental or physical integrity should be taken only with the free and informed consent of the person concerned.

Liberty, health and rehabilitation

The CRPD Committee has reaffirmed that involuntary or non-consensual commitment of persons with disabilities on health care grounds contradicts the total proscription on deprivation of liberty on the grounds of disabilities as well as the principle of voluntary and informed consent for health care (Articles 14(1)(b) and 25 CRPD).[33] In *X v Argentina*, the author also argued that his right to the enjoyment of the highest possible standard of health, without discrimination on the basis of his disability, was violated (Article 25 CRPD). Mr X contended that the authorities had failed to take his state of health into account when placing him in a central prison. The rehabilitation services provided there by the authorities were insufficient to allow him to be fully rehabilitated. No other inmates were in a similar state of health which made them dependent on the help of others to carry out basic daily tasks. Mr X therefore needed reasonable accommodations to be made for him to ensure his personal safety.

The rehabilitation programme prescribed by Mr X's physicians was interrupted owing to the failure to provide reasonable accommodations and this was alleged by Mr X to be a violation of his right to attain the highest possible standard of health without discrimination under Article 25 CRPD. Mr X also maintained that there had been a violation of his rights under Article 26 CRPD whereby States Parties are under an obligation to take effective and appropriate habilitation and rehabilitation measures to enable persons with disabilities to attain and maintain maximum independence for full inclusion and participation in all aspects of life.

The CRPD Committee held that appropriate measures to ensure access for persons with disabilities to health services, including rehabilitation as encompassed in Articles 25 and 26 CRPD, should be read in conjunction with Article 14(2) CRPD. The CRPD Committee recalled that 'States parties have a special responsibility to uphold human rights when prison authorities exercise significant control or power over persons with disabilities who have been deprived of their liberty by a court of law'.[34] If persons with disabilities are deprived of their liberty, they are entitled to guarantees in line with the objectives and principles of the Convention which must be taken to include the rights enshrined in Article 25 and 26 CRPD.

The CRPD Committee did not analyse the case of *X v Argentina* in the light of Article 10 ICCPR. In the cases of *Denis Yevdokimov and Artiom Rezanov v Russian Federation*, the HRC held that 'according to article 10, paragraph 3 of the [ICCPR], the penitentiary system shall comprise treatment of prisoners the essential aim of which shall be their reformation and social rehabilitation'. This is one of the United Nations Basic Principles for the Treatment of Prisoners.[35] The CRPD Committee, however, found in *X v Argentina* that the author had refused to undergo rehabilitation therapy on a number of occasions and that his application for the authorisation of house arrest or detention in hospital had been duly considered by the judicial domestic authorities. Accordingly, it was the view of the CRPD Committee that there had been no violation of Articles 25 and 26 CRPD in Mr X's case.

Conclusion

The case law above has illustrated the interdependence of civil rights of liberty and security of the person and other socio-economic rights which are enshrined in the Convention. Such economic rights include the rights to accessibility, health and rehabilitation (Articles 9, 25 and 26 CRPD). In *X v Argentina*, the CRPD Committee willingly reminded the State Party of its obligation to provide reasonable accommodation to prevent discrimination against a prisoner. The application of the reasoned principles of the HRC to the case of *X v Tanzania* signal an understanding of the critical relevance of torture that persons with disabilities are subject to in the twenty-first century. The cases of *Noble v Australia* and *X v Tanzania* both serve to illustrate the application of the international rule of law to the discourse of disability-based discrimination. In this way, the CRPD Committee continues to induce societal change regarding the nature and extent of the right to life, which will be discussed in the next chapter. However, as we shall see, the CRPD's perspective is as ever provocative and daring. We shall expose the controversy in the light of the proposed General Comment No.36 on the right to life of the HRC.

Summary of Concluding Observations and Recommendations

In a series of Concluding Observations to States Parties, the CRPD Committee has recommended a range of changes which are necessary at domestic level to ensure the liberty and security of persons with disabilities. Firstly, it has recommended that States Parties must adopt appropriate measures to ensure that, where persons with disabilities have been deprived of their liberty, that they can live independently in their places of detention, and participate fully in all aspects of life. The onus is upon States Parties to provide reasonable accommodation to facilitate these requirements; for example, to ensure that persons with disabilities can enjoy access to all facilities and services which are available within their place of detention on an equal basis with others. The CRPD Committee has also recommended the need for training on the scope of the Convention and its Optional Protocol for those involved in the administration of justice, including the judiciary, judicial officers and prison officers, with a view to enhancing awareness of the rights to liberty and security of persons with disabilities. In General Comment No.35 of the HRC, it was recommended that in cases of the arrest of persons with mental or other cognitive disabilities, notice of arrest, along with a statement of the reasons for it, should be provided directly to a designated person or an appropriate family member of the arrested person.

The CRPD Committee has called for the repeal of domestic legislation authorising the institutionalisation of persons with intellectual or psychosocial disabilities without their free and informed consent, including in cases where the approval of the concerned person has been substituted by that of a third party. Legal measures that permit the deprivation of liberty on the basis of disability should equally be prohibited. Persons with psychosocial or intellectual disabilities who are involved in criminal proceedings should be provided with the same substantive and procedural guarantees which are available to non-disabled persons. These guarantees include the presumption of innocence and the right to a fair trial.

In its General Comment No.35, the HRC also reminded States Parties of their obligations regarding the institutionalisation of persons with mental or psychosocial disabilities. There is a need to revise outdated laws and practices in the field of mental health in order to avoid the arbitrary detention of persons with mental or psychosocial disabilities. The HRC emphasised the inherent harm which is associated with the deprivation of liberty and the particular harm associated with involuntary commitment or hospitalisation. In cases where confinement is unavoidable, States Parties should ensure that less restrictive forms of confinement are available, such as community-based or social care services for persons with disabilities. The existence of a disability should not in itself be relied upon to justify a deprivation of liberty. Where a person with disabilities is deprived of his/her liberty, the deprivation must be necessary and proportionate for the purpose of protecting the individual in question from serious harm or, alternatively, for the purpose of preventing injury to others. In accordance with the requirement for proportionality, a person with disabilities must be deprived of his/her liberty only as a measure of last resort and for the shortest possible period of time. Any deprivation of liberty must be accompanied by adequate procedural and substantive safeguards which are established by law. Such procedures should respect the views of the person with disabilities concerned. They should also ensure that any representative who is appointed on behalf of a person with disabilities genuinely represents their wishes and defends their interests.

With reference to Articles 25 and 26 CRPD, the CRPD Committee has noted that States Parties are obliged to adopt appropriate measures to ensure that persons with disabilities who have been deprived of their liberty have access to medical and rehabilitation treatment. This is to ensure that they may, without discrimination, enjoy the highest possible standard of health. Persons with disabilities, whether in detention or not, should be free to either consent to or refuse medical treatment. They should have prompt access to appropriate health care services which are in keeping with their state of health, and access to regular rehabilitation therapy where necessary. Persons with disabilities should be able to access community-based rehabilitation services and programmes which are orientated towards social and community inclusion on an equal basis with others.

States Parties must offer programmes of treatment and rehabilitation to persons with disabilities who are institutionalised. Such programmes should be designed in light of the purpose of the person's detention. Deprivation of liberty and its ongoing necessity must be the subject of review and re-evaluation at appropriate intervals. Affected persons with disabilities must be supported in obtaining access to effective remedies in seeking to assert their rights. These include access to the judicial review of the lawfulness of a person's detention and also to remedies where conditions of detention are incompatible with international human rights norms.

States Parties must ensure that persons with disabilities, especially those with psychosocial or intellectual disabilities, have equal access to the best possible standard of health. There is a requirement to provide adequate and accessible health services for persons with disabilities and to provide suitable training for health care professionals and public health officials on the rights of persons with disabilities, including their right not to be detained in an institution or given medical treatment without their free and informed consent. Such awareness-raising is critical in ensuring that health care professionals and public health officials are fully versed with the rights of persons with disabilities under the Convention. There should be legislative provision for the development of comprehensive health care programmes specifically for persons with disabilities who require extensive support. Budgetary resources must be available to realise the right to health of persons with disabilities. Hospitals and health centres must be accessible to persons with disabilities. States Parties must also adopt plans and allocate resources to ensure that mainstream health services, including sexual and reproductive health services and information, are accessible to persons with disabilities.

Given the continuing prevalence of the medical models of habilitation and rehabilitation in some States Parties, the CRPD Committee has recommended that such States Parties should establish a framework to protect persons with disabilities from the imposition of habilitation or rehabilitation services without their free and informed consent. Such a framework is in line with the requirements of a human-rights orientated model of disability. The CRPD Committee was also concerned about the long waiting times for access to rehabilitation services for persons with disabilities, especially for those with severe forms of impairment. It therefore recommended that States Parties improve accessibility to habilitation and rehabilitation services and that they take measures to ensure their timely delivery.

In relation to Article 17 CRPD, the CRPD Committee has recommended that States Parties should amend their mental health laws to ensure that the free and informed consent of persons with disabilities, including those whose legal capacity has been revoked, is required as an essential precondition before any surgery or medical treatment is carried out, especially where such treatment is invasive, or its effects are irreversible, for example, sterilisation or surgical procedures which may be performed on intersex children. Where the conditions of detention of a person with disabilities are affected by a lack of accessibility or reasonable accommodation, State Parties must ensure that the detention does not become more onerous, or cause greater physical and psychological suffering to an extent that would constitute cruel, inhuman or degrading treatment, or that would undermine the person's physical and mental integrity.

Notes

1 HRC, General Comment No. 35 on Article 9 (Liberty and Security of the Person), 16 December 2014, CCPR/C/GC/35, para.3.
2 Ibid, para.9.
3 CRPD Committee, Concluding Observations on the Initial Report of Peru, 16 May 2012, CRPD/C/PER/CO/1.
4 CRPD Committee, Concluding Observations on the Initial Report of Denmark, 30 October 2014, CRPD/C/DNK/CO/1, para.36.
5 Accessibility is discussed in detail in Chapter 8.
6 See Article 4(2) CRPD.
7 *James Marlon Noble v Australia* (2016) CRPD/C/16/7/2012; See Chapter 4 for the facts.
8 Ibid, para.2.7.
9 Ibid, para.8.7.
10 Article 9(1) ICCPR.
11 Article 9(2) ICCPR.
12 Article 9(3) ICCPR.

13 *Robert John Fardon v Australia* (2010) ICCPR/C/98/D/1629/2007.
14 Ibid, para.7.4.
15 Article 15(1) ICCPR provides that:

> No one shall be held guilty of any criminal offence on account of any act or omission which did not constitute a criminal offence, under national or international law, at the time when it was committed. Nor shall a heavier penalty be imposed than the one that was applicable at the time when the criminal offence was committed. If, subsequent to the commission of the offence, provision is made by law for the imposition of the lighter penalty, the offender shall benefit thereby.

16 *X v Tanzania* (2017) CRPD/C/18/D/22/2014.
17 Article 1(1) CAT (emphasis supplied).
18 *X v Tanzania*, para.8.6.
19 Rashida Manjoo, Report of the Special Rapporteur on Violence against Women, its Causes and Consequences, 3 August 2012, A/67/227, para.38.
20 CRPD Committee, Concluding Observations on the Initial Report of Costa Rica, 12 May 2014, CRPD/C/CRI/CO/1.
21 Manfred Nowak, Interim Report of the Special Rapporteur of the Human Rights Council on Torture and other Cruel, Inhuman or Degrading Treatment or Punishment, 28 July 2008, A/63/175, para.49.
22 *X v Argentina* (2012) CRPD/C/11/D/8/2012.
23 *Fijalkowska v Poland* (2005) ICCPR/C/84/D/1061/2002.
24 See however *Fijalkowska v Poland* in Chapter 4 on the difference between legal capacity and mental capacity.
25 CRPD Committee, Concluding Observations on the Initial Report of the Republic of Korea, 29 October 2014, CRPD/C/KOR/CO/1, para.26.
26 HRC, Concluding Observations of the Sixth Periodic Report of the Russian Federation, 24 November 2009, CCPR/C/RUS/CO/6, para.19.
27 Juan E. Méndez, Report of Special Rapporteur on Torture and Other Cruel, Inhuman or Degrading Treatment or Punishment, 1 February 2013, A/HRC/22/53, para.69.
28 Article 19 CRPD provides that:

> States Parties to this Convention recognize the equal right of all persons with disabilities to live in the community, with choices equal to others, and shall take effective and appropriate measures to facilitate full enjoyment by persons with disabilities of this right and their full inclusion and participation in the community, including by ensuring that:
>
> (a) Persons with disabilities have the opportunity to choose their place of residence and where and with whom they live on an equal basis with others and are not obliged to live in a particular living arrangement;
> (b) Persons with disabilities have access to a range of in-home, residential and other community support services, including personal assistance necessary to support living and inclusion in the community, and to prevent isolation or segregation from the community;
> (c) Community services and facilities for the general population are available on an equal basis to persons with disabilities and are responsive to their needs.

29 HRC, General Comment No. 35 on Article 9 ICCPR, para.2.
30 *X v Argentina*, para.9, emphasis supplied.
31 CRPD Committee, General Comment No. 1 on Article 12 (Equal Recognition Before the Law), 11 April 2014, CRPD/C/GC/1, para.42.
32 Ibid.
33 CRPD Committee, Guidelines on Article 14 (The Right to Liberty and Security of Persons with Disabilities), September 2015, para.10.
34 *X v Argentina*, para.8.9.
35 *Denis Yevdokimov and Artiom Rezanov v Russian Federation* (2011) CCPR/C/101/D/1410/2005, para.7.4.

6

RIGHT TO LIFE

Introduction

Recent history serves to remind us of how the human mind may be corrupted by dogmatic ideologies based upon irrational beliefs. Nazism and other forms of extremism, sometimes based on religious convictions, have caused immense suffering in seeking the utilitarian objective of the greatest good for the maximum number of people. In 1933, in his obsessive quest for a perfect race, Adolf Hitler signed a decree for the sterilisation of 'genetically defective' citizens, thereby seeking to prevent the birth of people suffering from such defects. This resulted in the sterilisation of persons who were deemed to be genetically defective. All types of impairments fell within Hitler's definition of 'defective persons', including those who suffered from chronic alcoholism. The years that followed Hitler's rise to power saw the indiscriminate use of euthanasia against many persons with disabilities, regardless of their age. Hitler's regime of intentional killing reached such an intensity of violence that it had recourse to the gas chambers.

Throughout the history of the world, genocides and mass killings have devastated millions of lives. Between the fifteenth and twentieth centuries, many thousands of native Americans were assassinated by immigrants who stole their land by force. Between 1915 and 1923, the Armenian genocide resulted in the death of hundreds of thousands of ethnic Armenians living in the Ottoman Empire. The Rwandan genocide was perhaps the quickest killing rampage the world has ever witnessed, with approximately 800,000 Tutsis and Hutu moderates being massacred over a period of 100 days in 1994. The danger of genocide remains real today, and in many jurisdictions there are still attempts to eliminate persons with disabilities either before they are born or shortly after their birth. For instance, the CRPD Committee noted that persons with psychosocial and intellectual disabilities in 2017 Iran were more at risk than others of being subjected to the death penalty due to a lack of procedural accommodation.[1]

In some jurisdictions, for example in Iran, the right to life may be compromised due to compulsory genetic testing policies for couples prior to marriage.[2] The aim of these practices is to prevent the birth of children with disabilities. Other societies take the view that persons with disabilities are burdensome to tax-payers and ending their lives without mercy is common practice. Persons with disabilities are also regularly sacrificed in the name of religious beliefs.[3] It is against this background that the UN General Assembly adopted its World Programme of Action concerning persons with disabilities.[4] In its Report of the Advisory Committee on the International Year of Disabled Persons, the UN sent out a strong message that notwithstanding the protection afforded by international law to persons with disabilities, they continue to be denied equal treatment.

Faced with such human catastrophe, the UN has long sought to more closely define the meaning of the right to life. Whereas international law does not offer a definition of the right to life, academics and human rights activists have reflected upon its core elements. Articles 1 and 3 of the Universal Declaration of Human Rights (UDHR) emphasise that everyone has the right to life and that all human beings are born free and equal in terms of their dignity and rights. In accordance with these provisions, human dignity and the right to life are inseparably linked.

States Parties to the ICCPR are afforded a margin of appreciation with regard to the measures which must be taken to uphold the right to life. Whilst States Parties are under an international obligation to protect the right to life, they are also under a duty to arrest and punish the perpetrators of crimes and only under stringent conditions are they permitted to derogate from their obligation to protect the right to life. For instance, the Constitution of the Republic of Mauritius provides for a derogation from the right to life in order to effect a lawful arrest or to prevent the escape of a person who has been lawfully detained.[5]

The obligations of states concerning the right to life are at times conflictual, paradoxical and controversial. The most challenging areas include the imposition of the death penalty, the use of enforced disappearance, the rights of the unborn, abortion, euthanasia and assisted dying. This chapter seeks to examine these areas from the perspective of the CRPD. The incremental development of international law on the right to life has not been without criticism. The universality of the right to life has not been upheld and its inalienable characteristics have been downplayed. Nor has its interdependence with other rights been fully recognised. The absence of robust legal protection for the right to life results in its violation with the infliction of physical and mental suffering.

The arbitrary deprivation of life

In international law, the justiciability of the right to life was first enunciated in Article 6(1) ICCPR, which holds that every human being has the inherent right to life. Article 6(1) further requires that the right to life shall be protected by law and that no one shall be arbitrarily deprived of his life. Interference with the right to life is permissible only within the parameters of legally defined restrictions.[6] The preamble to the CRPD recalls the principles set out in the UN Charter in asserting that the fabric of society rests on the recognition of 'the inherent dignity and worth and the equal and inalienable rights of all members of the human family as the foundation of freedom, justice and peace in the world'.[7] Article 10 CRPD reaffirms the provisions enshrined in Article 6 ICCPR and sets out the obligation of States Parties to recognise that every human being has the inherent right to life and that all necessary measures must be taken to ensure its effective enjoyment by persons with disabilities on an equal basis with others.

In its draft General Comment No.36 on Article 6 ICCPR (Right to life), the HRC has sought to clarify the nature and scope of the right to life and also to provide guidance for States Parties regarding its implementation.[8] Proposed General Comment No.36 will replace General Comments Nos 6 (1982) and 14 (1984) and seeks to further elucidate the manner in which the right to life interrelates with other rights contained in the ICCPR. In its opening remarks to General Comment No.36, the HRC observed that the right to life represents the entitlement of individuals to be free from acts and omissions intended or expected to cause their unnatural or premature death. The right to life includes the right to enjoy one's life with dignity.[9] The CRPD's jurisprudence is consistent with this reasoning and one of the primary purposes of the CRPD Committee when hearing complaints concerning the right to life is to protect persons with disabilities, on an equal basis with others, from succumbing to an unnatural or premature death.

Both Article 6(1) ICCPR and 10(1) CRPD expressly prohibit the arbitrary deprivation of the right to life. In international law, the arbitrary deprivation of the right to life consists of 'a deliberate or otherwise foreseeable and preventable life-terminating harm or injury, caused by an act or omission'.[10] Such an act or omission must consist of more than a threat or injury to bodily or mental integrity. Whilst the formulation of General Comment No.36 has been the subject of criticism, its content is nonetheless informative, and, where pertinent, is drawn upon in the discussion which follows on the right to life from the perspective of the CRPD.

Right to life and freedom from torture

Article 10 CRPD provides that 'States Parties reaffirm that every human being has the inherent right to life and shall take all necessary measures to ensure its effective enjoyment by persons with disabilities'. States Parties may be held responsible for the violation of Article 10 CRPD, even in situations where the breach has not actually caused a loss of life. The state has a duty not merely to prevent the arbitrary deprivation of the right to life; it is also under an obligation to prohibit situations arising which, whilst not explicitly breaching Article 10 CRPD, nonetheless give rise to a reasonably foreseeable threat to the right to life. In such circumstances, the state must provide protection to individuals whose lives are threatened. States Parties must be mindful of the interrelated nature of the right to life of persons with disabilities with their rights to freedom from torture, exploitation, violence and abuse and to the protection of their mental and physical integrity (Article 7 ICCPR; Articles 15–17 CRPD).[11]

The rights to life (Article 10 CRPD) and to freedom from torture are sacrosanct (Article 15 CRPD). The scope of the Article 15 CRPD has already been examined in the previous chapter. In this chapter, from a CRPD perspective, we examine the interplay between the right to life and the right to freedom from torture through the case of *Vasily Yuzepchuk v Belarus*.[12] The key issues arising were whether Mr Yuzepchuk was a person with a disability, and, if so, what was the nature and extent of the State Party's obligations. Also at issue was the extent to which the international protection of the CRPD was relevant to the case. Mr Yuzepchuk submitted to the HRC that he had difficulty in recalling times and dates and that his memory was fading as a result of the physical brutality he had endured at the hands of the police. At the time when the HRC was examining Mr Yuzepchuk's communication, he was awaiting execution in Belarus. In an interim order, the HRC requested the State of Belarus not to execute Mr Yuzepchuk pending a determination by the HRC on the admissibility of his petition. However, the State Party disregarded the interim order and proceeded with Mr Yuzepchuk's execution. He was sentenced to death by the Domestic Court of Belarus upon being convicted of murder and robbery.

Mr Yuzepchuk was arrested in 2008 and placed in custody whilst awaiting trial until April 2009 when he was brought before a judge for the first time, almost 15 months after his initial arrest. According to Mr Yuzepchuk, he was tortured by police officers during his pre-trial detention in order to force him to confess to the charges against him. He claimed that he was kept in solitary confinement for prolonged periods and that he was denied food. Mr Yuzepchuk also alleged that the police had plied him with alcohol, that they had administered an unknown substance to him and that the effect of this combination 'impaired his ability to think clearly'. Mr Yuzepchuk further claimed that during his detention the police threatened to incarcerate close members of his family.

A medical expert concluded that the injuries complained of by Mr Yuzepchuk were consistent with the infliction of torture and ill-treatment in the manner which he had described. Mr Yuzepchuk made a complaint to the Prosecutor's Office. However, an investigation concluded that his injuries were self-inflicted. Mr Yuzepchuk argued that the Prosecutor's Office had failed to properly investigate his complaint of police ill-treatment; witnesses were not questioned; a medical examination was not requested, video surveillance footage from Mr Yuzepchuk's cell was not secured and diary book entries were not examined. Meanwhile, three appeals against Mr Yuzepchuk's conviction were lodged to the Supreme Court of Belarus between July and September 2009. However, these were all set aside and it was concluded that his conviction was fully supported by evidence.

The HRC held that there had been a violation of Mr Yuzepchuk's right to life under Article 6 ICCPR. He had been sentenced to death following an unfair trial and the State of Belarus had not complied with Article 6(2) of the ICCPR.[13] A death sentence may only be imposed in accordance with law which complies with the ICCPR and its procedural guarantees. These include the right to a fair hearing by an independent tribunal, the presumption of innocence, the observance of minimum guarantees for the defence, and the right to review by a higher tribunal. The HRC reiterated that the imposition of a death sentence upon the conclusion of a trial in the course of which Article 14 ICCPR had been breached amounted to a de facto violation of Article 6 ICCPR.

It is notable that the HRC failed to dwell upon Mr Yuzepchuk's evidence to the effect that he could not think clearly and could not remember times and dates. It did not seek further clarification regarding the nature of his impairment which the facts indicated was of a cognitive nature.[14] It appears that those who violently threatened Mr Yuzepchuk were responsible for the onset of his cognitive impairment and that his interaction with prison and court environments gave rise to barriers which prevented and 'disabled' him from properly defending himself. This is illustrated by the complete rejection of Mr Yuzepchuk's complaint that he had been assaulted.

It is open to question whether the HRC's reasoning ought to have taken into account the right of persons with disabilities to equal recognition before the law and to access to justice in line with Articles 12 and 13 of the CRPD respectively. Mr Yuzepchuk was denied his legal capacity in that he was not adequately represented and nor did he have the benefit of a fair trial. He was not able to cross-examine witnesses, 30 of whom were absent from the proceedings and the prosecution had even failed to disprove his alibi. He was denied his right to the legal protection to which he was entitled because the judge relied upon the uncorroborated evidence of only one witness.[15] The circumstances suggest that Mr Yuzepchuk may have been the victim of a miscarriage of justice. The HRC did not consider the need for reasonable or procedural accommodation in order to allow Mr Yuzepchuk to effectively access the justice system in line with Article 13(1) CRPD. Without the legal protections to which he was entitled, Mr Yuzepchuk's execution was unjustifiable and constituted a breach of his fundamental right to life (Article 10 CRPD). Mr Yuzepchuk's case illustrates how the right to a fair trial may have a significant bearing on one's right to life, especially in situations where the death penalty is possible.

Right to life and the death penalty

In its proposed General Comment No.36, the HRC has argued that a prohibition on the arbitrary deprivation of life in accordance with Article 6(1) ICCPR fetters States Parties seeking to apply the death penalty.[16] Article 6(1) ICCPR is an unambiguous provision and provides no grounds for the deprivation of life. However, the HRC went on to assert that Article 6(2)–(5) ICCPR tacitly endorse the ongoing use of the death penalty for the most serious of crimes provided that strict conditions are satisfied. Only those States Parties which have neither abolished the death penalty nor ratified the Second Optional Protocol to the ICCPR seeking to abolish the death penalty are affected.[17] To date, only 85 States Parties out of a total of 197 have ratified the Second Optional Protocol to the ICCPR.[18] The HRC has stressed that Article 6(2) ICCPR should be narrowly interpreted given 'the anomalous nature of regulating the application of the death penalty in an instrument enshrining the right to life'.[19] States Parties which have abolished capital punishment are prohibited from reintroducing it. Under international law, abolition of the death penalty is legally irrevocable.

In *Lubuto v Zambia*, the HRC considered whether the imposition of the death sentence on Mr Lubuto by the State of Zambia was unfair and disproportionate. It was the case that no one had been wounded or killed during a robbery for which Mr Lubuto had been convicted and the death penalty imposed.[20] Mr Lubuto was convicted and sentenced to death under a Zambian law which provided for the death penalty in cases of aggravated robbery using firearms. The HRC adopted a strict interpretation of the wording of Article 6(2) ICCPR which allows for the imposition of the death penalty for only 'the most serious crimes'. In the instant case, the imposition of the death sentence by the domestic court had been manifestly arbitrary and disproportionate because it should have taken into account the fact that the use of firearms in the robbery had not caused the death or wounding of any person.

The HRC also found in favour of Mr Lubuto regarding his allegations that there was a considerable delay in his trial proceedings between his initial arrest in February 1980 and the final ruling in the matter by the Zambian Supreme Court in February 1988. Article 14(3)(c) ICCPR sets out the minimum standards to be adhered to in respect of an accused person to ensure that he/she is tried without undue delay. In conformity with Article 14(5) ICCPR, the undue delay requirement applies equally to the right of review of conviction and sentence. In Mr Lubuto's case, the period of eight years between arrest and final sentencing amounted to a violation of Article 14(3)(c) ICCPR.

While Mr Lubuto did not per se bring a claim under Articles 6 and 14 ICCPR, the HRC nevertheless held that the right to life should be read in conjunction with the right to a fair trial. States Parties are under an obligation to ensure that an accused person avails himself of his right to a fair trial before or during the imposition of the death penalty.

In *Judge v Canada*, the HRC had to determine whether the detention of the author for ten years despite the fact that he faced execution at the end of his sentence and whether his proposed extradition by Canada to the US amounted to a violation of his right to life under Article 6 ICCPR.[21] The HRC reviewed the scope and contents of Article 6 ICCPR by reference to the Vienna Convention on the Law of Treaties according to which 'a treaty should be interpreted in good faith and in accordance with the ordinary meaning to be given to the terms of the treaty in their context and in the light of its object and purpose'.[22] Adopting a purposive approach to the wording of Article 6(2)–(6), the HRC held that in

> countries that have abolished the death penalty, there is an obligation not to expose a person to the real risk of its application. Thus, they may not

remove, either by deportation or extradition, individuals from their jurisdiction if it may be reasonably anticipated that they will be sentenced to death, without ensuring that the death sentence would not be carried out.[23]

The HRC has followed the same line of reasoning in its subsequent draft General Comment No.36:

> States parties that abolished the death penalty cannot deport or extradite persons to a country in which they are facing criminal charges that carry the death penalty, unless credible and effective assurances against the imposition of the death penalty have been obtained. In the same vein, the obligation not to reintroduce the death penalty for any specific crime requires States parties not to extradite or deport an individual to a country in which he or she is expected to stand trial for a capital offence, if the same offence does not carry the death penalty in the removing State, unless credible and effective assurances against exposing the individual to the death penalty have been obtained.[24]

It is a fundamental principle of the international rule of law that everyone is presumed to be innocent until a court of law finds otherwise. Capital punishment is a relic of the era of retributive justice and stands in stark contrast to a human rights-based approach to justice, envisioning the rehabilitation of persons rather than punishing them. The committing of horrendous crimes cannot be condoned or excused on any grounds. However, it is submitted that the death penalty can never benefit society at large. Capital punishment is the ultimate form of cruel, inhuman and degrading treatment and should be vehemently opposed in all circumstances. The injustice of capital punishment is paramount given that its practice is manifestly more harmful to vulnerable groups, including persons with intellectual and psychosocial disabilities who may not have the legal capacity to defend themselves.

According to Amnesty International, '[i]nternational law and standards on the use of capital punishment clearly state that the death penalty should not be imposed or carried out on people with mental or intellectual disabilities'.[25] In its resolution on the safeguards guaranteeing protection of the rights of persons facing the death penalty, the UN Economic and Social Council argued that the death penalty should not be carried out 'on persons who have become insane'.[26] In *Atkins v Virginia*, the US Supreme Court held that the imposition of the death penalty on persons with intellectual disabilities (then referred to as mentally retarded) was unconstitutional insofar as it amounted to a cruel and unusual punishment.[27] The Supreme Court reasoned that whilst criminals with intellectual disabilities may often be competent to stand trial, they nevertheless have diminished capacities to understand and process information, to reason logically or to control their impulses. Whilst their impairments were not such as to warrant an exemption from criminal liability, they did contribute to a reduction of their personal culpability.

Article 31.1(a) of the Rome Statute of the International Criminal Court 1998 recognises that criminal responsibility can be circumvented if a person with disability does not have the capacity 'to appreciate the unlawfulness or nature of his or her conduct, or capacity to control his or her conduct to conform to the requirements of law'. Persons with intellectual or psychosocial disabilities are likely to be more exposed to discriminatory practices excluding them from access to the justice system. They may not have the capacity to stand trial or to fully grasp the nature of the punishment that may be imposed on them. The position of the HRC was set out in draft General Comment No.36 as follows:

> States parties must refrain from imposing the death penalty on individuals who have limited ability to defend themselves on an equal basis with others, such as persons with serious psycho-social and intellectual disabilities, and on persons with or without disability that have reduced moral culpability.[28]

The HRC's position is based upon the spurious premise that States Parties should refrain from imposing the death penalty on persons with intellectual or psychosocial disabilities because they lack legal capacity owing to their limited mental capacity.[29] Instead, the HRC should have emphasised how the denial of fair trial guarantees and procedural accommodations to persons with psychosocial or intellectual disabilities constitutes discrimination. In the next section, the discordance in postures between the HRC and the CRPD Committee will be further highlighted. The right to life of the unborn with fatal genetic malfunctions and/ or cognitive impairments will be examined in tandem with the mother's right to abortion.

Right to life of the unborn and abortion

Every human being has the inherent right to life. However, the implications of this simple statement have been particularly controversial in the context of abortion. Whereas the inalienable nature of the right to life may be agreed by many, the question of when exactly a human being becomes human is more contestable. The nature of the right to life of the unborn may be approached alternatively as a matter of science, religion, philosophy or law. Whilst the point of conception may be regarded as the time when a new life emerges, its acquisition of the status of 'human being' may be differently defined by religious, cultural or ethical beliefs.

The right to life is sacrosanct and is a right to which every human being, born or unborn, is entitled. However, it should be recalled that the ICCPR provides for derogation from the right to life, most notably in the context of the death penalty, as has been seen above. On the face of it, in its proposed General Comment No.36, the HRC may be seen to take a pro-choice stance on the issue of abortion. Pro-life campaigners have long argued that the ICCPR does not provide grounds on which the HRC can interpret the right to life as compatible with a right to abortion.[30] The implicit protection of the unborn is, according to them, evident in Article 6(5) ICCPR which states in unambiguous terms that the death penalty 'shall not be carried out on pregnant women'.

However, the HRC is not committed to the view that the ICCPR confers a right to abortion or that it supports the denial of the right to life of the unborn. The HRC's position reflects its consideration of the rights of women alongside those of the unborn. However, its language in General Comment No.36 is disproportion-ate in relation to persons with disabilities. The HRC's key recommendation is that States Parties who have anti-abortion legislation in place should ensure that such measures 'must not result in violation of the right to life of a pregnant woman or of her other rights under the Covenant' as to do otherwise may amount to cruel, inhuman and degrading treatment or punishment.[31] The HRC seems to suggest that States should proportionately address the competing rights of women and the unborn. On the other hand, with regard to the issue of unsafe abortion, there is general consensus on the CEDAW Committee that:

> Unsafe abortion is a leading cause of maternal mortality and morbidity. As such, States parties should legalize abortion at least in cases of rape, incest, threats to the life and/or health of the mother, or severe foetal impairment, as well as provide women with access to quality post-abortion care, espe-cially in cases of complications resulting from unsafe abortions. States parties should also remove punitive measures for women who undergo abortion.[32]

Anti-abortion legislation which exposes women to psychological and emotional trauma may violate their right to freedom from cruel, inhuman and degrading treatment.[33] The CRPD's objection to the usage of terms such as 'severe foetal impairment' gains its support in the belief that the terms connote negative stereo-types of persons with disabilities. It is strongly recommended that international law should refrain from using this terminology as it is insulting to the dignity of women who choose to give birth to a child with impairment.

In the case of *Whelan v Ireland*, Mrs Whelan, who was pregnant, underwent an ultrasound scan in an Irish hospital. The obstetrician found that the unborn child had a congenital brain abnormality. Mr and Mrs Whelan were informed that the baby would not survive. They were also informed that abortion was illegal in Ire-land. Mrs Whelan was not given any further information on her treatment options, nor was she referred to anyone else in order to discuss the diagnosis. Mrs Whelan's options were either to carry the pregnancy to term, knowing that the child would most probably die prior to birth, or to voluntarily terminate the pregnancy abroad. Mrs Whelan argued that her physical and mental situation was exacerbated by the circumstances arising from the prevailing legislative framework in Ireland and by the treatment she received from some health care providers. As a result, she felt abandoned by the state and was required to gather her own information regarding the available medical options. Mrs Whelan was forced to choose between con-tinuing her non-viable pregnancy in Ireland or travelling to another country to undergo a termination at her own expense. Mrs Whelan suffered from the shame and stigma associated with the criminalisation of abortion in Ireland, and following her termination abroad, she had to leave the baby's remains in a foreign country. Upon her return to Ireland, Mrs Whelan did not receive appropriate bereavement counselling.

The HRC found that Mrs Whelan was in a highly vulnerable position upon learning that her pregnancy was not viable. The suffering she endured could have been mitigated had she been allowed to terminate her pregnancy in the familiar environment of her own country, under the care of her trusted health professionals. According to the HRC, Mrs Whelan's suffering was worsened due to the obstacles she faced in receiving information from her health care providers about the appropriate medical options available. The HRC found that she had suffered severe mental anguish owing to a combination of acts and omissions, in violation of the prohibition against cruel, inhuman or degrading treatment (Article 7 ICCPR). Legal restrictions on abortion must not endanger the lives of women nor subject them to mental or physical pain or suffering, otherwise States Parties may find themselves in violation of Article 7 ICCPPR. Whilst States Parties may implement measures to regulate abortion, these measures should not result in an infringement of the right to life of a pregnant woman or her other rights under the ICCPR.[34]

Whilst it is not the role of the UN or its treaty bodies to dictate to States Parties on the extent to which they can legislate to regulate the rights to life or to freedom from cruel, inhuman or degrading treatment, state sovereignty must nonetheless respect the parameters of international law. As the HRC has observed, any legal restrictions on abortion must not have the effect of jeopardising the lives of women or subjecting them to physical and mental pain in violation of Article 7 ICCPR.[35] In its Concluding Observations on the fourth periodic report of Ireland, the HRC noted 'the severe mental suffering caused by the denial of abortion services to women seeking abortions due to rape, incest, fatal foetal abnormality or serious risks to health'.[36]

It is clear that abortion on the ground of impairment runs counter to the human rights-based approach to disability espoused by the CRPD:

> Even if the condition is considered fatal, there is still a decision made on the basis of impairment. Often it cannot be said if an impairment is fatal. Experience shows that assessments on impairment conditions are often false. Even if it is not false, the assessment perpetuates notions of stereotyping disability as incompatible with a good life.[37]

However, in cases where the unborn child is not going to survive and where the continuing pregnancy puts the mother at risk of physical or mental harm, it is not apparent why a pregnant woman should not be given the right to an abortion. Such cases do not have a eugenic dimension whereby the unborn child is selected for abortion on the basis of 'undesirable' traits, with the right to life of the unborn being violated as a result of impairment. Globally, abortion law is developing incrementally, as feminists and human rights activists strive for the recognition of a woman's right to full autonomy over her body. More recently, issues of euthanasia and assisted dying have been the subject of controversy, as will be seen in the following section.

Right to life and euthanasia

The voluntary termination of life of persons with unbearable forms of physical impairment or of old people who develop impairments as a result of disease or other complications have been met with fierce resistance. Euthanasia is the intentional killing of a human being, either by an act or an omission, with a view to eliminating their pain and suffering. In considering the initial country report of Belgium, the CRPD Committee was particularly concerned with the rights of institutionalised persons with mental disabilities.[38] The high level of institutionalisation of services for persons with disabilities in Belgium presented the risk that euthanasia could be misused to terminate the lives of persons with intellectual and psychosocial disabilities. The CRPD Committee pointed out that the Belgian Act of 28 May 2002 on euthanasia did not make any distinction on the basis of disability as it catered for the possibility of every Belgian national being able to end his life. Although the legislative framework authorises assisted suicide under very stringent conditions, a patient could decide to terminate her life if she has the legal capacity to do so or if a doctor could certify that her decision was voluntary and that her written consent had been obtained. The CRPD Committee concluded that the safeguards were inadequate and that persons with disabilities were particularly vulnerable in that they could be arbitrarily deprived of their right to life by the state.

In the same vein, the ICESCR Committee has drawn attention to the relationship between the right to life and the right to health. Measures relating to the realisation of the right to health should also take into account care for chronically and terminally ill persons, sparing them avoidable pain and enabling them to die with dignity.[39] Recent case law demonstrates that domestic courts have been taking a proactive stance in recognising that euthanasia or physician-assisted dying does not infringe the right to life. In *Carter v Canada (Attorney General)*, the Supreme Court of Canada had to decide whether the criminal law which prohibited physician-assisted dying amounted to a violation of the rights to life, security and liberty of the person under Section 7 of the Canadian Charter of Rights and Freedoms.[40] Mrs Taylor was diagnosed with amyotrophic lateral sclerosis in 2009 and was told that there was a high probability that she would become paralysed within six months and die within a year. She decided to judicially challenge the prohibition on assisted suicide provided in paragraph 241(b) of the Canadian Criminal Code.

The Supreme Court held that the 'prohibition on physician-assisted dying deprived Mrs Taylor and others suffering from grievous and irremediable medical conditions of the right to life, liberty and security of the person.'[41] The right to life was engaged insofar as the law or state action imposed death or an increased risk of death on a person, either directly or indirectly. However, concerns about autonomy and quality of life have traditionally been treated as liberty and security rights.[42] The Supreme Court of Canada analysed the legal prohibition on assisted suicide and the manner in which it impinges on the right to life of the person who is coerced to take his/her own life 'prematurely'. This premature taking of life can occur due to the fear of not having the opportunity to end one's life by assisted suicide when one reaches a point where pain and suffering becomes too unbearable. The state can thus be held liable for arbitrarily depriving an individual of the right to life if one is denied assisted suicide. The Supreme Court also held that the right to liberty encompasses the right to make fundamental personal choices free from external state interference. On the other hand, the right to security of the person comprises

> a notion of personal autonomy involving . . . control over one's bodily integrity free from state interference [. . .] and it is engaged by state interference with an individual's physical or psychological integrity, including any state action that causes physical or serious psychological suffering.[43]

The Supreme Court of Canada concluded that the denial of the right to request a physician's assistance in dying interfered with one's ability to make decisions about one's own bodily integrity and medical care, which in turn impacts upon one's liberty. It further held that 'by leaving people like Ms. Taylor to endure intolerable suffering, it impinges on their security of the person'.[44]

Assisted suicide or consensual termination of life requires a strong legal and institutional framework protecting the rights of patients, and in this regard States Parties are bound to ensure that medical professionals are acting in accordance with the free, informed, and explicit consent of patients. Patients' decisions must be unambiguous and the decisions of professionals must be dictated by the overriding consideration of protecting patients from pressure and abuse.[45] The CRPD Committee has expressed concerns about legislation providing for medical assistance for the voluntary termination of life in Canada, including the lack of regulation for monitoring medical assistance in dying, the lack of data to assess compliance with procedural safeguards regarding such assistance and, finally, the absence of sufficient support to assist civil society's engagement in monitoring the voluntary termination of life.[46]

Right to life and enforced disappearance

In the case of *Kumari Katwal v Nepal*, Mrs Katwal complained to the HRC that her rights under Article 7 ICCPR had been violated and that those of her husband under Articles 6 and 7 ICCPR had also been violated.[47] On 13 December 2001, Mr Katwal, who worked as a teacher in Nepal, was taken to the office of the chief district officer, where he was illegally detained before being transferred to the army barrack, where he was subjected to torture. Mr Katwal presumably died as a result.

Mrs Katwal made several attempts to establish the whereabouts of her husband but her efforts were hampered by the authorities. She was herself arrested by soldiers and was repeatedly beaten, insulted and interrogated by military personnel concerning herself and her daughter's possible connection with the Maoist movement. As a result of her injuries, Mrs Katwal was hospitalised for two weeks and, following her release, she continued to experience physical and mental suffering. Mrs Katwal's daughter was also arrested by the army and was subjected to ill-treatment which also resulted in her hospitalisation. It had been reported that Mr Katwal was last seen in the hands of the authorities immediately after his disappearance. The circumstances of Mr Katwal's disappearance gave rise to a strong presumption that he had been unlawfully killed. It was upon this basis that Mrs Katwal claimed that her husband's enforced disappearance constituted a violation of Article 6(1) ICCPR.

The HRC held that there had indeed been a violation of Article 6 ICCPR in respect of the unlawful killing of Mr Katwal.[48] It further held that 'the acts of torture to which the author's husband was exposed and his incommunicado detention constitute a violation of article 7 of the Covenant'.[49] The breach by the State Party of Article 7 ICCPR arose for several reasons, including the ill-treatment and threats which Mrs Katwal had received; the misleading explanations given by the Nepalise authorities regarding her husband's whereabouts; the impossibility of obtaining Mr Katwal's remains; and the state's failure to provide Mrs Katwal with adequate reparation.[50]

The HRC held that the deprivation of Mr Katwal's liberty, followed by a period in which the authorities refused to acknowledge the deprivation and during which his true fate was concealed, amounted to an enforced disappearance.[51] The term 'enforced disappearance' is absent from the ICCPR, however the HRC established that enforced disappearance falls within the ambit of Articles 6 and 7 ICCPR. According to the HRC, in its draft General Comment No.36, enforced disappearance 'constitutes a unique and integrated series of acts and omissions representing a grave threat to life and may thus result in a violation of the right to life'.[52] It seems that the HRC was inspired here by the definition of 'enforced disappearance' contained in Article 2 of the International Convention for the Protection of All Persons from Enforced Disappearance, which stipulates that 'enforced disappearance' consists of

> the arrest, detention, abduction or any other form of deprivation of liberty by agents of the State or by persons or groups of persons acting with the authorization, support or acquiescence of the State, followed by a refusal to acknowledge the deprivation of liberty or by concealment of the fate or whereabouts of the disappeared person, which place such a person outside the protection of the law.

Enforced disappearances violate many substantive and procedural provisions of the ICCPR and are an aggravated form of arbitrary detention.[53] States Parties are under an obligation to conduct an effective and speedy inquiry to establish the fate of persons who have been subjected to enforced disappearance.[54] In light of its earlier jurisprudence in *Rubio v Colombia* (1983)[55] and its then General Comment No.6 on the right to life, the HRC has further elaborated on the international obligations of States Parties on the issue of enforced disappearance:

> States parties should also ensure that the enforced disappearance of persons is punished with criminal sanctions and introduce prompt and effective procedures to investigate cases of disappearances thoroughly, by independent and impartial bodies. They should bring to justice the perpetrators of such acts and omissions and ensure that victims of enforced disappearance and their relatives are informed about the outcome of the investigation and are provided with full reparation. Under no circumstances should families of victims of enforced disappearance be obliged to declare them dead in order to be eligible for reparation. States parties should also provide families of victims of disappeared persons with means to regularize their legal status in relation to the disappeared persons after an appropriate period of time.[56]

In the light of the above, the State of Nepal had failed to take adequate measures to prevent Mr Katwal's enforced disappearance. The HRC's proposed General Comment No.36 on the right to life signifies a positive duty on States Parties to harmonise their legislative frameworks in accordance with the requirements of Article 6 ICCPR and Article 10 CRPD. With regard to the protection of persons with disabilities against enforced disappearance, failure to act in situations of armed conflicts, humanitarian emergencies and of natural disasters may be critical. In these situations, persons with disabilities are much more vulnerable, a fact that is highlighted in Article 11 CRPD governing situations of risk and humanitarian emergencies.[57] Recently, the CRPD Committee welcomed the State of Luxembourg's commitment to foster high levels of development cooperation, including financial aid, to non-governmental organisations related to disability rights and its efforts to mainstream disability in its humanitarian action.[58]

In seeking to analyse the impact of Article 7 ICCPR, it is important to note that incommunicado detention may constitute torture of a detained person's relatives as well as torture of the detained person himself. The relatives' anguish in not knowing the whereabouts of their loved one, coupled with a lack of information and being subjected to reprisals, may amount to violation of the relative's rights under Article 7 ICCPR. Article 15 CRPD is wide-ranging in scope and covers a multitude of situations previously envisaged by the drafters of the ICCPR. In *Noble v Australia*, Mr Noble claimed that his right under Article 15 CRPD was violated because he was subjected to inhuman or degrading treatment.[59] Mr Noble, an innocent person with a disability, had complained that he had been indefinitely detained with criminals. The CRPD Committee held as follows:

> Taking into account the irreparable psychological effects that indefinite detention may have on the detained person, the Committee considers that

the indefinite detention to which [Mr Noble] was subjected amounts to inhuman and degrading treatment. The Committee therefore considers that the indefinite character of the author's detention and the repeated acts of violence to which he was subjected during his detention amount to a violation of article 15 of the Convention by the State party.[60]

Conclusion

The CRPD Committee's objection to proposed draft General Comment No.36 goes to the very roots of the adoption of the CRPD. It adopts a twin approach with a view to respect, promote and protect the rights of both women and persons with disabilities. While a decision to terminate or not to terminate a pregnancy must be the exclusive province of the autonomy of women, perceived or actual understanding of what constitutes a viable pregnancy should not rest upon arbitrary medical pronouncement. Although it is the youngest of the human rights treaty bodies, the CRPD Committee, through its jurisprudence, has served to broaden the scope of application of the rights to life and to freedom from torture. It has done this by extracting principles from previously established human rights treaty bodies and applying them to novel situations. On the other hand, the CRPD Committee's unique contribution has been to offer a legal analysis of human rights, including the right to life from a disability perspective.

In 2016, a total of 117 UN Member States voted in favour of a Resolution calling for a universal moratorium on the use of the death penalty.[61] Meanwhile, the categories of persons who cannot be subject to the death penalty have been extended to include persons suffering from mental disorders, including psychosocial disabilities. Whilst such a widening of the categories is to be welcomed, persons with disabilities still regularly suffer from a form of double jeopardy whereby the recourse to substituted decision-making on their behalf results in a denial of their right to a fair trial. This issue will remain a challenge for persons with disabilities in the future.

Summary of Concluding Observations and Recommendations

Persons with disabilities, including those with psychosocial and intellectual disabilities, are entitled to special measures of protection so as to ensure their effective enjoyment of the right to life on an equal basis with others. Such measures should include reasonable accommodation of public policies which are necessary to ensure the right to life, such as ensuring access for persons with disabilities to essential goods and services, and the adoption of special measures designed to prevent excessive use of force by law enforcement agencies against persons with disabilities.

In relation to the specific issue of abortion, States Parties should ensure that the legislative framework applicable to voluntary termination of pregnancy is in line

with the Convention. This includes ensuring effective, timely and accessible procedures for pregnancy termination. Safe access to abortion is essential to protect the
life and health of pregnant women. The problem is more acute in situations where
carrying a pregnancy to term causes substantial pain or suffering to a woman, or
where a pregnancy is the result of rape or incest, or when the unborn child suffers
from a fatal cognitive impairment.

States Parties may not regulate pregnancy or abortion in a manner that runs
contrary to their obligation to guarantee that women do not have to undergo
hazardous abortions. The application of criminal sanctions to women who have
undergone abortion or their application against physicians assisting women in such
circumstances may be expected to significantly increase recourse to unsafe abortions. States Parties should therefore take measures to ensure that health care providers are in a position to supply full information regarding the availability of safe
abortion services without fear of being subjected to criminal sanctions.

The absence of criminal sanctions does not prevent States Parties from imposing humiliating or unreasonably burdensome requirements upon women seeking
to terminate a pregnancy. The duty to protect women against the health risks
associated with unsafe abortion, and to ensure that safe abortion is available in cases
where the unborn child has a fatal impairment requires States Parties to take certain
practical measures. These include ensuring access for men and women to information and education regarding their reproductive options. States Parties must also
ensure that men and women have access to a wide range of contraceptive methods
and that adequate prenatal and post-abortion health care plans are deployed where
necessary.

With regard to euthanasia, the CRPD Committee recommends that States
Parties ensure that persons seeking an assisted death have access to information
regarding alternative courses of action. Examples of alternative forms of support
which may be made available to such persons include the provision of appropriate palliative care, disability support, home care and other social measures that
support human happiness. The collection of information about all requests for
medical assistance in dying and details of any subsequent intervention should be
regulated by specific legal measures. Reporting duties with regard to such data
collection should also be the subject of legal regulation. National data standards
must be identified, along with an effective and independent mechanism to ensure
regulatory compliance. It is a matter of paramount importance that persons with
disabilities must never be subjected to external pressure to end their lives. The
CRPD Committee has argued that the use of substituted decision-making in matters concerning life termination or the withdrawal of life-sustaining treatment or
care is inconsistent with the right to life of persons with disabilities. The CRPD
Committee recommends that States Parties adopt action plans to challenge the
perception that persons with disabilities do not have a good and decent life. Given
that persons with disabilities form an integral part of human diversity, society must
acknowledge them as equal to others.

The CRPD Committee has also recommended that States Parties take effective legal and administrative measures to prohibit involuntary commitment or hospitalisation and forced medical treatment. In particular, forced psychiatric treatment on the basis of impairment should be avoided. States Parties should provide sufficient community-based alternatives where the need arises. In a similar vein, in 2008, the UN Special Rapporteur on Torture addressed the institutionalisation of persons with psychosocial and intellectual impairments. He proposed that States Parties should adopt clear and unambiguous guidelines, in keeping with international human rights treaties including the ICCPR and the CAT, on what is meant by 'free and informed consent' in such cases. Complaints procedures must be readily accessible. Independent human rights monitors, such as national human rights institutions, national anti-torture preventative bodies and members of civil society should regularly oversee institutions where persons with disabilities may reside. These include prisons, social care centres, orphanages and mental health care institutions. The establishment of an independent mechanism to monitor residential centres for persons with disabilities may serve to prevent acts that constitute torture or other cruel, inhuman or degrading treatment or punishment. Laws which permit guardians or legal representatives to consent to medical research or experiments on behalf of persons with disabilities should also be abolished.

The CRPD Committee has expressed concerns about the lack of investigation into reports of cruel and degrading treatment of persons with disabilities in 'shelters'. Such investigations should be undertaken with a view to establishing administrative and criminal responsibility. Investigations must be impartial, speedy and effective so that perpetrators can be prosecuted in a timely manner. Persons with disabilities who have been exposed to torture and ill-treatment should have access to independent complaint mechanisms. Victims of such abuse should be legally entitled to redress and adequate compensation. Redress should also include support in terms of rehabilitation which may be necessary to enable persons with disabilities to live independently, or in any event to live as fully an independent life as possible given their individual circumstances.

The CRPD Committee has recommended that States Parties intensify their efforts to investigate alleged executions of persons with disabilities in situations of armed conflict. In such cases, States Parties should establish criminal responsibility, which should also apply in cases of enforced disappearance. Measures should be adopted to restore the dignity of victims and to grant reparations to their families.

The CRPD Committee has highlighted the scant dissemination of its views on the part of States Parties. Such inaction is most disappointing given that there is an obligation on the part of States Parties to widely circulate the Committee's views in accessible formats, so that they might be available to all sectors of the population. In order to address harmful practices affecting the human rights of persons with disabilities, there is a need for awareness-raising campaigns based on the human rights model of disability. A particularly acute need for such awareness-raising has arisen recently in some African states, where the human rights of persons with albinism are routinely abused.

Notes

1 CRPD Committee, Concluding Observations on the Initial Report of the Islamic Republic of Iran, 10 May 2017, CRPD/C/IRN/CO/1.
2 Duke Initiative for Science & Society, Iran: Premarital Genetic Testing Mandatory, 13 February 2017. Available at http://scipol.duke.edu/content/iran-premarital-genetic-testing-mandatory, accessed 21 March 2018.
3 See *X v Tanzania* (2017) CRPD/C/18/D/22/2014 in Chapters 1 and 5.
4 World Programme of Action concerning Disabled Persons, available at https://www.un.org/development/desa/disabilities/resources/world-programme-of-action-concerning-disabled-persons.html, accessed 21 March 2018.
5 Constitution of Mauritius, Section 4(2)(b).
6 Article 6(1)–(6) ICCPR.
7 Preamble CRPD, para.(a).
8 HRC, Draft General Comment No. 36 on Article 6 ICCPR (Right to Life) available at http://www.ohchr.org/Documents/HRBodies/CCPR/GCArticle6/GCArticle6_EN.pdf, accessed 21 March 2018.
9 HRC, Draft General Comment No.36, para.3.
10 HRC, Draft General Comment No.36, para.6.
11 For a discussion of Article 17 CRPD see Chapter 5. For a discussion of Article 16 CRPD see Chapter 3.
12 *Vasily Yuzepchuk v Belarus* (2014) CCPR/C/112/D/1906/2009.
13 Article 6(2) ICCPR states 'In countries which have not abolished the death penalty, sentence of death may be imposed only for the most serious crimes in accordance with the law in force at the time of the commission of the crime and not contrary to the provisions of the present Covenant and to the Convention on the Prevention and Punishment of the Crime of Genocide. This penalty can only be carried out pursuant to a final judgement rendered by a competent court.'
14 See Preamble, CRPD para.(e); Article 1 CRPD.
15 See Article 9 ICCPR.
16 HRC, Draft General Comment No.36, para.5.
17 Ibid, para.20.
18 OHCHR, Status of Ratification of International Human Rights Treaties, available at http://indicators.ohchr.org/, accessed 21 March 2018/
19 HRC, Draft General Comment No.36, para.37.
20 *Lubuto v Zambia* (1995) CCPR/C/55/D/390/1990/Rev.1.
21 *Judge v Canada* (2003) CCPR/C/78/D/829/1998.
22 Ibid, para.10.4.
23 Ibid.
24 HRC, Draft General Comment No.36, para.38.
25 Amnesty International, 2014, World Day Against The Death Penalty: Protecting People with Mental and Intellectual Disabilities from the Use of Death Penalty, https://www.amnesty.org/download/Documents/4000/act510052014en.pdf accessed 21 March 2018.
26 ECOSOC, Safeguards Guaranteeing Protection of the Rights of those Facing the Death Penalty, 25 May 1984, Resolution 1984/50.
27 *Atkins v Virginia* 536 U.S. 304 (2002).
28 HRC, General Comment No.36, para.53 (footnote omitted).
29 See Chapter 4 on the difference between 'mental capacity' and 'legal capacity'.
30 See European Centre for Law and Justice, 'The Right to Life is not the Right to Kill', 2017, https://eclj.org/abortion/un/protgez-toute-vie-humaine-, accessed 21 March 2018.
31 HRC, General Comment No.36, para.9.
32 CEDAW Committee, Statement of the Committee on the Elimination of Discrimination against Women on Sexual and Reproductive Health and Rights: Beyond 2014 ICPD review, 10–28 February 2014.

33 See *Amanda Jane Mellet v Ireland* (2016) CCPR/C/116/D/2324/2013; *Karen Noelia Lla-ntoy Huamán v Peru* (2005) CCPR/C/85/D/1153/2003; *Siobhan Whelan v Ireland* (2017) CCPR/C/119/D/2425/2014.

34 HRC, Draft General Comment No.36, para.9.

35 Ibid.

36 HRC, Concluding Observations on the Fourth Periodic Report of Ireland, 19 August 2014, CCPR/C/IRL/CO/4, para.9.

37 CRPD Committee, Comments on the Draft General Comment No.36 of the Human Rights Committee on Article 6 of the International Covenant on Civil and Political Rights, para.1 (on file with the author).

38 CRPD Committee considers the Initial Report of Belgium, 19 September 2014, available at http://www.ohchr.org/EN/NewsEvents/Pages/DisplayNews.aspx?NewsID=15 073&LangID=E, accessed 21 March 2018.

39 CESCR, General Comment No.14 on Article 12 ICESCR (The Right to the Highest Attainable Standard of Health), 2000, E/C.12/2000/4, para.25.

40 *Carter v Canada (Attorney General)* 2015 SCC 5.

41 Ibid, para.70.

42 Ibid, para.62.

43 Ibid, para.64.

44 Ibid, para.66.

45 HRC, Concluding Observations on Report of Netherlands, 2009, para.7.

46 CRPD Committee, Concluding Observations on the Initial Report of Canada, 8 May 2017, CRPD/C/CAN/CO/1.

47 *Yuba Kumari Katwal v Nepal* (2015) CCPR/C/113/D/2000/2010.

48 Ibid, para.11.5.

49 Ibid, para.11.6.

50 Ibid, para.11.7.

51 Ibid, para.11.2.

52 HRC, Draft General Comment No.36, para.8.

53 Ibid, para.17.

54 Ibid, para.8.

55 *Herrera Rubio v Colombia* (1990) CCPR/C/31/D/161/1983; HRC, General Comment No.6 on Article 6 (The Right to Life), 30 April 1982.

56 Ibid, para.8.

57 Article 11 CRPD provides that 'States Parties shall take, in accordance with their obligations under international law, including international humanitarian law and international human rights law, all necessary measures to ensure the protection and safety of persons with disabilities in situations of risk, including situations of armed conflict, humanitarian emergencies and the occurrence of natural disasters.'

58 CRPD Committee, Concluding Observations on the Initial Report of Luxembourg, 10 October 2017, CRPD/C/LUX/CO/1.

59 See *James Marlon Noble v Australia* (2016) CRPD/C/16/7/2012 in Chapter 5.

60 Ibid, para.8.10.

61 UN General Assembly, 6th Resolution Calling for a Universal Moratorium on Executions, 19 December 2016, A/RES/71/187.

7

PARTICIPATION IN POLITICAL AND PUBLIC LIFE

Introduction

The ability to hold and express opinions, and to cause those opinions to be translated into actions that are respectful of others, guided by conscience and within the bounds of acceptable morals, is at the heart of what it means to be free. The rights to freedom of opinion, expression, association and peaceful assembly are the cornerstones upon which a democratic society is built. These four rights are closely interconnected and collectively they are the bridge which holds the organs of state accountable.

Article 21 CRPD, which provides for the right to freedom of expression and opinion and access to information, glosses on Article 19(1) and (2) ICCPR which contain the right to freedom of opinion and of expression. With its express reference to the right to access information using all forms of communication, Article 21 CRPD brings a disability perspective to these rights. Freedom of opinion and freedom of expression form the basis for the enjoyment of a multitude of other human rights. States Parties are under an international obligation to respect these freedoms and to ensure that non-state actors do likewise. According to the HRC, '[a]ll branches of the State (executive, legislative and judicial) and other public or governmental authorities, at whatever level—national, regional or local—are in a position to engage the responsibility of the State party'.[1]

Likewise Article 29 CRPD, which provides for the right of persons with disabilities to participate in political life, touches on various other Articles of the ICCPR containing the rights to peaceful assembly, freedom of association, to participate in public affairs, to vote and to be elected. Article 29(a) CRPD requires States Parties to ensure 'that persons with disabilities can effectively and fully participate in political and public life on an equal basis with others, directly or through freely chosen representatives, including the right and opportunity for persons with disabilities to vote and be elected'. Article 29(b) CRPD requires States Parties to actively promote 'an environment in which persons with disabilities can effectively and fully participate in the conduct of public affairs, without discrimination and on an equal basis with others'. It also requires States Parties to encourage the participation of persons with disabilities in public affairs. The right of every citizen to take part in public and political life on an equal basis with others includes the right to express one's opinion, including to freely choose and vote for candidates in elections. These provisions require States Parties to ensure that citizens have an effective opportunity to freely determine their political status. The right of persons with disabilities to access public services and public information on an equal basis with others is a prerequisite if the rights enshrined in Article 29(a) and (b) CRPD are to have effect.

Notwithstanding the provisions of international law described above, persons with disabilities have had to fight relentlessly for equal recognition of their rights to freedom of expression and opinion and of their right to participate in political and public life. To date, persons with disabilities still do not enjoy these rights on an equal basis with others and the struggle for equal recognition is ongoing. During the 1990s, disability rights movements organised protests through direct action, seeking to vindicate the civil and political rights of persons with disabilities. In essence, these protesters were saying that they were no longer passive spectators, but active participants at every level of the community.

Persons with disabilities form the largest minority group in the world. However, prior to the adoption of the CRPD, their participation in political and public life was not always guaranteed. Persons with disabilities could not always express themselves on issues which might affect their daily living conditions and they wanted their government and world political leaders to acknowledge them as equal citizens before and under the law. There were increasing calls for an internationally binding covenant which would recognise the civil and political rights of persons with disabilities. Such a covenant would also need to provide for the establishment of an international monitoring mechanism to adjudicate on the rights of persons with disabilities to vote, to assemble freely in associations and to participate in political and public life on an equal basis with others. Persons with disabilities and their representative organisations also called for the harmonisation of domestic law and policy with the provisions of such a covenant.

States have frequently responded to the peaceful protests of persons with disabilities with the arbitrary arrest and imprisonment of human rights disability activists. Such protests have called for affirmative government action to ensure a place at the negotiating table for persons with disabilities in matters pertaining to their participation in political and public life. Peaceful assemblies by persons with disabilities have regularly been banned and members of the British Council of Disabled People, with its illustrious history of campaigning to promote full equality and participation of persons with disabilities in the UK, were arrested in the 1990s.[2] More recently, persons with disabilities in the Republic of Korea were 'impeded from participating in assemblies by police immobilising or obstructing their assistive devices, sometimes physically removing them from assemblies against their will'.[3]

Freedom of opinion and expression

Freedom of opinion and freedom of expression are essential prerequisites for persons with disabilities to fully-fledged members of society. The two freedoms are closely intertwined, as freedom of expression is the avenue through which opinions and ideas may be freely exchanged. Together, freedom of opinion and freedom of expression form the basis of a democratic society. Freedom of opinion, as enshrined in Article 19(1) ICCPR, is a negative freedom in the sense that it is a right which should not be infringed in any circumstances. On the other hand, Article 21 CRPD imposes a positive obligation upon States Parties to ensure that the right to freedom of opinion and of expression, including the freedom to seek, receive and impart information and ideas, is fully extended to persons with disabilities on an equal basis with others. It elaborates both the obligations and the means by which these rights should be respected.

The right to freedom of expression, as laid down in Article 19(2) ICCPR, is not absolute. Article 19(3) ICCPR qualifies this right by stipulating that its exercise carries with it special duties and responsibilities. Article 21 CRPD is not expressly subject to the same qualification as Article 19(3) ICCPR. However, it should not be assumed that as a result of this omission persons with disabilities can deliberately defame others or make statements without impunity or which compromise the security of the state. It can be argued that the principles contained in Article 19(3) ICCPR will also apply to the interpretation of the rights enshrined in Article 21 CRPD. This is because the rights to freedom of opinion, expression and access to information must be exercised by persons with disabilities on 'an equal basis with others' and non-disabled persons presumably cannot make such statements without impunity. Restriction of the rights contained in Article 19(2) ICCPR can be justified only in the following circumstances under Article 19(3):

- the restriction is provided for by law;
- the restriction is for the protection of public order or for the respect of the rights of other individuals; and
- the restriction is necessary and proportionate.[4]

In *Viktorovich Shchetko and Vladimir Vladimirovich v Belarus*, it was claimed that the State of Belarus had violated the rights of Mr Shchetko and Mr Vladimirovich by fining them for distributing leaflets calling for the boycott of a general election.[5] The State of Belarus argued that the fine which had been imposed upon Mr Shchetko and Mr Vladimirovich was effected under the Administrative Offences Code and, as such, it was a lawful restriction, in accordance with Article 19(3) ICCPR. According to the HRC, in principle, the application of laws which prohibit intimidation or coercion of voters may constitute a lawful limitation of freedom of expression. However, any situation in which voters are subject to intimidation and coercion must be distinguished from a situation in which voters are encouraged to boycott an election without any form of intimidation. The State of Belarus merely argued that the restrictions were provided for by law, without any actual justification of the measures in the particular circumstances of the case. The HRC concluded that the fine which had been imposed on Mr Shchetko and Mr Vladimirovich was not justified under any of the criteria set out in Article 19(3) ICCPR.

In *Svetik v Belarus*, Mr Svetik claimed that his right to freedom of expression under Article 19(2) ICCPR had been violated as he was subjected to an administrative penalty 'for the sole expression of his political opinion'.[6] The HRC had to decide whether punishing a call to boycott an election was a permissible limitation on Mrs Svetik's freedom of expression. The HRC held that voting was not compulsory in Belarus at that time and that the declaration signed by Mrs Svetik did not affect the possibility of voters' freely deciding whether or not to participate in that particular election. Mrs Svetik's rights under Article 19(2) had been violated because 'the limitation of the liberty of expression did not legitimately serve one of the reasons enumerated in article 19, paragraph 3'.[7] The reasons by which a State Party may seek to might justify such a restriction on the right to freedom of expression are: respect for the rights or reputations of others or for the protection of national security, public order, health or morals.[8]

In *Olechkevitch v Belarus*, Mr Olechkevitch claimed that the application of the Public Events Act 1997 had resulted in an unjustified restriction of his right to impart information under Article 19 ICCPR.[9] The 1997 Act prohibited the production and dissemination of information about public events before prior authorisation for an event had been granted. Mr Olechkevitch had been arrested and fined by the police when distributing leaflets inviting people to attend two unauthorised meetings with a representative of the political opposition in Belarus. The HRC recalled that all restrictions imposed upon freedom of expression must conform with strict tests of necessity and proportionality. Such restrictions must be 'applied only for those purposes for which they were prescribed' and must be 'directly related to the specific need on which they are predicated'.[10] The HRC held that the onus was upon the State Party to prove that the restrictions were necessary. Even if a State Party 'is in a position to implement a system designed to achieve a balance between individuals' freedom to impart information and the general interest in preserving public order in a particular area, this system's functioning must be compatible with article 19 of the Covenant'.[11] Given that a local court had refused to examine the issue of whether the restriction on Mr Olechkevitch's right to impart information was necessary, the HRC concluded that there had been a violation of Article 19(2) ICCPR by the State of Belarus.

The above case law illustrates that the HRC has examined the circumstances in which restrictions of the right to freedom of expression set out in Article 19(3) ICCPR may be justified. The HRC's reasoning as reflected in the case law can be applied to cases involving alleged breaches of Article 21 CRPD, which protects the right of persons with disabilities to freedom of expression. The HRC has stressed that Article 19(2) ICCPR protects all forms of expression and means of dissemination including the spoken and written word, sign language and non-verbal expressions such as images and artefacts.[12] An effective means of ensuring that persons with disabilities enjoy freedom of expression is through providing access to both information and communication, as required by Article 21 CRPD. As will be seen in the next section, accessibility to different forms of communication, especially sign language, is essential to guarantee the right of persons with disabilities to freedom of expression.

Freedom of expression and official interactions

Article 21 CRPD sets out the responsibility of States Parties to ensure that persons with disabilities 'can exercise the right to freedom of expression and opinion, including the freedom to seek, receive and impart information and ideas on an equal basis with others and through all forms of communication of their choice'. This responsibility requires States Parties, in the course of official communications, to accept and facilitate 'the use of sign languages, Braille, augmentative and alternative communication, and all other accessible means, modes and formats of communication of their choice by persons with disabilities in official interactions'.[13] Persons with disabilities usually have to overcome administrative obstacles which inhibit their access to information or their freedom of expression or opinion. The lack of regulations governing access to procedures, including access to official forms in accessible formats, is a particular cause of concern.

In *Gauthier v Canada*, Mr Gauthier, although a journalist, was not a member of a private press organisation responsible for the accreditation of its members, such accreditation being necessary to gain access to parliament.[14] Mr Gauthier was refused access to parliament, and nor was he allowed to take notes on its proceedings. The HRC held that Canada had allowed a private organisation to control access to the parliamentary press facilities, without intervention. The scheme which had been adopted did not ensure an absence of arbitrary exclusion from access to the parliamentary media facilities. This was held to be a violation of Mr Gauthier's rights under Article 19(2) and (3) ICCPR.

In the cases of *Michael Lockrey v Australia* and *Gemma Beasley v Australia*, the CRPD Committee considered the rights to freedom of expression and opinion enshrined in Article 21(b) CRPD.[15] The issue in these two cases was whether the failure to provide reasonable accommodation for deaf persons who had been called for jury service, in the form of either a sign-language interpreter or real-time stenocaptioning, amounted to a violation of Article 21(b) CRPD. The CRPD Committee noted that, in essence, Article 21(b) was subject to progressive realisation. However, it also noted that Article 21(b) places an obligation on States Parties to ensure that persons with disabilities can exercise their rights to freedom of expression or opinion on an equal basis with others, using the form of communication of their choice.[16] The CRPD Committee held that a juror or judicial officer was a person with public responsibility for the administration of justice; a role which necessitates 'interactions with other persons'. Such interactions constituted 'official interactions' within the meaning of Article 21(b) CRPD. The CRPD Committee therefore found that the refusal to provide Mrs Beasley and Mr Lockery with the form of communication which they needed to perform jury duty violated their right under Article 21(b) to express themselves in official interactions.

Even if the right to freedom of expression, opinion and access to information (Article 21 CRPD) and the right to participate in political and public life (Article 29 CRPD) are conceptually distinct from one another, they are in fact indissolubly linked. Article 29(a)(iii) bridges the gap between these two rights by declaring that States Parties should guarantee 'the free expression of the will of persons with disabilities as electors'. Freedom to express one's political views through voting is essential if persons with disabilities are going to participate fully and effectively in political life on an equal basis with others. The right of persons with disabilities to participate in political life is discussed further below.

Participation in political life (the rights to vote and to be elected)

The rights to vote and to be elected significantly impact on the lives of persons with disabilities. They provide persons with disabilities with the same opportunity as their non-disabled counterparts to fully and effectively participate in the democratic process. Through voting, persons with disabilities assert their individual autonomy. They are their own persons. The right to vote is not restricted to being able to vote in the formal sense. It requires States Parties to actually provide an opportunity for persons with disabilities to enjoy the right to vote on an equal basis with others. States Parties are under an obligation to implement positive measures to provide an accessible physical environment where persons with disabilities may exercise their right to vote. Such positive measures may include making polling stations accessible to wheelchair users.

In its General Comment No.25, the HRC stated that it is unreasonable for States Parties 'to restrict the right to vote *on the ground of physical disability* or to impose literacy, educational or property requirements'.[17] However, the HRC subsequently did not extend the right to vote to persons with psychosocial and intellectual disabilities. The medical model of disability was still prevalent in 1996 when the HRC's General Comment No.25 was adopted. Persons with psychosocial and intellectual disabilities were routinely denied the right to exercise their vote as they were presumed to lack the legal capacity to do so. However, the advent of the CRPD and the evolving jurisprudence of the CRPD Committee is bringing about a paradigm shift whereby the traditional medical model of disability is gradually being replaced by a human rights–based model of disability. For example, in its Initial Report of Canada, the CRPD Committee noted that despite the implementation of programmes and strategies to facilitate the right to vote of persons with disabilities, such measures did not specifically include persons with psychosocial or intellectual disabilities.[18]

It is frequently the case that persons with intellectual or psychosocial disabilities are denied the right to vote as a direct consequence of having been deprived of their legal capacity. This was illustrated in the Initial Report of Lithuania.[19] In its Concluding Observations, the CRPD Committee stated that the Constitution of Lithuania denied persons with disabilities the right to vote and to stand for election in circumstances where they have been declared legally incapable.[20] The CRPD Committee recommended to the State of Lithuania that it should repeal or amend any legal or constitutional provision which 'denied the right of persons with disabilities to vote and stand for election'. Such measures should include removing the possibility of persons with disabilities being declared 'legally incapable on the ground of disability'.[21]

In *Bujdoso et al v Hungary*, the CRPD Committee had the opportunity to explore the normative contents of the right of persons with psychosocial and intellectual disabilities to vote as enshrined in Article 29(a) CRPD.[22] In that case, persons with psychosocial disabilities were denied the right to vote in accordance with Article 70(5) of the Constitution of Hungary. The State of Hungary attempted to remedy the structural discrimination embedded in the constitution by introducing an assessment procedure to determine the eligibility for enfranchisement of intellectually disabled persons. This assessment of eligibility to vote was based upon the medical condition of the persons concerned.

Harvard University intervened as a third party on behalf of the authors. It submitted that a person loses his right to vote if a court finds that he lacks the capacity to vote. The assessments in question only affect persons with psychosocial or intellectual disabilities under guardianship.[23] New legislation which purported to provide for an assessment of eligibility to vote continued to allow for the disenfranchisement of persons with psychosocial or intellectual disabilities. This was because the eligibility assessment proceeded on the basis of a lack of legal capacity for persons with intellectual or psychosocial disabilities. The authors' representative argued that Article 29(a) CRPD provides for an unconditional right to vote for all persons with disabilities and that it does not provide for restrictions on the basis of real or perceived disability. The denial of the right to vote on the basis of disability constitutes direct discrimination. This is because denial of this right is founded upon a stereotypical view of persons with intellectual or psychosocial disabilities as being incapable of having political views.

The CRPD Committee held that Article 29(a) CRPD does not provide for any reasonable restriction or exception of the right to vote. To deny the right to vote on the basis of a perceived or actual psychosocial or intellectual disability, including where the restriction on the right to vote is based upon an assessment of an individual, constitutes discrimination on the basis of disability, in accordance with Article 2 of the CRPD.[24] The legislation which permits the judiciary to deprive persons with an intellectual disability of their right to vote and to be elected amounts to a violation of Article 29(a) CRPD. The CRPD Committee further held that the grounds of the assessment were not legitimate, nor was the assessment proportional to the aim of preserving the integrity of the State Party's political system. For these reasons, it was held that the assessment of the legal capacity of persons with intellectual and psychosocial disabilities was discriminatory.

Article 29(a) CRPD sets out the necessary conditions for persons with disabilities to be able to exercise their right to vote. While Article 25(b) ICCPR prohibits 'unreasonable restrictions' on the right to vote, thereby implying that the right may be curtailed in particular circumstances, the CRPD does not provide for any exceptions to the right of persons with disabilities to vote.[25] Article 29 CRPD requires that persons with disabilities must be able fully and effectively to exercise their right to vote. Prior to the ruling in *Bujdoso et al v Hungary*, it could be argued that that the right to vote in the context of the CRPD was subject to progressive realisation, but that theory has since lost ground. With regard to their positive obligation to fulfil human rights, States Parties do indeed enjoy 'a margin of appreciation in identifying the measures which should be adopted to ensure that persons with disabilities have an actual opportunity to participate in the conduct of the public affairs of their country on an equal basis with others'.[26] However, this does not absolve the State Party from its responsibility to fully realise this right and failure to do so would be a breach of the right of persons with disabilities to participate in political and public life on an equal basis with others. Based on the reasoning in *Bujdoso et al*, Article 29 CRPD arguably affords greater protection for the rights of persons with disabilities than those which arise under Article 25(b) ICCPR. This is particularly illustrated by the most recent communication, *Fiona Given v Australia*, in which the CRPD Committee had the opportunity to examine the cross-cutting issues of discrimination and the right to secret voting.[27]

In this case, the author, although she was accompanied by her assistant so that she could vote, requested the help of the electoral officer under Article 234 of the Australian Commonwealth Electoral Act 1918. As a person with cerebral palsy, she needed support as she did not want to disclose the secret content of her vote to her personal assistant. Article 234 of the Electoral Act permitted persons with physical disabilities to request the polling booth's presiding officer to assist them with marking the ballot papers according to their instructions, fold them and deposit them in the ballot box. The electoral officer refused to help her, arguing that he was very busy and that she could have recourse to her personal assistant. The author submitted that her rights under Articles 5, 9 and 29 CRPD were violated. She averred that an electronic voting system was in place to allow blind and visually-impaired persons to cast their vote independently and in complete secrecy but that the same system was not accessible to her as a person with cerebral palsy.[28] She also argued that the rights under Article 29 CRPD were derived from Article 25 ICCPR and that they were immediately realisable at and from the entry into force of the CRPD in Australia. She thus contended that denial of access to an electronic voting system constituted discrimination under Article 5 CRPD against her as a person with disability.

The CRPD Committee had to assess whether Australia had violated the rights of the author by failing to provide her with accessible voting procedures and facilities and the right to vote by secret ballot used assistive technology, per Article 29(a)(i–ii) CRPD. The CRPD Committee, following a similar line of reasoning as in *Bujdoso et al v Hungary*, held that Australia had violated the rights of the author under Article 29(a)(i–ii) read in conjunction with Article 5(2) and Article 9(1) insofar as access to the use of an electronic voting system would have enabled the author to cast an independent and secret ballot in the manner of her choice and on an equal basis with others. Article 29 CRPD places an obligation on States Parties to adapt their voting procedures by ensuring that they are 'appropriate, accessible, and easy to understand and use'. The CRPD Committee thus concluded that Australia had to take adequate measures to ensure that the author has access to voting procedures and facilities which will enable her to vote by secret ballot in future domestic elections and referendums.

Article 29 CRPD does not elaborate on what constitutes 'full and effective participation in political or public life'. However, these terms should be given their ordinary meaning and 'participation' should be taken to include involvement in all areas of political and public life. This is not only an objective in itself but it is also essential for the effective enjoyment of other rights.[29] The push for full inclusion of persons with disabilities and their representative organisations in policy and decision-making processes represents a seismic shift for society whereby the voices of persons with disabilities are heard, their priorities are recognised and their interests are considered on an equal basis with others.

Right to participate in public life

The ability to exercise one's rights to freedom of association and peaceful assembly 'constitutes a key component in the empowerment of marginalized communities and individuals'.[30] Such marginalised communities include persons with disabilities and Article 29(b) CRPD reaffirms their rights to freedom of assembly and of association. It includes the right to participate in non-governmental organisations concerned with the public and political life of the state and also in the activities and administration of political parties. There is also a right to form and join organisations representing persons with disabilities at international, national, regional and local levels. Persons with disabilities are often excluded from organising and participating in peaceful gatherings. Domestic legislation and policies do not adequately reflect the importance of reasonable accommodation and accessibility for the full and effective participation of persons with disabilities in the conduct of public affairs. There are physical barriers to be contended with, such as a lack of access to public buildings and amenities, including transportation, distances to be travelled to officially sanctioned protest sites and a lack of accommodation for facilitated communication, including in the online environment.[31] All of these factors serve to deny persons with disabilities the opportunity of peaceful assembly.

Article 29(b) CRPD recognises that the denial of the rights of persons with disabilities to fully and effectively participate in the conduct of public affairs constitutes discrimination. For instance, in *Gemma Beasley v Australia*, the failure by the State Party to provide either Auslan interpretation or steno-captioning to enable a deaf person to perform jury duty on an equal basis with others constituted disability-based discrimination (Article 5(1) and (3), Article 29(b) CRPD). Within the Australian justice system, following *Gemma Beasley v Australia*, the requirement for the full and effective participation of persons with disabilities in the conduct of public affairs includes not only claimants, victims and defendants, but also extends to jurors.

As the violation of Article 29(b) in *Gemma Beasley v Australia* was contingent upon the violation of other Articles of the Convention, the CRPD Committee did not have the opportunity in that case to explore the normative contents of Article 21 CRPD. It is interesting to note how the HRC has interpreted the rights to freedom of association and freedom of peaceful assembly (Articles 22, 21 ICCPR). The HRC jurisprudence in this regard provides a tantalising glimpse of how the CRPD Committee may construe these rights in relation to persons with disabilities in future.

Freedom of association

Article 22(1) ICCPR provides that everyone shall have the right to freedom of association. Similar to the right to freedom of expression set out in Article 19(1) ICCPR, the right to freedom of association is not absolute. Three conditions must be satisfied where a State Party seeks to derogate from the right to freedom of association. First, the restriction must be prescribed by law. Second, the restriction can be imposed only if it is either in the interest of public order or for the protection of the rights and freedoms of others. Finally, the restriction on the right to freedom of association must be necessary in a democratic society and proportionate in nature. Article 22(2) ICCPR replicates nearly all the conditions found in Article 19(3) ICCPR so that the protection afforded to the twin rights of freedom of association and of expression is almost identical. The only difference is that Article 22(2) ICCPR makes specific reference to the need for any restriction of one's right to freely associate to be necessary 'in a democratic society'. The jurisprudence of the HRC sheds more light on what the notion of 'democratic society' entails as far as breaches of the right to freedom of association are concerned.

In *Vladimir Romanovsky v Belarus*, Mr Romanovsky claimed that the refusal by the Ministry of Justice to register the public association 'Elderlies' was an arbitrary restriction on his right to freedom of association.[32] Mr Romanovsky contended that the reasons put forward by the Ministry were not provided for in legislation, thereby rendering the refusal to register the 'Elderlies' group as arbitrary. The HRC held that the Ministry's justifications were disproportionate and unnecessary for reasons of security, public order, or for the protection of health, morals or the rights and freedoms of others. The *Romanovsky* ruling suggests that the existence of associations, including those which peacefully promote ideas that are not necessarily favourably viewed by the government or the majority of the population, is fundamental in a democratic society.[33] Consequently, it is for States Parties to prove that restrictions on the right to freedom of association are justified in every case. The HRC held that even though the reasons given by the Ministry were prescribed by law, the State Party had not expanded on 'why' they were necessary in the interests of one of the purposes listed in Article 22(2) ICCPR, nor on why the refusal to register the association was proportionate. In the circumstances, the HRC concluded that Mr Romanovsky's right to freedom of association had been breached.

Freedom of assembly

The right to peaceful assembly allows one to organise, and/or to participate in, a peaceful picket or demonstration. It also includes the right to protest at a public setting. The right to peaceful assembly in conformity with Article 21 ICCPR is limited in nature. There should be no restriction of the exercise of this right except when permitted by law and when the restriction is necessary in a democratic society in the interests of national security, public safety, public order, the protection of public health or morals or for the protection of the rights and freedoms of others. The conditions for a permissible restriction on the right to peaceful assembly are the same as those pertaining to the right to freedom of association set out in Article 22(2) ICCPR. However, in its case law on freedom of assembly, the HRC has constantly stressed that States Parties should first and foremost seek to uphold the rights of citizens to freely assemble:

> When a State party imposes restrictions with the aim of reconciling an individual's right to assembly and the aforementioned interests of general concern, it should be guided by the objective of facilitating the right, rather than seeking to impose unnecessary or disproportionate limitations on it.[34]

States Parties are therefore under an obligation to justify any limitation of the right to peaceful assembly protected by Article 21 ICCPR. In *Valentin Evrezov v Belarus*, freedom of assembly was defined as 'a fundamental human right that is essential for public expression of one's views and opinions and indispensable in a democratic society'.[35] As the jurisprudence of the HRC illustrates, the right to peaceful assembly is closely linked with the right to freedom of expression and opinion.

In *Evgeny Basarevsky and Valery Rybchenko v Belarus*, the authors alleged that their right to freedom of expression under Article 19 ICCPR and also to freedom of peaceful assembly under Article 21 ICCPR had been arbitrarily restricted. They argued that the domestic municipal authorities of Belarus had refused them permission to organise pickets and to publicly express their opinions, and that the refusal was unjustified.[36] The HRC had to determine whether the restriction imposed on Mr Basarevsky's and Mr Rybchenko's rights was justified under either Article 19(3) or 21 ICCPR. The application to hold a picket was treated by the court as an application to hold a public event and was rejected because the concept of 'political persecution' was not defined in the Belarus Criminal Code. Furthermore, the locations which had been selected for the picket were not among those permitted by the town's executive.[37] However, the prohibition of a protest against political persecution for such reasons did not meet the standards of necessity and proportionality under Article 19(3) ICCPR. The State of Belarus and its national courts had failed to provide any justification for such restriction, nor had it demonstrated how the authors' pickets would violate the interests of national security, public safety, public order, the protection of public health or morals or the protection of the rights and freedoms of others. The HRC held that, even though the restrictions were prescribed by law, they were in clear violation of Mr Basarevsky's and Mr Rybchenko's right to impart information and ideas of all kinds and also their right to freedom of assembly in line with Article 19(2) and 21 ICCPR.

Conclusion

The ICCPR jurisprudence illustrates the application of the principles upon which the right to vote is based and it will undoubtedly inform the CRPD Committee going forward, in seeking to apply those same principles with regard to persons with disabilities. In *Yevdokimov and Rezaov v Russia*, the HRC held that denial of the right to vote to Mr Yevdokimov and Mr Rezaov, who had been denied their liberty under court sentence, constituted an unreasonable restriction of their right to vote in accordance with Article 25(b) ICCPR.[38] It will be interesting to see how a similar case might be decided before the CRPD Committee, if in the future it is asked to consider an alleged breach of the right to vote. Would the CRPD Committee, in such a situation, be prepared to hold that there has been a breach of rights under both Articles 5 and 29(a) CRPD, in that States Parties have a duty to provide reasonable accommodation to allow the prisoner with disabilities the opportunity to vote on an equal basis with others? It is to be hoped that in such a case the CRPD Committee's answer would be in the affirmative, given that the right to vote is the foundation of any free and democratic society.

The paternalistic attitudes which continue to prevail regarding the right of persons with disabilities to freedom of expression and to participate in political and public life are a cause of serious concern. This is so, notwithstanding the optimism which followed the CRPD Committee's decision in *Budjoso et al v Hungary*. Even the most democratic of societies still seek to act on behalf of persons with disabilities without consultation. It is appalling that this remains the case, notwithstanding ten years' of reminders to States Parties in the form of the Concluding Observations regarding their obligations in line with Articles 4(3) and 33(3) CRPD.

Summary of Concluding Observations and Recommendations

The CRPD Committee has regularly addressed the right of persons with disabilities to participate in political and public life in the Concluding Observations of its State Parties' Reports. Of primary concern to the Committee have been national measures serving to disenfranchise persons with disabilities and the failure of States Parties to provide adequate means for the dissemination of public information or to communicate in a manner which meets the needs of persons with disabilities.

In its Concluding Observations on Hungary, the Committee highlighted the need to ensure that national legislation enables persons with disabilities to exercise their right to vote and to participate in public and political life on an equal basis with others.[39] A similar recommendation was made in 2015 regarding Ukraine, where the Committee urged the State Party to amend its national legislation to enable persons with disabilities to enjoy the right to vote and to be elected regardless of the effect of guardianship or other regimes.[40]

The systematic denial of the right to vote to persons with psychosocial or intellectual disabilities has also been addressed by the CRPD Committee. In 2016, the Committee noted the need for legal and constitutional reform in Lithuania to ensure that persons with disabilities were not deprived of their right to vote on the basis of a declaration of legal incapacity or by virtue of a disability.[41] It also urged the State of Lithuania to restore the right to vote to persons with disabilities who have been excluded from the electoral register and to ensure that all persons with disabilities have the right to assistance where necessary to facilitate their vote. The Committee further requested that Lithuania collect statistics on the level of participation of persons with disabilities in the electoral process, both in their capacity as voters and also as candidates for election. In 2016, the Committee urged the State of Bolivia to repeal its domestic legislation which restricted the right to vote on grounds of legal capacity, and to ensure that persons with psychosocial or intellectual impairments were both registered to vote and eligible to stand as candidates for election.[42]

In 2017, the Committee highlighted the need for legal reform in Bosnia and Herzegovina to ensure that persons with disabilities can participate in the electoral process on an equal basis with others and that they have unhindered access to the voting process.[43] In 2017, the Committee also urged the State of Canada to ensure access for persons with psychosocial or intellectual disabilities to every level of the electoral process.[44] It also recommended that the State of Honduras ensure that its voting procedures are fully accessible to persons with disabilities, and that such persons are legally entitled to assistance from a person of their choice when voting.[45]

The lack of access to sign language interpreters for persons with disabilities, and its impact upon their right to participate in political and public life, has been a recurring theme of the CRPD Committee in recent years. In 2016, the Committee recommended that the State of Slovakia significantly increase the availability of trained sign language interpreters in the broadcasting, legal and other public sectors.[46] The same year, it made a similar observation with regard to the State of Bolivia, whom it urged to expedite recognition of Bolivian sign language as an official language of the state, to increase the availability of Bolivian sign language interpreters and to introduce a scheme for their accreditation.[47] With regard to Guatemala, the Committee found that there was a need to improve access to information for persons with disabilities in the natural languages of its indigenous communities.[48] It also called for the official recognition of Guatemalan sign language and Braille as the basis of an official reading and writing code for blind and deaf-blind persons, and urged the State of Guatemala to ensure that sufficient numbers of ballot papers in Braille were available for such persons at election time.

In 2017, the Committee reminded the state of Bosnia and Herzegovina of its responsibility to ensure the full recognition of sign language and Braille.[49] It also highlighted the need for public broadcasters and telecommunications service providers in Bosnia and Herzegovina to make information available in a variety of formats, including Easy Read, to meet the needs of persons with disabilities. With regard to Cyprus, the Committee noted that there was a need to ensure that sufficient financial resources were made available for sign language interpretation services, and for the State of Cyprus to take steps to recognise and promote Cypriot sign language and forms of tactile communication.[50] It also called for state support for the development of augmentative and alternative modes of communication, especially for use by persons with psychosocial or intellectual disabilities. In 2017, the Committee urged the State of Canada, working in conjunction with organisations of deaf persons, to recognise American and Québec sign languages as official languages of the state, to promote their use in schools and to establish a quality control mechanism for sign language interpretation services.[51] It also called for the promotion of Easy Read and other accessible information formats, and for the provision of information and communications technology (ICT) in the form of software and assistive devices for persons with disabilities.

In 2011, in its thematic study on participation in political and public life by persons with disabilities, the OHCHR drew attention to the need to interpret Article 25 ICCPR in light of developments in human rights law pertaining to persons with disabilities.[52] It also highlighted the need for the HRC to review its General Comment No.25 (1996) on the right to participate in public affairs, voting rights and the right of equal access to public services in line with international human rights law.[53] The OHCHR considered the measures which States Parties may adopt to facilitate persons with disabilities in the exercise of their vote, such as the use of postal voting or voting at special polling stations. It stated that the appropriateness of such measures must be assessed against the need to include persons with disabilities in society, and to promote their independence, autonomy and dignity. Such measures should not be generally relied upon, and should be contemplated only in cases where it is extremely difficult or impossible for persons with disabilities to vote in regular polling stations.

Notes

1 HRC, General Comment No.34 on Article 19 (Freedoms of Opinion and Expression), 12 September 2011, CCPR/C/GC/34, para.7.
2 See Shakespeare, Tom, 'Disabled People's Self-Organisation: A New Social Movement?', 8:3 Disability, Handicap and Society 1993.
3 OHCHR, Report of the Special Rapporteur on the Rights to Freedom of Peaceful Assembly and of Association on his Mission to the Republic of Korea, 15 June 2016, A/HRC/32/36/Add.2, para.44.
4 For a full account of the application of Article 19 (3) ICCPR, see HRC, General Comment No.34 on Article 19 ICCPR, paras 21–36.
5 *Viktorovich Shchetko and Vladimir Vladimirovich v Belarus* (2006) CCPR/C/87/D/1009/2001.
6 *Leonid Svetik v Belarus* (2004) CCPR/C/81/D/927/2000, para.7.2.
7 Ibid, para.7.3.
8 Article 19(3) ICCPR.
9 *Andrei Olechkevitch v Belarus* (2013) CCPR/C/107/D/1785/2008.
10 Ibid, para.8.3.
11 Ibid, para.8.5.
12 HRC, General Comment No.34 on Article 19 ICCPR, para.12.
13 Article 21 (b) CRPD.
14 *Gauthier v Canada* (1999) CCPR/C/65/D/633/1995.
15 *Michael Lockrey v Australia* (2016) CRPD/C/15/D/13/2013; *Gemma Beasley v Australia* (2016) CRPD/C/15/D/11/2013.
16 Article 2 provides that 'communication' includes languages, display of text, Braille, tactile communication, large print, accessible multimedia as well as written, audio, plain-language, human-reader and augmentative and alternative modes, means and formats of communication, including accessible information and communication technology.
17 HRC, General Comment No.25, Article 25 (The Right to Participate in Public Affairs, Voting Rights and the Right of Equal Access to Public Service), 12 July 1996, CCPR/C/21/Rev.1/Add.7, para.10 (emphasis supplied).
18 CRPD Committee, Concluding Observations on the Initial Report of Canada, 8 May 2017, CRPD/C/CAN/CO/1, para.51.
19 CRPD Committee, Concluding Observations on Initial Report of Lithuania, 11 May 2016, CRPD/C/LTU/CO/1, para.57.
20 Ibid.
21 Ibid, para.58.
22 *Bujdoso et al v Hungary* (2013) CRPD/C/10/D/4/2011.
23 See ibid, paras 5.1–5.11.
24 Article 2 CRPD defines discrimination on the basis of disability as 'any distinction, exclusion or restriction on the basis of disability which has the purpose or effect of impairing or nullifying the recognition, enjoyment or exercise, on an equal basis with others, of all human rights and fundamental freedoms in the political, economic, social, cultural, civil or any other field. It includes all forms of discrimination, including denial of reasonable accommodation'.
25 Article 25 (b) ICCPR provides that 'To vote and to be elected at genuine periodic elections which shall be by universal and equal suffrage and shall be held by secret ballot, guaranteeing the free expression of the will of the electors.'
26 OHCHR, Thematic Study on Participation in Political and Public Life by Persons with Disabilities, 21 December 2011, A/HRC/19/36, para.16.
27 *Fiona Given v Australia* (forthcoming).
28 For an elaboration on the breach on Article 9 (accessibility), see Chapter 8.
29 *Fiona Given v Australia*, para.18.
30 Maina Kiai, Report of the Special Rapporteur on the Rights to Freedom of Peaceful Assembly and of Association, 14 April 2014, A/HRC/26/29, para.15.
31 Ibid, para.40.

32 *Vladimir Romanovsky v Belarus* (2015) CCPR/C/115/D/2011/2010.
33 Ibid, para.7.2; See also *Katsora et al. v. Belarus* (2010) CCPR/C/100/D/1383/2005, para.8.2.
34 *Valentin Evzrezov v Belarus* (2016) CCPR/C/117/D/2101/2011, para.8.4; See also *Sergei Androsenko v Belarus* (2016) CCPR/C/116/D/2092/2011, para.7.6.
35 *Valentin Evrezov v Belarus* (2015) CCPR/C/114/D/1988/2010, para.7.4.
36 *Evgeny Basarevsky and Valery Rybchenko v Belarus* (2016) CCPR/C/117/D/2108/2011-CCPR/C/117/D/2109/2011.
37 Ibid, para.9.2.
38 *Denis Yevdokimov and Artiom Rezanov v Russian Federation* (2011) CCPR/C/101/D/1410/2005.
39 CRPD Committee, Concluding Observations on the Initial Report of Hungary, 22 October 2012, CRPD/C/HUN/CO/1.
40 CRPD Committee, Concluding Observations on the Initial Report of Ukraine, 2 October 2015 CRPD/C/UKR/CO/1.
41 CRPD Committee, Concluding Observations on the Initial Report of Lithuania, 11 May 2016, CRPD/C/LTU/CO/1.
42 CRPD Committee, Concluding Observations on the Initial Report of Bolivia, 4 November 2016, CRPD/C/BOL/CO/1.
43 CRPD Committee, Concluding Observations on the Initial Report of Bosnia and Herzegovina, 2 May 2017, CRPD/C/BIH/CO/1.
44 CRPD Committee, Concluding Observations on the Initial Report of Canada, 8 May 2017, CRPD/C/CAN/CO/1.
45 CRPD Committee, Concluding Observations on the Initial Report of Honduras, 4 May 2017, CRPD/C/HND/CO/1.
46 CRPD Committee, Concluding Observations on the Initial Report on Slovakia 17 May 2016 CRPD/C/SVK/CO/1.
47 CRPD Committee, Concluding Observations on the Initial Report of Bolivia, 4 November 2016, CRPD/C/BOL/CO/1.
48 CRPD Committee, Concluding Observations on the Initial Report of Guatemala, 30 September 2016, CRPD/C/GTM/CO/1.
49 CRPD Committee, Concluding Observations on the Initial Report of Bosnia and Herzegovina.
50 CRPD Committee, Concluding Observations on the Initial Report of Cyprus, 8 May 2017, CRPD/C/CYP/CO/1.
51 CRPD Committee, Concluding Observations on the Initial Report of Canada.
52 OHCHR, Thematic Study on Participation in Political and Public Life by Persons with Disabilities, 21 December 2011, A/HRC/19/36, para.71.
53 Ibid.

PART III

Economic, social and cultural rights

8

ACCESSIBILITY

Introduction

An often forgotten part of the aftermath of the two World Wars are the millions of war casualties who were left with a range of physical and mental impairments. Millions more people have incurred life-long disabilities in the course of over 230 outbreaks of regional and civil wars since the Second World War.[1] In response to this human tragedy, governments introduced welfare benefits systems and established segregated institutions for persons with disabilities. For instance, in relation to financial benefits, following the independence of Mauritius in 1968, the Government announced and implemented a social protection measure known as 'basic invalidity pension', and since then this benefit has not been renamed. The overriding perception of persons with disabilities was that they were functionally limited. Those who were disabled for reasons unrelated to the theatre of war—for example, people who were disabled from birth or who acquired a disability as a result of an accident or illness—were afforded a similar fate, apart from the patriot salutes reserved for war veterans. In the hierarchy of persons with disabilities, the war heroes undoubtedly enjoyed a higher ranking than their non-military counterparts. However, one common denominator amongst all persons with disabilities was that they were taken from their families to be marginalised through hospitalisation or institutionalisation.

In the post-war era, many countries invested heavily in infrastructures which are accessible only to persons without disabilities. Such limits to accessibility significantly contributed to the side-lining of people with disabilities, which in turn led to disproportionate rates of poverty and marginalisation amongst persons with disabilities. The freedom of persons with disabilities to move in and around their own countries and to access public and private buildings was significantly restricted, and in some instances was completely denied. However, at the same time, approximately half of the countries in the world had become Contracting Parties to both the UDHR and ICCPR. Article 13 UDHR and Article 12 ICCPR both reaffirm the right of citizens to freedom of movement and residence within their country borders. Article 5(f) CERD requires States Parties to prohibit and to eliminate racial discrimination in all its forms and to guarantee the right of access of everyone, without distinction as to race, colour, or national or ethnic origin to any place or service intended for use by the general public, such as transport, hotels, restaurants, cafes, theatres and parks. It can be argued that a precedent has been established in the international human rights legal framework for viewing the right to access as a right in and of itself. Admittedly, for members of different racial or ethnic groups, the barriers to free access to places and services open to the public were the result of prejudicial attitudes and a readiness to use force in preventing access to spaces that were physically accessible.

These three important international provisions have been the inspiration for advocates in the disability rights movement, particularly with regard to Article 9 CRPD. Article 9(1) CRPD provides that:

> To enable persons with disabilities to live independently and participate fully in all aspects of life, States Parties shall take appropriate measures to ensure to persons with disabilities access, on an equal basis with others, to the physical environment, to transportation, to information and communications [. . .]

During the final phase of drafting the CRPD, many States Parties were reluctant to incorporate accessibility as an innovative ground for justiciable rights within the Convention. Some stakeholders believed that accessibility as defined by Article 9 would create new rights which were not included within other international covenants. Opponents argued that the scope of Article 9 was far too wide. In the absence of a definition of the word 'accessibility' in the Convention, there was a possibility that the concept would be applied purposively. The risk of purposive interpretation was all the greater because Article 9(1) makes specific reference to the phrase 'all aspects of life'. The financial resources which would be required to allow persons with disabilities to benefit from universally-designed goods, products and services would be extremely burdensome on taxpayers. Opponents were finally reassured by the belief that accessibility falls within the ambit of economic rights, and in that case, Article 4(2) CRPD would afford States Parties the leeway to 'progressively fulfil their obligation'. They would also have a margin of discretion regarding the manner and form of the implementation of Article 9.

In this chapter, the question whether the accessibility rights which are enshrined in Article 9 are of an economic or civil nature will be explored at length. The analysis which follows relies upon the case law of the CRPD Committee, its Concluding Observations, and its General Comment No.2 on Article 9 (Accessibility). According to the CRPD Committee, accessibility to the built environment, transportation and information and communication technologies (ICT) is a precondition for persons with disabilities to be able to live independently, as provided for in Article 19 of the Convention.[2] Article 19, which sets out the right to live independently and be included in the community, must be viewed in tandem with Article 9 (accessibility), because independent living requires that community services and facilities which are available to persons without disabilities should be also available to be enjoyed by persons with disabilities.[3] To deny access to the same facilities and services to persons with disabilities which are otherwise available to the public may amount to discrimination and constitute a violation of Article 9. In accordance with Article 4(1)(b), States Parties are under an obligation to modify or abolish existing laws, regulations, customs and practices that breach the rights of persons with disabilities.

States Parties' obligations in relation to Article 9

In *Szilvia Nyusti and Péter Takács v Hungary*, the authors were both severely visually-impaired individuals who had contracted services agreements with OTP Bank (a private banking institution) for the provision and use of banking cards.[4] Ms Nyusti and Mr Takacs both needed the assistance of third parties in order to access automatic teller machines (ATMs), and as such, they received fewer services for the same fees compared to their non-visually impaired counterparts. In 2005, their legal representatives wrote to OTP requesting the bank to retrofit the ATMs situated in the vicinity of the authors' places of residence. However, OTP refused to do so. In August 2015, Ms Nyusti and Mr Takács raised the matter before the Metropolitan Court, arguing that OTP had violated their personal right to equal treatment, which effectively constituted direct discrimination under the Equal Treatment and Promotion of Equal Opportunities Act 2003. OTP argued that the court could not impose an obligation upon it as to do so would be tantamount to interfering with a contract between private individuals. They further argued that the accessibility requirements of the Built Environment Act did not apply to the case at hand because ATMs were not 'buildings' and did not fall within the scope of the Act.

The Metropolitan Court held that the right to equality imposes an obligation upon service providers to provide equal services for equal fees to all customers and that OTP had directly discriminated against Ms Nyusti and Mr Takács. OTP's obligation to provide equal services for equal fees did not necessarily mean that services had to be provided to every client in the same way. A different means of service provision was required to ensure that clients with visual impairments could access ATMs without assistance. OTP was held liable for failing to retrofit its ATMs following the coming into force of the Equal Treatment Act 2003. The court ordered OTP to retrofit a number of its ATMs, including four machines which were situated in the districts where the authors resided. OTP appealed and the decision was subsequently reversed by the Metropolitan Court of Appeal on the ground that the authors' civil claim did not fall within the scope of Hungarian disability legislation. It was held that OTP was free to amend or conclude its contracts in the manner of its choosing and that the court could not interfere with contractual terms and conditions at the request of just one of the parties to a contract. It further held that the retrofitting of OTP's ATMs posed an increased risk to the safety of others.

Ms Nyusti and Mr Takács applied to the Supreme Court for a judicial review of this decision. However, their request was denied and the Supreme Court upheld the judgment of the Metropolitan Court of Appeal. The Supreme Court stated that the disadvantaged situation of blind and visually impaired persons with regard to the use of ATMs was induced by the fact that there was no Braille facility on the ATMs nor was there voice assistance support available when using the machines. The parties had entered into a contract for current account services, the content of which may be freely established by the parties. Ms Nyusti and Mr Takács had taken note of the contractual terms, and by their conduct they had impliedly agreed to them, including their limited use of facilities. The Supreme Court also upheld the decision of the Metropolitan Court of Appeal that OTP was exempt from the provisions of the Equal Treatment Act 2003.

When the matter came before the CRPD Committee, the issue to be determined was whether the State of Hungary had failed to fulfil its duties in denying persons with visual impairments access to banking card services on an equal basis with others. Article 4(1)(e) of the Convention provides that States Parties must 'take all appropriate measures to eliminate discrimination on the basis of disability by any person, organization or private enterprise'. In accordance with Article 9(2)(a), they must develop, promulgate and monitor the implementation of minimum standards and guidelines for the accessibility of facilities and services open or provided to the public. Services open to the public include those offered by both public and private institutions. States Parties must therefore ensure that private entities which offer facilities and services to the public take into account all aspects of accessibility for persons with disabilities.

The CRPD Committee held that Hungary had failed to fulfil its obligation under Article (9)(2)(b) in that it had not ensured that OTP had made its entire network of ATMs accessible for persons with visual impairments. The decision in *Szilvia Nyusti and Péter Takács v Hungary* is significant because despite the reluctance of the domestic courts to disturb the doctrine of privity of contract, it was held that discrimination on the basis of disability is sufficient ground for judicial intervention to vary the terms and conditions of a contract. The decision also confirmed the obligations of States Parties in accordance with Article 5 of the Convention to ensure that the practices of private providers of goods, services and products are non-discriminatory.

Reasonable accommodation and accessibility

In Chapter 2, 'reasonable accommodation' and 'accessibility' were distinguished as two different concepts within the purview of the Convention. The concept of reasonable accommodation is applied to individuals whereas accessibility is applied to groups of individuals. In *Szilvia Nyusti and Péter Takács v Hungary*, the CRPD

Committee highlighted the fact that the authors' complaint did not relate to the non-provision of reasonable accommodation in that OTP had failed to provide them with the means to access the ATMs. Instead, it was the need to retrofit some of the ATMs within the proximity of the authors' homes so that they became accessible for persons with visual impairments which was at issue in the case.[5] As such, the claim instead fell under the scope of Article 9 since it was framed in broader terms than the need to provide reasonable accommodation. The issue before the Committee was whether the State Party had taken appropriate measures to ensure the accessibility of OTP's banking card services across its entire ATM network for persons with visual impairments. It follows that the claim by Ms Nyusti and Mr Takács fell within the scope of Article 9 of the Convention.[6]

Accessibility relates to groups, and as such it is an *ex ante* duty, which means that States Parties are under an obligation to ensure accessibility prior to the receipt of an individual request to enter or use a place of service.[7] In the case of *Szilvia Nyusti and Péter Takács v Hungary*, the authors chose to ground their action on Article 9 of the CRPD which imposes an unconditional obligation upon States Parties to ensure accessibility. The case predated the publication of the CRPD Committee's General Comment No.2, which confirmed the unconditional nature of the State Parties' duty in that regard:

> the entity obliged to provide accessibility may not excuse the omission to do so by referring to the burden of providing access for persons with disabilities. The duty of reasonable accommodation, contrarily, exists only if implementation constitutes no undue burden on the entity.[8]

The duty to provide reasonable accommodation can therefore be considered as an *ex nunc* duty, i.e. a duty which becomes enforceable from the moment an individual with an impairment requires reasonable accommodation in a given situation such as a workplace or school, in order to enjoy his/her rights on an equal basis in that situation.[9] According to General Comment No.2,

> reasonable accommodation can be used as a means of ensuring accessibility for an individual with a disability in a particular situation. It seeks to achieve individual justice in the sense that non-discrimination or equality is assured, taking the dignity, autonomy and choices of the individual into account.[10]

Based on the above, it would appear that the CRPD Committee has created more confusions than it has attempted to resolve. The distinction between the two concepts of accessibility and reasonable accommodation rests on policy considerations which enable domestic courts to choose between the two concepts without having recourse to reasoned legal principles. In *Szilvia Nyusti and Péter Takács v Hungary*, the Committee's decision implied that the authors' claim was a group action and, as such, it was based on accessibility. However, the authors had individual contracts with OTP Bank and accordingly had a right to seek reasonable accommodation. The domestic courts in Hungary had examined the issue of reasonable accommodation and the CRPD Committee implicitly endorsed its reasoning in that regard. However, irrespective of whether the reasoning in the case was policy-orientated or based on international public law principles, it can be argued that even if Ms Nyusti and Mr Takács had individual contracts with OTP, their action was a group one nonetheless. The distinction between the concepts of accessibility and reasonable accommodation became even more confusing in the case of *Jungelin v Sweden*.[11]

Ms Jungelin was a visually impaired person who claimed that she was denied the reasonable adaptation and support measures which were necessary to guarantee her right to employment. Upon applying for work, Ms Jungelin requested her potential employer, the Social Insurance Agency, to equip her computer with a screen reader and a Braille display to enable her to perform most of the tasks associated with the advertised post. The Social Insurance Agency refused to do so. Ms Jungelin therefore referred the matter to the Ombudsperson and also to the Swedish Labour Court, but her claim was rejected. The Labour Court determined that the measures proposed by the Ombudsman to the Social Insurance Agency which required the latter to adjust its computer systems and to provide other aids for Ms Jungelin were neither reasonable nor proportionate. Ms Jungelin contended that this decision was discriminatory. When the CRPD Committee examined the case, it held that since the State Party had a margin of discretion in the interpretation of the concept of 'reasonable accommodation', there was no violation of Article 5(3) of the Convention in Ms Jungelin's case. This was especially so given that the domestic court had carefully and objectively considered the different alternatives available in the case.

However, six members of the CRPD Committee expressed a minority view in Ms Jungelin's case, stating that whilst in principle reasonable accommodation is an individual measure, the benefit for other employees with disabilities must also be taken into account when assessing reasonableness and proportionality. Therefore, both Articles 5 and 9 of the Convention were applicable to Ms Jungelin's case. The minority expanded on the reasonableness and proportionality test for reasonable accommodation as follows:

> 'Reasonable accommodation' must be analysed on a case-by-case basis, and the reasonableness and proportionality of the measures of accommodation proposed must be assessed in view of the context in which they are requested. In the present case, the accommodation was required in a professional context. The test of reasonableness and proportionality should therefore ensure, inter alia, that (i) the measures of accommodation were requested to promote the employment of a person with a disability, with the professional capacity and experience to perform the functions corresponding to the position for which he or she applied; and (ii) the public or private company or entity to which the candidate applied can reasonably be expected to adopt and implement accommodation measures. It was never questioned that the author had

the professional capacity and work experience required to perform the duties of the position for which she had applied. One of the specific objectives of 'reasonable accommodation' is to compensate for factual limitations with a view to promoting the employment of persons with disability, so that the lack of factual capacity to perform such functions can therefore not be considered as the main obstacle to the employment of a person.[12]

The Labour Court had failed to take account of the potential benefit of the measures suggested by the Ombudsman on the future employment prospects of other persons with visual impairments in his assessment of the requested accommodation measures. The duty to ensure accessibility at the outset when designing a computer system, by installing specialist software which could be of benefit not only to the applicant, but also to other blind and visually-impaired persons, was one which related to accessibility, and as such Ms Jungelin's case should have fallen squarely under an Article 9 CRPD claim. Perhaps, Ms Jungelin's action might have met with more success had she grounded her action on Article 9 in conjunction with Article 5(1) of the Convention. *Fiona Given v Australia* seems to have an answer to this question and in a very tacit manner endorses the minority view in *Jungelin v Sweden*. It will be recalled that the CRPD Committee stated that Ms Given was discriminated on the grounds of her disability in contrast to blind and visually-impaired persons who had access to electronic voting. Relying on Article 9 as a bridge between Article 5 and 29, the CRPD Committee held that the failure to provide the author with access to an electronic voting platform resulted in a denial of her rights under all the aforementioned Articles.

As will be seen in *F v Austria*, 'the obligation to implement accessibility is unconditional, i.e. the entity obliged to provide accessibility may not excuse the omission to do so by referring to the burden of providing access for persons with disabilities'.[13] The CRPD Committee in *Fiona Given v Australia* accepted the State Party's submission that barriers to accessing existing objects and services should be removed gradually, taking into account limited resources and that significant increase in cost can constitute a disproportionate burden. The Committee, however, noted that an electronic voting option could have been made available in the 2013 Federal Election, as such an option was provided to persons with visual impairments and as an electronic voting system had been used in New South Wales elections since 2011. Australia did not provide any specific information as to why such an electronic voting option could not have been made available in the federal election for persons with cerebral palsy. This is especially so considering the fact that such an option had been available in New South Wales state elections since 2011. Article 29 CRPD places an obligation on States Parties to the Convention not only to uphold the right to vote of persons with disabilities by ensuring that voting procedures, facilities and materials that are appropriate, accessible and easy to understand and use are provided to them, but also that electronic voting options are made available and accessible to enable persons with disabilities to vote by secret ballot through the use of assistive technologies.

General Comment No.2 elaborates further on the obligations of States Parties and further curtails their margin of discretion with regard to the manner and form of the implementation of Article 9 of the Convention. It states that '[a]ccessibility of information and communication, including ICT, should [. . .] be achieved from the outset because subsequent adaptations to the Internet and ICT may increase costs'.[14] It is hence more economical for States Parties to incorporate mandatory ICT accessibility features from the first stages of design and production.'[15]

Real-time information and access to transport

In the case of *F v Austria*, the issue was whether the denial of access to real-time information via a digital system constituted discrimination on the basis of disability, where the denial had the consequence of preventing Mr F from boarding a tram.[16] Mr F averred that, in March 2004, the tram company Linz Linien GmbH started to equip tram stops in the city of Linz with a digital audio system, which reproduced the written text on a digital information display in audible form at the press of a button. The digital audio system provided Mr F with real-time information about the arrival and departure times of trams and their direction of travel. It also provided information about the disruption of services. Prior to June 2009, over 40 digital audio systems were installed in Linz which enabled persons with visual impairments to use the tram system independently. In August 2011, Linz Linien GmbH extended the railway network of tram Line 3. However, none of the stops along the extension was equipped with the digital audio system. Mr F was therefore compelled to rely on passers-by to get access to information regarding trams, and this made it difficult for him to find his way when using the new stops, thus also preventing him from using them.

Mr F argued that the State Party's failure to install the digital audio system on the extension to Line 3 violated the two-senses principle of accessibility. According to this principle, all information, including guidance aids, must be perceptible by a minimum of two senses out of three (hearing, sight and touch) to enable visually-impaired and hearing-impaired persons to access important information independently. The lack of an audio system on the extension to Line 3 prevented Mr F from accessing information which was available only in visual form. This communication barrier, he contended, amounted to discrimination because it deprived him of the use of the transport service on the extended tram line on an equal basis with others, in breach of Articles 5 and 9 of the Convention.

The question before the CRPD Committee was whether Austria had taken sufficient measures to ensure that information about transport services which was provided to persons without disabilities was also provided, on an equal basis, to persons with visual impairments. The Committee noted that none of the new stops was equipped with the digital audio system. The system was known to the service providers and it could have been installed at limited cost during the initial construction of the extension to Line 3. The Committee further noted that the digital audio system would have provided Mr F and other persons with visual impairments with immediate access to real-time information on an equal basis with others. The existing alternatives for information which might have been availed of by persons with disabilities—including the different applications which are accessible via the internet or mobile telephone—and the line message system did not provide accessibility on an equal basis with others. Austria's failure to install the digital audio system on the extension to Line 3 resulted in a denial of access to ICTs and also to facilities and services open to the public on an equal basis with others. The State Party's inaction thus amounted to a violation of Articles 5(2) and 9(1), (2)(f) and (h) of the Convention.

Article 9(2)(h) requires States Parties to promote the design, development, production and distribution of accessible ICTs and systems at an early stage so that they become accessible to persons with disabilities at minimum cost. In General Comment No.2, the Committee recalled that new technologies 'can be used to promote the full and equal participation of persons with disabilities in society, but only if they are designed and produced in a way that ensures their accessibility'.[17]

Following *F v Austria* (2014), the requirement to ensure accessibility may be extended, by analogy, to the built environment. For instance, States Parties must ensure accessibility for a wheelchair user who is unable to access an ATM service because the machine is at an inaccessible height; or for a wheelchair user who cannot access a court to perform his jury service due to unsuitable steps or the lack of an elevator. According to the UNDESA Forum on Disability Inclusion and Accessible Urban Development:

> Integrated transportation facilities and services not only provide accessibility for all but are also reliable and affordable. They drive sustainable and inclusive growth and change. Inclusive transportation requires continuity of accessibility throughout travel chains, meaning all elements of a journey from the starting point to the final destination include accessible entranceways.[18]

The obligation to provide accessibility for persons with disabilities is not limited to transport but extends to other aspects of the built environment so that they can exercise their freedom of movement in accordance with their rights under Article 12 CRPD (Equal recognition before the law) and Article 13 CRPD (Access to justice). General Comment No.2 provides further guidance for States Parties seeking to ensure that persons with disabilities enjoy accessibility without discrimination and on an equal basis with others.

The CRPD Committee recognises that movement and orientation within buildings and other public spaces poses challenges for persons with disabilities if there is inadequate signage, accessible information and communication or support services.[19] Buildings and other places open to the public should have signage in Braille and Easy Read formats and live assistance and intermediaries, including guides, readers and professional sign-language interpreters should be provided to facilitate accessibility. Without such signage, 'accessible information and communication and support services, orientation and movement in and through buildings may become impossible for many persons with disabilities, especially those experiencing cognitive fatigue'.[20]

Sweden provides an excellent example of good legislative practice with regard to accessibility. In its initial county report in 2012, Sweden made reference to the Swedish Planning and Building Act 2010 which

> includes accessibility and usability for persons with impaired movement or orientation as one of nine technical requirements for construction works. The requirements apply to buildings, plots, public locations and areas with facilities other than buildings. Swedish building regulations also contain detailed requirements regarding accessibility in housing. In all new and converted accommodation, for example, there must be accessible wet rooms. All new buildings must, for example, have accessible entrances, and newly built accommodation must have a turning area for indoor wheelchairs. The building regulations also require lifts in new and converted housing buildings of more than three floors, and for storage areas, mailboxes, laundry rooms, waste areas, refuse disposal and other accommodation supplements to be accessible and usable. The requirement for lifts also exists for buildings that contain working premises to which the general public have access, as well as public premises.[21]

States Parties are also under an obligation to implement Article 9 CRPD in line with the requirement of universal design as is enshrined in Article 2 CRPD. The concept of universal design is legitimately owned by persons with disabilities and it has had growing influence in international law.

Universal design

Article 2 CRPD defines universal design as 'the design of products, environments, programmes and services to be usable by all people, to the greatest extent possible, without the need for adaptation or specialized design'. The term 'to the greatest extent possible' suggests that States Parties may have some latitude in fulfilling their obligation under Article 9. However, their discretion is fettered by the requirement immediately following in the definition of Article 2 that '"universal design" shall not exclude assistive devices for particular groups of persons with disabilities where this is needed'. Article 4(1)(f) places a particular obligation on States Parties as follows:

> To undertake or promote research and development of universally designed goods, services, equipment and facilities, as defined in article 2 of the Convention, which should require the minimum possible adaptation and the least cost to meet the specific needs of a person with disabilities, to promote their availability and use, and to promote universal design in the development of standards and guidelines.

General Comment No.2 expands on the scope and normative contents of the novel concept of universal design as strictly applying to all new goods, products, facilities, technologies and services. States Parties are under an obligation to ensure full, equal and unrestricted access for all potential consumers, including persons with disabilities:

> Persons with disabilities and other users should be able to move in barrier-free streets, enter accessible low-floor vehicles, access information and communication, and enter and move inside universally designed buildings, using technical aids and live assistance where necessary [. . .] While the initial application of universal design is more economical, the potential cost of subsequent removal of barriers may not be used as an excuse to avoid the obligation to remove barriers to accessibility gradually.[22]

Article 30(1) of the CRPD requires States Parties to take appropriate measures to ensure that persons with disabilities:

a) Enjoy access to cultural materials in accessible formats;
b) Enjoy access to television programmes, films, theatre and other cultural activities, in accessible formats;
c) Enjoy access to places for cultural performances or services, such as theatres, museums, cinemas, libraries and tourism services, and, as far as possible, enjoy access to monuments and sites of national cultural importance.

A gradual, progressive or incremental approach to this right has been taken by both the CRPD Committee and States Parties. General Comment No.2 clarifies the interrelationship between the provisions contained in both Articles 2 and 30 of the Convention and also highlights the myriad forms which discrimination may take regarding accessibility:

> Everyone has the right to enjoy the arts, take part in sports and go to hotels, restaurants and bars. However, wheelchair users cannot go to a concert if there are only stairs in the concert hall. Blind persons cannot enjoy a painting if there is no description of it they can hear in the gallery. Hard of hearing persons cannot enjoy a film if there are no subtitles. Deaf persons cannot enjoy a theatrical play if there is no sign language interpretation. Persons with intellectual disabilities cannot enjoy a book if there is no easy-to-read version or a version in augmentative and alternative modes.[23]

The CRPD Committee noted that providing access to cultural and historical monuments that are part of national heritage may often present challenges. However, States Parties must gradually seek to widen access to such sites. Many monuments and sites of national cultural importance have been made accessible in a way that preserves their cultural and historical identity and uniqueness. The interrelated nature of State Parties' obligations under Articles 9 and 30 of the Convention was further highlighted by the Committee in its country report on Belgium.[24] With regard to Article 30, the Committee was concerned that Belgium had not yet ratified the Marrakesh Treaty, which facilitates access to published material for blind and visually-impaired persons.[25]

Research continues to show that there are sound economic, social and cultural arguments for investing in accessibility for persons with disabilities. According to the Forum on Disability Inclusion and Accessible Urban Development, cities which have a significant tourist economy will pay a high opportunity cost if they fail to address the problems caused by inaccessible infrastructure for tourists with disabilities and their families.[26] In economic terms, such failure could result in an opportunity loss of 15–20 per cent of the global tourism market share.[27]

Conclusion

Following the initial adoption of the CRPD, accessibility was considered to be a general obligation upon States Parties which should be incrementally and gradually fulfilled, and its scope was considered to be too wide to be subject to review by domestic courts. Ten years following the adoption of the CRPD, perceptions of accessibility have significantly changed. Today, accessibility is more than a mere economic right which is justiciable within defined boundaries. The duties of States Parties concerning accessibility are perceived to be much more onerous under Article 9 of the CRPD. The policy-orientated approach of the CRPD Committee has served to fetter the discretion of States Parties regarding the manner and form of implementation of Article 9 of the Convention. While it cannot be decisively concluded that accessibility as a general obligation upon States Parties has been elevated to the status of a civil right, it continues to build a bridge between the two traditional sets of civil and economic rights. As such, accessibility is a hybrid right, the conception of which continues to develop. In that process, it makes a growing contribution in protecting the rights of persons with disabilities.

Summary of Concluding Observations and Recommendations

According to the Report of the Forum on Disability Inclusion and Accessible Urban Development (2015), accessibility is a collective good, which benefits everyone.[28] Accessibility is a fundamental component of good policy for sustainable urban development as it allows for the full participation and inclusion of everyone in society. As the Report observed, a city that is well designed is well designed for everyone. Without accessibility, it is not possible for persons with disabilities to achieve economic, social, cultural and political empowerment. An accessible and disability-inclusive urban development agenda can be realised everywhere, provided there is a strong and genuine commitment to establish inclusive and disability-responsive urban policy frameworks. These must be accompanied by the establishment of appropriate regulatory structures, the adoption of a 'design for all' approach to planning and design, and the availability of adequate resources. The attainment of an accessible and disability-inclusive urban development agenda is premised upon the genuine participation of persons with disabilities and their representative organisations, as rights-holders, throughout the entire urbanisation process.

The scope of the concept of accessibility has been interpreted to include products, services, built environments and ICTs that relate to the needs and interests of a wide range of people, including persons with disabilities. The commitment of the UN Sustainable Development Goals (SDG) agenda 'to leave no one behind' seeks to ensure that SDG targets are achieved for all of society, including persons with disabilities in urban areas. In order to achieve a truly inclusive New Urban Agenda, persons with disabilities and their representative organisations must form part of a holistic and people-centred approach which seeks to inform and engage society as a whole regarding urban development, and especially regarding the need to provide adequate accessible housing. The New Urban Agenda should also further the goal of accessibility to the built environment, public spaces, transportation, facilities, services and ICTs for the estimated one billion persons with disabilities worldwide. A truly inclusive New Urban Agenda can be realised only if it reflects the needs and rights of persons with disabilities.

Housing as a key element of inclusive cities

The Report of the Forum on Disability Inclusion and Accessible Urban Development (2015) has highlighted the need to place accessible housing at the centre of an inclusive urban development policy, reflecting an integrated approach that also encompasses environmental sustainability, diversity and the availability of adequate financial resources. It is essential that an inclusive urban development policy should also be responsive to human rights, including those of persons with disabilities. Designs and plans for new built environments must reflect the principle of universal design, and plans for the renovation of existing buildings and facilities must also ensure accessibility for all. To that end, building standards regulations must contain effective enforcement mechanisms to ensure accessibility to both housing and public services, especially for persons with disabilities.

Transportation and public services

The development of integrated transportation facilities and services provides accessibility for persons with disabilities as well as being both reliable and affordable. Integrated transportation facilities and services enable the realisation of sustainable and inclusive growth. A truly inclusive transportation service requires continuous accessibility at all points of a travel chain, so that all points of entry and exit on the journey's route include accessible passageways. Integrated urban transportation policies must identify and rectify such gaps, just as building policies must remove barriers to accessibility in the built environment. In accordance with equity, the cost of accessible transportation and public services should not be fully borne by service users because accessibility is necessary to ensure the full and effective participation by persons with disabilities in all aspects of social, economic, cultural and political life.

ICTs for building inclusive, resilient smart cities

According to the Report of the Forum on Disability Inclusion and Accessible Urban Development (2015), governments should develop accessible ICTs, including mobile applications. It is also necessary for government websites, public kiosks and automated teller machines to make use of accessible ICTs. Provisions for the use of accessible ICT services should be included in all urban development plans.

Owing to the fast pace of development and innovation in the sphere of ICTs, assistive and adaptive devices and technologies which are used by persons with disabilities are not always compatible with new ICTs, and the cost of gaining access to innovative technologies can be prohibitive. This is especially the case in many low- and middle-income countries. Governments should promote and facilitate research and development into accessible ICT products and services. This can be encouraged through the inclusion of accessibility requirements when procuring ICT products and services to be used by public organisations, their customers or staff. It is notable that many national telecommunication authorities have adopted universal service goals which recognise the right of their consumers to access telecommunications networks at an affordable price. To conclude; the Report of the Forum on Disability Inclusion and Accessible Urban Development (2015) has highlighted the need for accessibility to be adopted as a third universal service goal.

CRPD Committee, General Comment No.2 on Article 9 (Accessibility)

Given that a lack of accessibility frequently arises owing to insufficient awareness and lack of technical know-how, States Parties must provide training for all stakeholders on accessibility for persons with disabilities (Article 9(2)(c) CRPD 2007). Whilst Article 9 does not offer an exhaustive list of such stakeholders, it includes engineers, designers, architects, urban planners, transport authorities, service providers, academics, persons with disabilities and their representative organisations. The authorities responsible for the issuance of building permits and ICT licences are also stakeholders for the purposes of Article 9 of the Convention. Accessibility training should be provided for designers and producers of goods, products and services. A deeper understanding of the existing needs of persons with disabilities can be achieved by their greater involvement in product development. Such a move would also enhance the efficacy of accessibility tests. In the final analysis, it is the actions of the builders on the construction site which determine whether or not a building is accessible for persons with disabilities, so it is essential that builders also receive adequate accessibility training, and that there are robust monitoring systems in place to ensure compliance with accessibility standards.

Access to information and communication is a prerequisite if persons with disabilities are to enjoy freedom of thought and expression, and many other basic rights and freedoms. Article 9 provides that States Parties should 'provide forms of live assistance and intermediaries, including guides, readers and professional sign language interpreters, to facilitate accessibility to buildings and other facilities open to the public.' (Article 9(2)(e) CRPD (2007)). States Parties are also required, through the adoption of mandatory accessibility standards, to promote other appropriate forms of assistance and support to persons with disabilities to ensure their access to information, and to promote their access to new ICTs and systems, including the Internet.

Information and communication should be accessible in easy-to-read formats and in augmentative and alternative modes for persons with disabilities.

To conclude, it is notable that in its initial country report for Latvia (2017), the CRPD Committee highlighted the absence in Latvia of a comprehensive national legal, policy and strategic framework accompanied by the necessary monitoring mechanisms in the State Party to ensure compliance with accessibility standards based on universal design that guarantee persons with disabilities access, on an equal basis with others, to all facilities and services open or provided to the public throughout the territory of the State Party, including access to information, means of communication and transport.[29]

Notes

1 UK Disability History Month, War and Impairment: The Social Consequences of Disablement (2014). Available at http://ukdhm.org/v2/wp-content/uploads/2014/09/UK-Disability-history-month-2014-Broadsheet.pdf last accessed 22 March 2018.
2 CRPD Committee, General Comment No. 2 on Article 9 (Accessibility), 11 April 2014, CRPD/C/GC/2, para.23.
3 Article 9(3) CRPD.
4 *Szilvia Nyusti and Péter Takács v Hungary* (2013) CRPD/C/9/D/1/2010.
5 *Szilvia Nyusti and Péter Takács v Hungary*, para.9.2.
6 Ibid.
7 General Comment No.2, para.25.
8 General Comment No.2, para.25.
9 General Comment No.2, para.26.
10 General Comment No.2, para.26.
11 *Marie-Louise Jungelin v Sweden* (2014) CRPD/C/12/D/5/2011.
12 *Ibid*, Joint dissenting opinion of Committee members Carlos Rios Espinosa, Theresia Degener, Munthian Buntan, Silvia Judith Quan-Chang and Maria Soledad Cisternas Reyes, para.4.
13 *F v Austria* (2015) CRPD/C/14/D/21/2014, para.8.4.
14 General Comment No.2, para.15.
15 Ibid.
16 *F v Austria*.
17 General Comment No.2, para.20.
18 Report on Forum on Disability Inclusion and Accessible Urban Development, Co-organized by DESA and UN-Habitat, supported by the African Disability Forum,

28 to 30 October 2015, UN Convention Center, Nairobi, Kenya. Available http://www.un.org/disabilities/documents/2015/report-desaforum-disability-inclusion-Nairobi.pdf, accessed 22 March 2018.
19 General Comment No.2, para.20.
20 Ibid, with reference to Art.9(2)(d) CRPD.
21 CRPD Committee, Concluding Observations on the Initial Report of Sweden, 18 September 2012, CRPD/C/SWE/1, para.65.
22 General Comment No.2, para.15.
23 Ibid, para.13.
24 CRPD Committee, Concluding Observations on the Initial Report of Belgium, 28 October 2014, CRPD/C/BEL/CO/1, para.40.
25 Marrakesh Treaty to Facilitate Access to Published Works for Persons Who Are Blind, Visually Impaired, or Otherwise Print Disabled, adopted in 2013 by the World Intellectual Property Organization.
26 Secretariat for the Convention on the Rights of Persons with Disabilities and UNDESA, Accessibility and Disability Inclusion in Urban Development.
27 Ibid.
28 Report on Forum on Disability Inclusion and Accessible Urban Development, Co-organized by DESA and UN-Habitat, supported by the African Disability Forum, 28 to 30 October 2015, UN Convention Center, Nairobi, Kenya. Available http://www.un.org/disabilities/documents/2015/report-desaforum-disability-inclusion-Nairobi.pdf, accessed 22 March 2018.
29 CRPD Committee, Concluding observations on the Initial Report of Latvia, 10 October 2017, CRPD/C/LVA/CO/1.

9

RIGHT TO EDUCATION

Introduction

The dominant capitalist ideology of the post-war era is premised upon utilitarian calculus. With regard to education, as long as there is maximum benefit for the maximum number of people, education achieves its goal of reproducing an educated class for the smooth and effective running of the economy. From a capitalist perspective, education systems are controlled by the elite class, which has authority over policies for curricular development, research and teacher training. School forms a central part of the substructure through which the elite ideology is promulgated, and the economic superstructure is thereby safeguarded and rendered financially stable. Capitalism utilises the education system as a means of defending and promoting the economy, irrespective of the exclusion of minorities within the system. Persons with disabilities are relegated to a class of persons who are unable to adapt to the system. In different parts of the world, a similar relegation of persons with disabilities is achieved through different ideologies. For many decades, education systems which are patriarchal in substance and paternalistic in application have been promoting the segregation of life-long learners with disabilities.

The utilitarian calculus of the greatest possible good appears to rest upon the doctrine of fairness, premised as it is upon the idea that hard work and the ability to compete are rewarding in themselves. It is argued herein that this form of social organisation is structurally discriminatory, because it assumes that alternative models, such as the inclusion of all in the education system, are both unrealistic and irrational. The utilitarian-based education system discriminates against non-disabled children, because it legitimises the acceptance of their future role as passive agents of the system. Human beings, living in the system, generally become good, obedient workers for the capitalist society. More broadly, the education systems of several ideologies commonly display several features including the passive subservience of pupils to tyrannical orders, the subordination of individuality and the acceptance of hierarchy, in the absence of motivation to enjoy the diversity of humanity. Across the ideologies, instead of being motivated to enjoy diversity, pupils are being encouraged to seek future extrinsic satisfaction through the reward of good grades and in due course, big wages. All ideologies reproduce the same alienating results for persons with disabilities. All ideologies have miserably failed persons with disabilities. They do not promote the universal values which education systems ought to inculcate in learners. They do not reflect the view that education should enable all persons to participate effectively in a free society. Nor do they promote the values enshrined in the UN Declaration on Human Rights Education and Training, which are; understanding, tolerance and friendship among all nations and all racial, ethnic or religious groups, and the maintenance of peace.[1]

Persons with disabilities, universally, have struggled to access their right to education. For example, according to UNICEF, in rural China the lack of access for persons with disabilities to education and other social services is a significant problem:

> Most children with disabilities live in poverty in rural areas. Local health care workers may not be qualified to provide rehabilitation services. Teachers may lack training in special needs education. Children with disabilities also suffer discrimination. Schools may refuse to enroll them, communities may shun them, and some families even consider them a shame or burden. The lack of community-based family support and social services results in a heavy childcare burden for parents, which contributes to a high rate of abandonment. As many as 90% of children in institutional care are disabled.[2]

Irrespective of social norms or prevailing ideology, governments everywhere have always argued that there are barriers hindering inclusive education for persons with disabilities. Ironically, States Parties appear to forget that these barriers exist as a consequence of their deliberate acts and omissions, and, in some instances, States Parties themselves have actively constructed barriers. They equally lose sight of the fact that disability only manifests itself when people with impairments interact with ideologically driven, dogmatic systems, which have long since been rationalised, legitimised and set into motion.

The origin of the right to education

The right to education finds its origin in numerous international treaty bodies and declarations including, among others, Article 26(1) UDHR which holds that:

> Everyone has the right to education. Education shall be free, at least in the elementary and fundamental stages. Elementary education shall be compulsory. Technical and professional education shall be made generally available and higher education shall be equally accessible to all on the basis of merit.

In accordance with Article 13(1) ICESCR, States Parties must recognise the universal right to education. Education must be directed to 'the full development of the human personality and the sense of its dignity, and shall strengthen the respect for human rights and fundamental freedoms'.

Article 23 CRC was the first treaty body provision to offer a disability perspective on the right to education. It requires States Parties to ensure that children with disabilities receive an education and that they have effective access to the education system. In the same vein, Article 24 CRPD recognises the right of persons with disabilities to education and requires that the right to education should be realised without discrimination. The basis of the right to education for persons with disabilities is equality of opportunity throughout the life-long learning cycle, within an inclusive education system. However, Article 24 CRPD goes further and places onerous obligations on States Parties regarding the right of persons with disabilities to education.

Barriers to inclusive education

According to the OHCHR, the inclusion of persons with disabilities in mainstream education is a process which requires action on several fronts. First, there is a need to recognise that barriers which restrict or ban the participation of persons with disabilities in mainstream education must be eliminated. Culture, policy and practice in mainstream schools must also adapt to properly accommodate the needs of all, including students with disabilities.[3] It follows that inclusive education may be defined as 'a child-centred pedagogy' capable of successfully educating all children, including those with disabilities.[4]

In its General Comment No.4 on the right to education, the CRPD Committee considered the multitude of barriers facing inclusive education. The Committee sought to determine the extent to which such barriers are real or imaginary, and in so doing it identified a total of seven common obstacles facing persons with disabilities and their right to education. First, the Committee noted a general failure to embrace the human rights-based model of disability, whereby barriers are perceived to exist due to the nature of society within, rather than as a result of the impairments of persons with disabilities. There are also problems of persistent discrimination against persons with disabilities, which is exacerbated by isolation in the case of long-term residents of institutions and by low expectations of the potential of persons with disabilities in mainstream settings. Such discrimination allows prejudice and fear of persons with disabilities to develop and strongly militates against their inclusion in mainstream education. There is a cluster of issues which together serve to fuel fears and negative stereotypes surrounding inclusive education, in particular that it will lead to a reduced quality of education generally, or otherwise negatively impact upon mainstream education. These include poor knowledge of the nature of inclusive, quality education, and misunderstandings about the value of diversity in education.

There has been a lack of involvement and outreach to parents, coupled with poor responses to requests for support for students with disabilities, whose requirements are frequently left unmet. Sadly, there is often a lack of political will and technical knowledge and capacity which is necessary to make the right to education a reality for persons with disabilities. Nor is there sufficient education of teachers regarding the needs of students with disabilities and their right to education. Existing funding mechanisms for inclusive education are often inadequate and they are frequently inappropriate in light of the needs of students with disabilities. Funding schemes also fail to provide effective incentives for educational institutions to provide reasonable accommodations for the inclusion of students with disabilities. There is a further problem of a lack of effective legal remedies and mechanisms for students with disabilities to claim redress when their right to education is violated. Finally, there is the perennial issue of a lack of disaggregated data and research, which prevents the development and design of effective policies and interventions to ensure inclusive and quality education for all.[5]

The list of issues identified by the CRPD Committee in its General Comment No.4 is not exhaustive. A myriad other factors which may negatively impact upon the process of inclusive education may also be added to their list. However, the CRPD Committee's list is notable in that there are several common denominators amongst their seven common obstacles to inclusive education which help to account for the lack of progress to date. The first is the effect of prevalent capitalist, economic models, as discussed previously. This tends to objectify human beings, and rather than economies responding to human needs, workers are expected instead to respond to economic variables. In such a climate, the education system is inextricably linked with the capitalist economic model, and is in turn driven by its requirements. Secondly, capitalist systems worldwide find it difficult or impossible to accommodate a human rights-based model of disability and they naturally tend to perpetuate inequality and discrimination. Lack of knowledge and understanding of the human rights model of disability is also problematic and there is a worrying lack of interest in exploring the long-term economic and social benefits of inclusive education. Finally, the myth that inclusion of persons with disabilities in mainstream education would lower the quality of education generally for non-disabled children serves to perpetuate segregation and institutionalisation. This is regrettable, given that evidence has shown that inclusive, quality education is of long-term, economic benefit to society.[6]

For decades, people with disabilities have been advocating tirelessly for inclusive education, notwithstanding the ratification of numerous international human rights treaties on the right to education. And whilst the origin of the right to education dates back to 1948, progress to date has been minimal. However, it must be noted that domestic courts have played a prominent role in seeking to progressively secure the universal right to education.

The obligations of States Parties under Article 24 CRPD

Article 24 CRPD sets out the measures which States Parties must take to fulfil their obligation to safeguard the right of persons with disabilities to education. It explicitly states that persons with disabilities have the right to inclusive education.

Article 24 CRPD also expands upon the nature of States Parties' obligations. States Parties are required to ensure an inclusive education system at all levels of life-long learning. The right to inclusive education is a fundamental one and it is only through its realisation by States Parties that the inherent dignity and autonomy of life-long learners can be respected. This entails creating an inclusive education environment for the full and effective participation of the entire society which fosters respect for differences and acceptance of persons with disabilities as an integral part of human diversity. It also includes promoting respect for the evolving capacities of children with disabilities. Article 24 CRPD tackles the issue of education from an empirical functionalist perspective. It looks at society as a whole as opposed to examining the education system in isolation.

In order to achieve compliance with Article 24 CRPD, States Parties should adopt, without discrimination, legislative and administrative policies and programmes promoting equality and non-discrimination in societies and, in particular, within education systems. States Parties should also abolish laws and policies which are discriminatory by nature, or which have similarly negative effects upon the implementation of inclusive education policies. Article 24 CRPD also requires States Parties to carry out research to ensure the development of high quality services and should also make available access to evolving information and communication technologies (ICT) and assistive devices which are required for the effective participation of students with disabilities in the education system.

In seeking to fulfil their obligations under Article 24 CRPD, States Parties must closely consult with persons with disabilities and their representative organisations. They must also be mindful of their duty to provide accessible information; a duty which extends to the provision of information for parents and legal guardians. States Parties must also provide protection against discriminatory practices and ensure that there is an effective system of remedies in cases of violation of rights under Article 24 CRPD. States Parties must also provide non-discriminatory services, and their duty in that regard is not limited to matters pertaining to the education system, but includes a wider array of social and other services.

The obligation to progressively realise Article 24 CRPD

In recent decades, the right to education has become increasingly justiciable, that is to say it is a right the violation of which is subject to remedy before a national court. However, given that the right to education falls within the category of economic, social and cultural rights (rights which are not subject to immediate realisation), States Parties are free to decide the manner and form in which to implement the right of persons with disabilities to education. At the supranational and international level, human rights bodies have traditionally been reluctant to adjudicate on the right to education, primarily because it is a right which is subject to progressive realisation. However, in 2003, the European Committee on Social Rights (ECSR) broke free from this tradition in the case of *International Association Autism Europe (IAAE) v France*.[7]

In *IAAE v France*, the ECSR had to decide whether France had disregarded its obligation, in accordance with the European Social Charter, to advance the right to education of children and adults with autism. It was argued by the IAAE that France's failure to advance their right to education was a clear violation of the rights of persons with disabilities as it was discriminatory in principle. The IAAE further argued that France had failed to provide adequate special education institutions and services, and that it was hiding behind legal technicalities in order to deny funding for the education of children with autism. It was claimed that France did not consider the education of persons with disabilities to be a public service which the state was under an obligation to provide in conformity with the Finance Act (France).

The ECSR held that, given the lack of improvement in the area of education, France had failed to ensure that the right to education of children and adults with autism was protected, a failure which de facto amounted to discrimination under the European Social Charter. The ECSR held as follows:

> When the achievement of one of the rights in question is exceptionally complex and particularly expensive to resolve, a State Party must take measures that allow it to achieve the objectives of the Charter within a reasonable time, with measurable progress and to an extent consistent with the maximum use of available resources. States Parties must be particularly mindful of the impact that their choices will have for groups with heightened vulnerabilities [. . .] Nevertheless, [the Committee] considers, as the authorities themselves acknowledge, and whether a broad or narrow definition of autism is adopted, that the proportion of children with autism being educated in either general or specialist schools is much lower than in the case of other children, whether or not disabled. It is also established, and not contested by the authorities, that there is a chronic shortage of care and support facilities for autistic adults.[8]

According to General Comment No.4, Article 4(2) CRPD confers an obligation upon States Parties to adopt measures to uphold economic, social and cultural rights, to the maximum extent possible, in light of available resources. Where necessary, States Parties must also engage with the framework of international cooperation in order to progressively achieve the full realisation of the right of persons with disabilities to education. Progressive realisation means that States Parties have a specific obligation 'to move as expeditiously and effectively as possible' towards the full realisation of Article 24 CRPD. It should be noted that this requirement is not compatible with maintaining two systems of mainstream and special education. The requirement for 'progressive realisation' must be interpreted according to the overall objective of the Convention which includes a need to establish clear obligations for States Parties regarding the full realisation of the rights set out in the Convention. Similarly, States Parties are encouraged to redefine budgetary allocations for education, including transferring budgets to develop inclusive education.

Any deliberately retrogressive measures in that regard must not disproportionately target learners with disabilities, and must be a temporary measure, limited in duration to the period of crisis. Deliberately retrogressive measures must be necessary and proportionate. They must not be discriminatory and they must consist of all possible measures to mitigate inequality.

The law in this area lacks clarity, and confusion abounds, in particular regarding the concept of 'special education', which is used by States Parties to convey a message that they are using the maximum available resources to ensure quality education for persons with disabilities. General Comment No.4 has identified three different types of education system: exclusion, segregation and integration, none of which completely complies with international standards.

Defining exclusion, segregation and integration

In the context of education, exclusion arises 'when students are directly or indirectly prevented from or denied access to education in any form'.[9] From this perspective, exclusion occurs when a student with disabilities is prevented from accessing the education system on the grounds of his age, development or diagnosis, and instead is placed in a social welfare or health-care setting, with no access to education.[10] The CRPD Committee has consistently called upon States Parties either to legislate or adopt other policy measures to prevent children with disabilities from being denied their right to education. For instance, in its Concluding Observations on the initial report of Mexico, the CRPD Committee expressed its concern that some children with disabilities in Mexico were not receiving education.[11]

Segregation arises when students with disabilities are educated in separate environments, which may be designed to respond to their needs in light of their particular impairments, in isolation from non-disabled students.[12] The CRPD Committee has noted with concern that in Moldova, a large number of children with psychosocial or intellectual disabilities are separated for the purpose of education from their non-disabled counterparts. They remain in segregated educational institutions, including special schools. Moldovan students with disabilities were also more likely to be segregated by being placed in 'special classes' and were also more likely than their non-disabled counterparts to receive home education.[13] The prevalence of negative attitudes towards students with disabilities and a lack of knowledge of inclusive education amongst administrative and teaching staff often result in children with disabilities being refused admission to mainstream schools.[14] The Committee has also expressed concern that in Gabon, children with disabilities were confined to segregated schools and that they were unable to access inclusive, quality education within mainstream schools.[15]

The process of integration requires persons with disabilities to be placed in mainstream educational settings, on the understanding that they are able to adjust to the standardised requirements of such settings.[16] The integration approach is focused upon enhancing the ability of students with disabilities to comply with established standards in mainstream educational settings.[17] For instance, the CRPD

Committee has noted with concern that in Tunisia, many integrated schools were not equipped to cater for children with disabilities and that the training of teachers and administrators regarding disability issues was inadequate.[18]

It seems that issues of segregation and integration are frequently a source of confusion for States Parties; some are of the view that segregation is a good thing, whilst others endeavour to hide behind integrative approaches, in an effort to demonstrate that their policies are inclusive. However, it remains a reality that many States Parties have failed to meet their obligations regarding the right of students with disabilities to access education. To develop a deeper understanding of the rights and obligations concerning inclusive education from the perspective of public international law, it is instructive, first, to consider how States Parties' domestic courts have approached cases involving segregation and integration in the context of education.

Segregation and integration

In *Western Cape Forum for Intellectual Disability v South Africa*, the right to education of children with severe intellectual disabilities in the Western Cape, South Africa, was considered.[19] The Western Cape Forum for Intellectual Disability (WCFID) contended that the level of state provision for children with severe intellectual disabilities was much less than for other children, and that the allocated funds were inadequate to cater for the educational needs of the children concerned. The WCFID also complained that funding was made available only to non-governmental organisations who provided educational facilities for students with disabilities. It was argued that, in the circumstances, the policy and practice of the State of South Africa infringed upon the right to education of children with psychosocial disabilities.[20]

The High Court of South Africa held that the state had violated the rights of the students with severe intellectual disabilities through its failure to fund their basic educational needs, and also through its failure to admit the students concerned to a special school or other institutional setting. According to the court, the infringement of the affected students' right to education, and of their right to equality, could not be justified:

> [The children's] rights to dignity have been infringed since they have been marginalised and ignored and in effect stigmatised. The failure to provide the children with education places them at the risk of neglect for it means that they often have to be educated by parents who do not have the skills to do so and are already under strain.[21]

It was held that the state must take reasonable measures to provide for the educational needs of severely intellectually disabled children in the Western Cape region. Such measures should include the provision of adequate funds to organisations providing education for severely intellectually disabled children at special care centres. The purpose of such funding was to enable special care centres to provide adequate facilities, to hire sufficient suitably trained staff and to provide appropriate transport for students attending the special care centres.[22]

The judgment in *Western Cape Forum for Intellectual Disability v South Africa* exemplifies the misunderstanding which commonly surrounds the concepts of 'special education' and 'inclusive education'. Whilst the court held that there had been a violation of the right to education of children with intellectual and psycho-social impairments, its judgment was not wholly in accordance with the human rights model of disability. In holding that the State of South Africa must take reasonable measures to ensure that special care centres were fully operational, the court endorsed the 'special education' paradigm. This promotes 'segregated educa-tion that leads to the development of separate educational systems: one for persons with disabilities, often referred to as "special schools"; and one for those without disabilities, or "mainstream" schools'.[23]

The UN Special Rapporteur on the right to education has observed the toxic effect of the perception of persons with disabilities as 'uneducable' and a burden on the mainstream education system.[24] The special school system is the natural result of such flawed reasoning, and it is a system which is inflexible, and incapable of meeting the individual learning needs of persons with disabilities. The negative impact of such perceptions is apparent in the design of many national and interna-tional educative assessments. Such negative reasoning causes mainstream schools to exclude those students whose scores fail to meet performance goals, a reluctance to include students with disabilities and a tendency to expel students who are deemed 'difficult to teach'. Furthermore, the practice of separation or segregation of students with disabilities increases their social marginalisation, which is already a significant factor in driving discrimination against persons with disabilities. On the other hand, it has been demonstrated that inclusive education limits the mar-ginalisation effect.

There are hopeful signs that some States Parties are successfully embracing the inclusion process. For example, in its Concluding Observations on the initial report of Spain, the CRPD Committee commended Spain's efforts to ensure that the schooling of students with special educational needs was governed by the prin-ciple of inclusion. Spain has also prohibited discrimination in education, with the result that most children with disabilities are included in the mainstream education system.[25] The Committee also expressed its approval of the new legislative frame-work on education, the Organic Act of Education 2/2006:

> [The Act] obliges the education authorities to provide specialist teachers, qualified professionals and the necessary materials and resources, as well as the laws that oblige schools to make necessary curricular adjustments and diversi-fications for pupils with disabilities.

However, in light of reported cases in Spain of failures to provide reason-able accommodation, the CRPD Committee has expressed concern that the implementation of the Spanish law is inadequate.[26] There were also reports of ongoing exclusion and segregation of students with disabilities in Spain. The Committee was also aware of children with disabilities in Spain being placed in special education against their parents' wishes, and that there was no availability of an appeal against such decisions. Often, parents' only alternatives were either to educate their child at their own expense or to personally foot the cost of providing reasonable accommodation for their child in the mainstream system.

In Case No.6868/2012 of 27 January 2014, the Constitutional Court of Spain declined to recognise that the State of Spain had not fulfilled its international obligations pertaining to the right of children with disabilities to inclusive education, in line with Article 24 CRPD. The Constitutional Court also declined to acknowledge that Spain's domestic legislative framework was incompatible with the requirements of the CRPD. In that case, the parents of a child with disabilities had objected to his placement in a special school. They argued that their child should be provided with reasonable accommodation to pursue his education in a mainstream school on an equal basis with non-disabled students.

The Constitutional Court rejected the parents' claim on the ground that a special school education was in the best interests of their child. It held that the child's unique educational needs could be better met in a special educational setting, outside the mainstream education system. The Constitutional Court expressed the view that it was neither unreasonable nor discriminatory to segregate the child in a special school. The decision to deny the specific adaptation measures to the child was consistent with the requirements of the Convention, because to require the school to provide the specific adaptation measures would constitute a disproportionate and undue burden upon the State Party. It was further held that the decision was in accordance with Spanish domestic legislation, which permitted the segregation of students with disabilities in special schools, in cases where their needs could not be met within the mainstream education system.[27]

It is difficult to reconcile the Constitutional Court's reasoning in Case No.6868/2012 with international legal norms. The primary difficulty is that the normative contents of the right to inclusive education, as enshrined in Article 24 CRPD, did not form an integral part of the judicial analysis in the case. Another problem with the case arose due to the analysis of the child's educational needs in accordance with the medical model. The effect of this was to legitimise the medical model of disability, whilst also shifting focus away from the child as a right-holder.

It is a fundamental principle, enshrined in Article 1 of the Convention, that persons with disabilities are rights-holders. It is also a core universal value, which international jurisprudence unequivocally endorses, to ensure respect for the dignity of children and life-long learners. The judgment of the Constitutional Court did not choose to offer an analysis of the concept of reasonable accommodation as compared to the notion of a disproportionate or undue burden. Instead, it was assumed that in cases where a disability was classified as 'severe', the only alternative was to segregate the child. Furthermore, notwithstanding the fact that Article 7 CRPD requires that, in all actions concerning a child with disabilities, the best interests of the child shall be a primary consideration, there was a routine failure to consult children with disabilities in the course of the evaluation process. Finally, it is arguable that the evidence on record did not necessarily support the view that the child's educational needs in a mainstream setting could not be reasonably met by the State Party, or that to do so would amount to an undue burden.

The proposition that the segregation of children with disabilities does not constitute discrimination is a flawed premise from which to reason. It fails to recognise children with disabilities as being equal to their non-disabled counterparts before the law. It also offers a rationale to the education inspectorate to justify the imposition of their decisions upon students and parents who do not opt for segregated schooling. A child's life experience is irreversibly damaged as a result of segregation, which potentially impacts upon his/her ability to live independently in the community, to obtain employment in the open labour market and to fully participate in society. Even if the term 'inclusive education' has gained wide currency in both academic and popular debate, there remains confusion regarding its interpretation at national level, as the domestic case law considered above has demonstrated. General Comment No.4 offers some clarity regarding the concept of 'inclusive education', as discussed in the following section.

The meaning of inclusive education

In its General Comment No.4, the CRPD Committee interpreted the right to education as being a right to 'inclusive education'. It requires education services and facilities, from pre-primary to tertiary education, to include persons with disabilities. Students with disabilities must have access to all educational and physical environments where learners receive their education, socialise with other individuals or participate in extracurricular activities. Inclusive education systems are fundamental to supporting persons with disabilities towards both independent living and inclusion in the wider community. Inclusive education requires recognition of the right of persons with disabilities to live within the community and enjoy inclusion and participation in the community as encompassed in Article 19 CRPD. The relationship between inclusive education and independent living has recently been highlighted in the CRPD Committee's General Comment No.5 on the right to independent living.

> Inclusion of persons with disabilities in the mainstream education system generates further inclusion of persons with disabilities in the community. De-institutionalization also entails the introduction of inclusive education. States parties should note the role that exercising the right to inclusive education will play in building the strengths, skills and competencies necessary for all persons with disabilities to enjoy, benefit from and contribute to their communities.[28]

The right to education has a direct bearing on the right of persons with disabilities to a family life. However, where independent living is not possible, or where family life is not an alternative for a person with a disability, care within a community setting must be made available (Article 23 CRPD). Children in the care of a State Party, for example those who are resident either in foster care or care homes, also have the right to inclusive education, including the right to appeal against decisions of the State Party which has allegedly violated their right to inclusive education. In its General Comment No.5, the CRPD Committee further observed that:

> [t]oo many persons with disabilities live in long-term institutional care, without access to community-based services, including education, consistent with their right to, inter alia; family life, community living, freedom of association, protection from violence and access to justice.'[29]

In light of these observations, the CRPD Committee recommended that inclusive education in a local community setting must be available, coupled with a strategic commitment to end the practice of segregating persons with disabilities in separate educational institutions.[30] The Committee's approach supports the view of disability as a relative concept. For instance, a person may be perceived to have a disability in one society, but not in another. A person's living experience of disability often depends upon the level of support services and facilities available. Moreover, given the evolving concept of disability, inclusive education systems tend to foster a greater understanding of diversity, its value and importance.

It is a matter of concern that stakeholders in both the public and private education sectors do not yet clearly understand the meaning of inclusive education. Inclusion can be realised only when there is systematic change, adjustment and modification of the education environment. Changes must be made at the level of both the curriculum and teaching methodologies, in order to overcome the barriers faced by students with disabilities in accessing their right to education. Suitable adjustment strategies must also be implemented to ensure that the system is capable of responding to the individual needs of students with disabilities. Inclusive education only becomes a reality when barriers to education are removed, so that all learners have an equitable opportunity to participate in a non-discriminatory environment. Access for all to a shared learning experience, in a shared environment, is the best way to ensure that the barriers facing persons with disabilities in all aspects of living will finally become a thing of the past.

In General Comment No.4, the CRPD Committee emphasised that the process of inclusion requires non-discriminatory access to high-quality, formal and informal education:

> Inclusion involves access to and progress in high-quality formal and informal education without discrimination. It seeks to enable communities, systems and structures to combat discrimination, including harmful stereotypes, recognize diversity, promote participation and overcome barriers to learning and participation for all by focusing on well-being and success of students

with disabilities. It requires an in-depth transformation of education systems in legislation, policy, and the mechanisms for financing, administration, design, delivery and monitoring of education.[31]

It is clear that understanding and implementation of the core principle of inclusive education requires a real transformation in social culture. Non-discrimination in an inclusive mainstream education institution guarantees equality in diversity to all children, including those without disabilities. It must be remembered that children without disabilities equally have the right to experience diversity in all sectors of life, including education, and they have the right to enjoy the companionship and share the experiences of their fellow students with disabilities.

Many States Parties, by virtue of their constitutions, have directly incorporated the provisions of the CRPD into their domestic legal systems following ratification by the States Parties. However, ratification in itself is not sufficient to meet their international obligations. To date, the interpretation by Constitutional Courts of the right to inclusive education has to a considerable extent failed to take into account the normative contents of Article 24, or the guidance contained in General Comment No.4. Instead, Constitutional Courts have tended to focus upon the assessment of children with disabilities, without giving due consideration to the duty of the State Party to provide reasonable accommodation. In recent years, however, the social right to education has become increasingly justiciable. Domestic courts have avoided examining the social right to education in isolation, and instead they have sought to analyse it within the wider spirit of the Convention, taking account of the pervasive effect of discrimination, both within the education environment and beyond it.

For instance, in the case of *César Alan Rodríguez v Argentina*, the Tax and Administrative Court of Buenos Aires held that the right to education of Mr Rodriguez, a student with a disability, had been violated when an educational institution failed to issue him with an official certificate upon completion of his secondary education.[32] The certificate had not been issued to Mr Rodriguez even though he had met all the requirements of his personalised education project, and his results were within the minimum threshold required for the award of a certificate. The court established that persons with disabilities have the right to inclusive education on an equal basis with others. This includes the right to have their abilities and capabilities certified on equal conditions. 'On an equal basis' with others does not mean equal conditions of appraisal, but instead 'conditions of equality' require that all students, regardless of whether or not they have a disability, should be appraised according to the parameters imposed on them.

Reasonable accommodation

As illustrated above, a State Party is under an immediate obligation to realise the right to reasonable accommodation, and the onus to establish that a requested measure constitutes a disproportionate or undue burden rests upon the State Party.

There is a lack of clear guidance concerning resource allocation for the needs of children with disabilities, and in its absence, evidence suggests that the right to reasonable accommodation is not being protected in line with the requirements of Article 5(3) CRPD.

In *Moore v British Columbia*, the Supreme Court of Canada upheld a decision of a lower court, which had found that a School District Board of Education had denied a child with severe dyslexia access to education.[33] The Supreme Court held that education was a service normally available to the public, the denial of which was contrary to the British Columbia Human Rights Code. The case arose as result of the decision to close a facility providing intensive services and individualised assistance to students with severe learning disabilities. Although the School District of Vancouver faced severe subsidy controls, in deciding to close the facility it was found not to have acted with a bona fide and sensible justification, which could have provided a defence to the claim. Although *Moore v British Columbia* predates the Spanish Case No.6868/2012 which was considered earlier, it appears that the judges of Spain's Constitutional Court were neither inspired by the ruling of the Canadian Supreme Court in *Moore v British Columbia*, nor did they appreciate that the interpretative rules concerning the provision of reasonable adjustment, discrimination and accessibility have evolved since Spain's ratification of the Convention.

In many jurisdictions, when considering the provision of reasonable accommodation, neither the opinion of the child nor of the parents concerned is taken into account in the course of the assessment process. It is often the case that the school to which the child is assigned does not have the resources to cater for the child's special needs. Also, schools frequently fail to ask for additional resources, as such requests are considered to be a waste of time. Children are often assigned to schools which are long distances from their residence, preventing them from enjoying the companionship of their neighbours and peers. National education systems are often so bureaucratic and unfriendly that parents are compelled to accept the segregated schooling assigned to their child, and they are often deterred from lodging administrative complaints in respect of such decisions.

The administrative complaint procedures available to parents are often long-winded and tedious and, frequently, the child concerned must attend the assigned school pending the outcome of mediation or conciliation. In the event that a child fails to attend the assigned school, it is not uncommon for education authorities to threaten or initiate prosecution of parents, given that school attendance is generally mandatory until the age of 16. Some parents can have their child removed from their care, pending the outcome of an administrative complaint procedure, and others can even be prosecuted for abandonment. In the event that a complaint is dismissed—and this is usually the case—parents must continue to deal with the education authorities regarding their child's future education. It is a matter of concern that, notwithstanding the CRPD Committee's General Comment No.2 on Article 9 (Accessibility), education authorities are generally not legally mandated to scrutinise accessibility-related legislation.

Access to justice

In situations where parents wish to pursue the domestic administrative complaint procedure, or where they wish to make a complaint to a national human rights institution, it does not necessarily follow that a child is entitled to stay at home, pending a final decision concerning where they may access their right to education. Whilst legal aid may sometimes be available to pursue an appeal to an administrative decision, parents do not necessarily have access to a lawyer of their choice, and those lawyers who are available do not necessarily have expertise in the field of human rights and inclusive education. Consequently, many court cases are funded by parents themselves. The judicial system is complex. Different remedies may be available at different stages of proceedings, and final determination of the case may take up to three years.

Justice delayed is justice denied, and this is particularly so in cases concerning the right to inclusive education, given the irreversible prejudice caused to a child with a disability and her parents, where the right to inclusive education is violated. There is a need to revisit procedural and evaluation criteria pertaining to inclusive education for children with disabilities. Current systems often serve to alienate students with disabilities and are discriminatory in their effect. Whilst in some cases wealthy parents can pay for private education for their child, children with disabilities are more frequently forced to receive their education in segregated units, in breach of their right to inclusive education (Article 24 CRPD). It should be recalled that the immediate obligations of States Parties in relation to Article 24 are to ensure non-discrimination regarding access to education and reasonable accommodation for persons with disabilities. States Parties must also make available compulsory, free, primary education to all children, regardless of ability or disability. It is clear that States Parties have an ongoing obligation to move expeditiously towards the full realisation of inclusive education.

Conclusion

The various treaty bodies which have considered the right of children with disabilities to education have unanimously called for their inclusion in mainstream education and life-long training. The general focus of such bodies has been on attaining equality of opportunity for persons with disabilities on an equal basis with others. Notwithstanding the clear understanding which has emerged internationally regarding the progressive nature of economic, cultural and social rights, it remains the case that States Parties are bound by legal obligations with immediate effect, and these include a duty to provide education for all. The benchmark by which to judge how well States Parties have met their obligation to provide universal education on an equal basis for all is the extent to which they have embraced the process of inclusive education. Engagement in inclusive education enables States Parties to provide good quality education for persons with disabilities, whilst also facilitating their social development.

This chapter has considered several obstacles to inclusive education for persons with disabilities, including a resistance to accept a paradigm shift in human rights discourse on disability, from a medical to a human rights-based model. Political ideologies and processes of indoctrination are other factors which prevent access to inclusive education in many jurisdictions. The model of inclusive education which has been consistently promoted by the international community over the years has gained increasing support, as evidenced by the growing numbers of international covenants propounding the right to education for all. Domestic courts have played a valuable role in the inclusive education process. However, their rulings have not always been underpinned by an awareness of what inclusive education entails for society. The process of inclusive education is ongoing, and provided progress continues, the cycle of exclusion, segregation and isolation of persons with disabilities may at last be broken.

Summary of Concluding Observations and Recommendations

In many education systems around the world, the relationship between Article 24 and other provisions of the CRPD is manifested in the form of multiple breaches of the Convention. Frequently, breaches of the right to education occur in situations where there is also evidence of a failure to adhere to the general principles of the Convention, such as respect for the inherent dignity of persons with disabilities and a commitment to non-discrimination (Article 3(1) and (2) CRPD). Breaches of the right to education also arise alongside breaches of other general principles, such as the right to full and equal participation in society and the right to accessibility (Article 3(3) and (6) CRPD). The failure of States Parties to respect the evolving capacities of children with disabilities in accordance with Article 3(8) CRPD may also be associated with breaches of the right to education.

Where States Parties fail to meet their general obligations under the Convention, as enshrined in Article 4 CRPD, it seems that the right to education is also more likely to be breached. In accordance with Article 4(2) CRPD, States Parties are required to take measures, as far as possible in light of their available resources, to progressively realise economic, social and cultural rights. Where States Parties fail to adhere to the provisions of Article 4(2) CRPD, the breach of the right to education of persons with disabilities is more likely to occur. Likewise, breaches of States Parties' obligations to engage in awareness-raising programmes, to ensure accessibility for persons with disabilities or to guarantee their equal recognition before the law, may also be associated with the denial of the right to education (Articles 8, 9 and 12 CRPD).

Where persons with disabilities, and other persons, have been subjected to discrimination on the basis of disability, States Parties must ensure that they have easy access to mechanisms through which to challenge such discrimination. The establishment of bodies for the promotion of non-discrimination, and for the investigation of complaints, which have enforcement powers to effectively pursue and remedy breaches, is an effective means for States Parties to address the ongoing problem of discrimination. With regard to the right to inclusive education, effective mediation services should be made available so that students with disabilities and educational institutions can directly engage with one another in the inclusive education process. Where discrimination is found to have occurred, sanctions must be sufficient to deter such behavior. This requires effective enforcement by legal authorities, including the establishment of effective inspection regimes to ensure adherence to accessibility codes. In the case of breaches of Article 24 CRPD, suitable penalties and fees must be imposed, with the award of damages also being available where appropriate.

States Parties should also establish a legally binding code of practice for the provision of reasonable accommodation. Such a code should be the subject of ongoing review. States Parties must ensure that the rights of persons with disabilities to confidentiality and autonomy are always respected. All education providers must apply policies to ensure non-discrimination and equality of opportunity, in accordance their legal obligations to provide inclusive education for students with disabilities.

In its General Comment No.4 on the right to inclusive education, the CRPD Committee reflected upon the obligations of States Parties in light of the UN Sustainable Development Goals.[34] The Committee stated that the States Parties should increase their efforts towards inclusive education, through the adoption and implementation of strategies and action plans to achieve inclusive education within the mainstream system. Such strategies and action plans must have clearly defined time frames, indicators and monitoring and evaluation frameworks, to ensure their effectiveness. States Parties must also ensure that they collect data on the level of participation of children with disabilities in mainstream education. They must also ensure that mainstream educational institutions are accessible, and that where necessary, there are clearly defined time frames in which to provide accessibility, reasonable accommodation and individual support. The requirement to ensure accessibility includes a duty to ensure accessible environments and accessible educational materials. Where necessary, educational materials must also be adapted to meet the individual needs of students with disabilities. Curricula in all education institutions must be inclusive of the educational needs of students with disabilities. The Committee further recommended that States Parties should revise their systems of assessment for school enrolment, to ensure that they do not discriminate against children with disabilities seeking to access inclusive education. States Parties should also require mandatory training for all teachers, and others engaged in the provision of education, regarding inclusive, quality education, and they should make available the necessary resources in that regard.

In order to ensure the right of persons with disabilities to inclusive education, the Committee also recommended that States Parties should develop comprehensive education policies, and they should ensure that sufficient financial resources are available for their effective implementation. In particular, States Parties must ensure that all children with disabilities receive a complete, compulsory education, in accordance with domestic legislative provisions. The particular needs of indigenous peoples and those in rural areas with regard to inclusive education must be considered. States Parties should develop programmes for the transfer of students with disabilities from special schools to inclusive settings, and ensure that reasonable accommodation is provided within the mainstream education system.

Notes

1 United Nations Declaration on Human Rights Education and Training, 19 December 2011, A/RES/66/137.
2 UNICEF, Children with Disabilities, available at http://www.unicef.cn/en/child-protection/children-with-disabilities/, accessed 23 March 2018; See also Jessie Li, Pulitzer Center Project China: Students With Disabilities, available at https://pulitzercenter.org/projects/china-children-education-disabilities, accessed 23 March 2018.
3 OHCHR, Thematic Study on the Right of Persons with Disabilities to Education, 18 December 2013, A/HRC/25/29, para.7.
4 UNESCO, Salamanca Statement and Framework for Action on Special Needs Education, Spain, 7–10 June 1994, para.3.
5 CRPD Committee, General Comment No.4 on Article 24 (Right to Inclusive Education), 2016, CRPD/C/GC/4, para.4.
6 Oliver Walton, *Helpdesk Research Report: Economic Benefits of Disability-Inclusive Development*, Governance and Social Development Resource Centre, 6 September 2012; Lena Morgon Banks and Sarah Polack, *The Economic Costs of Exclusion and Gains of Inclusion of People with Disabilities: Evidence from Low and Middle Income Countries*, International Centre for Evidence in Disability, London School of Hygiene & Tropical Medicine.
7 *International Association Autism Europe v France*, ECSR Complaint No.13/2002, 4 November 2003.
8 Ibid, paras 53 and 54.
9 General Comment No.4, para.11.
10 OHCHR, Thematic Study on the Right of Persons with Disabilities to Education, para.4.
11 CRPD Committee, Concluding Observations on the Initial Report of Mexico, 27 October 2014, CRPD/C/MEX/CO/1, para.47.
12 General Comment No.4, para.11.
13 CRPD Committee, Concluding Observations on the Initial Report of the Republic of Moldova, 18 May 2017, CRPD/C/MDA/CO/1.
14 Ibid.
15 CRPD Committee, Concluding Observations on the Initial Report of Gabon, 2 October 2015, CRPD/C/GAB/CO/1, para.52.
16 General Comment No.4, para.11.
17 OHCHR, Thematic Study on the Right of Persons with Disabilities to Education, para.4.
18 CRPD Committee, Concluding Observations on the Initial Report of Tunisia, 13 May 2011, CRPD/C/TUN/CO/1, para.31.
19 *Western Cape Forum for Intellectual Disability v South Africa*, (2011 (5) SA 87 (WCC)) [2010] ZAWCHC 544; 18678/2007 (11 November 2010).
20 Ibid, para.4.
21 Ibid, para.46.
22 Ibid, para.52.
23 Vernor Muñoz, The right to education of persons with disabilities—Report of the Special Rapporteur on the right to education, 19 February 2007, A/HRC/4/29, para.11.
24 Ibid.
25 CRPD Committee, Concluding Observations on the Initial Report of Spain, 19 October 2011, CRPD/C/ESP/CO/1, para.43.

26 Ibid.
27 The Organic Act on Education 2/2006 (Spain).
28 CRPD Committee, General Comment No.5 on Article 19 (independent living and being included in the community), 2017, CRPD/C/GC/5, para.88.
29 Ibid.
30 Ibid.
31 General Comment No.4, para.9.
32 *César Alan Rodríguez v Argentina*, Tax and Administrative Court – Chamber No. 1 of Buenos Aires, 24 October 2016.
33 *Moore v British Columbia (Education)*, 2012 SCC 61.
34 UN Sustainable Development Goals 4.5 and 4.8.

10

RIGHT TO WORK AND EMPLOYMENT

Introduction

Social attitudes towards the full inclusion of persons with disabilities in the mainstream workforce have not always been positive. Persons with disabilities have traditionally been perceived as being non-productive and their contribution to the economy considered to be insignificant. However, there was a need to keep them busy with some kind of occupation, and historically, the establishment of segregated workshops had been the solution. These were institutions where persons with disabilities were confined and their prescribed occupations generally consisted of handicrafts, such as basket-making, making greeting cards or assisting with the repair of electrical goods.

Following sustained efforts by persons with disabilities to prove their talents, abilities and skills, society has become more aware of how it has been undervaluing their potential socio-economic contribution. In response to pressure from disability activists, governments have started to introduce legislation and policy to compel the private sector to recruit persons with disabilities. For example, sections 10 and 11 of the UK Disabled Persons (Employment) Act 1944 introduced a quota system for the employment of persons with disabilities, but these provisions were repealed by the Disability Discrimination Act 1995.[1] By that time, persons with disabilities worldwide were unanimously calling for the opportunity to prove their willingness and ability to participate in the open labour market and governments were beginning to take note. As a result, recent decades have seen the introduction of legislation embracing the right to work of persons with disabilities. However, States Parties still have a significant role to play in seeking to remove barriers in the workplace.

At this juncture it is useful to note the place of disability within domestic legislative frameworks. Constitutional law is for most countries the highest form of domestic law which is binding on all state authorities. It frequently reflects the importance afforded to the employment of persons with disabilities. Australia, Hong Kong, China, Mauritius and the Philippines, amongst others, have adopted civil and labour laws regarding the employment rights of persons with disabilities and the approach appears to have worked well over the years.

The medical model to assess the ability and willingness of persons with disabilities to work was first used after the Second World War. It was for medical professionals to determine the suitability and fitness of persons with disabilities to be in the workplace. Where a person's ability to work was in question, he was frequently certified as being unfit to work, even though willing to do so. As a result of the medical model, States Parties needlessly restricted employment opportunities for persons with disabilities through the issuance of disability certificates, which are still in use today in several jurisdictions. For example, section 2 of the Mauritius Training and Employment of Disabled Persons Act 1996 (repealed in 2012) provided that 'disabled person' must be interpreted as someone 'who is able and willing to work'.

Following the adoption and ratification of the CRPD in 2007, there is still a disparity between the percentage of persons with disabilities in employment compared to their non-disabled counterparts. Furthermore, even when persons with disabilities are in employment 'they are more likely to be in low-paying jobs, at lower occupational levels and with poor promotional prospects and working conditions' compared to their non-disabled counterparts.[2] For instance, in its Concluding Observations on the Initial Report of Ethiopia, the CRPD Committee observed that the rate of employment of persons with disabilities was so low that it was a contributory factor in poverty and segregation.[3] The Committee was also concerned about the low rate of employment of persons with disabilities in Kenya, which was currently about 1% of the whole workforce in a population of almost 50 million people.[4] Similarly, in relation to Denmark, the Committee has noted as follows:

> while the Act on the Prohibition of Discrimination in the Labour Market prohibits direct and indirect differential treatment on the grounds of disability, neither the general labour legislation nor collective labour agreements stipulate clear obligations on employers to afford reasonable accommodation in the labour market, which may be among the sources of a prevailing employment gap between persons with disabilities (44 per cent of whom are working) and persons without disabilities (78 per cent of whom are working).[5]

With regard to Canada, the CRPD Committee has criticised the high rate of unemployment amongst persons with disabilities and the lack of programmes to ensure that persons with disabilities were able to retain their jobs at a time of economic crisis.[6] It was also concerned about the lack of strategies to end the use of sheltered workshops in Canada and the state's failure to ensure access to the open labour market for persons with disabilities, especially for women and young persons. The Committee also noted that there had been a gradual increase in the number of complaints of discrimination in employment relating to disability.

The fundamental right to work is enshrined in numerous international treaties. Article 23(1) UDHR provides that '[e]veryone has the right to work, to free choice of employment, to just and favourable conditions of work and to protection against unemployment'. Article 6(1) ICESCR further stipulates that States Parties should recognise and safeguard the right to work of every person, including the right to an opportunity to gain a living by work which is freely chosen or accepted. However, while these provisions recognised the right to work and employment for all, they did not specifically refer to persons with disabilities.

The origin of the right to work of persons with disabilities

In 1981, The International Year of Disabled People was instrumental in gaining wider recognition of the right of persons with disabilities to work and employment.[7] Its theme was 'full participation', which was defined as the right of persons with disabilities to take part fully in the life and development of their societies, enjoy living conditions equal to those of other citizens, and have an equal share in improved conditions resulting from socio-economic development. The UN called for specialised agencies and other UN bodies to adopt measures to improve employment opportunities for persons with disabilities at all levels within their own organisations. It also called upon such organisations to improve access to their buildings and facilities for persons with disabilities and to ensure that their information sources are fully accessible.[8] In 1989, the UN General Assembly adopted the Tallinn Guidelines for Action on Human Resources Development in the Field of Disability. The Guidelines provided a framework for the promotion, training and employment of persons with disabilities across all government departments, as well as for securing their involvement at all levels of policy-making.[9]

Several instruments of international law have contributed to the creation of job opportunities for persons with disabilities. In particular, the International Labour Organisation (ILO), through the introduction of systems for standard-setting and supervision, has made a significant contribution to the promotion of equal employment opportunities for persons with disabilities. A number of ILO Conventions have been particularly valuable in seeking to improve working conditions and opportunities for persons with disabilities.[10] The UN Standard Rules on the Equalisation of Opportunities for Persons with Disabilities and, more recently, Article 27 CRPD have also made valuable contributions to the international legal framework governing the right to work of persons with disabilities. In accordance with Article 1(2) of the ILO Convention on Vocational Rehabilitation and Employment (Disabled Persons), 'each Member shall consider the purpose of vocational rehabilitation as being to enable a disabled person to secure, retain and advance in suitable employment and thereby to further such person's integration or reintegration into society'.[11] The ILO Convention was adopted in response to the International Year of Disabled Persons. Although its scope was somewhat limited in terms of the specific obligations it imposed upon States Parties, it nonetheless started a process of sensitising States Parties about the need to create training and employment opportunities for persons with disabilities. Rule 7 of the Standard Rules on the Equalization of Opportunities for Persons with Disabilities moreover stipulates that:

> States should recognize the principle that persons with disabilities must be empowered to exercise their human rights, particularly in the field of employment. In both rural and urban areas they must have equal opportunities for productive and gainful employment in the labour market.[12]

Notwithstanding the non-binding nature of the Standard Rules, they serve as a model for good practice and have been a valuable tool for disability activists seeking to secure the right to work and employment for persons with disabilities.

The scope of Article 27 CRPD

International and domestic discrimination law concerning the right of persons with disabilities to employment has evolved to include employment contracts, which are currently governed both by principles of public international law and domestic statute. Article 27(1) CRPD imposes numerous obligations upon States Parties, including an obligation to introduce measures to ensure that persons with disabilities enjoy the right to earn a living by work which is freely chosen or accepted in the open labour market. It also requires States Parties to guarantee that the work environment is inclusive and accessible, including an obligation to protect workers who acquire a disability in the course of employment. States Parties are called upon to immediately prohibit discrimination on the grounds of disability and to protect the rights of workers with disabilities on an equal basis with others through the adoption of appropriate policy and legislative measures. They must encourage and assist persons with disabilities to join a trade union of their choice and must continuously consult with persons with disabilities and their representative organisations with regard to legislation and policy.

States Parties are also under an obligation to guarantee effective access to technical and vocational guidance programmes and placement services for persons with disabilities, which includes a commitment to promote employment and career advancement opportunities for persons with disabilities. They must ensure that persons with disabilities are able to establish themselves as self-employed persons, and also that they are given the opportunity to engage in entrepreneurship. Article 27(1) also requires States Parties to promote the employment of persons with disabilities in the private sector and to ensure that they are provided with reasonable accommodation at their request. They must also promote vocational and professional rehabilitation and establish job retention and return-to-work programmes for persons with disabilities. Article 27(2) CRPD reinforces the principles previously enshrined in Article 8 ICCPR and places an obligation on States Parties to ensure that persons with disabilities are not subject to slavery or servitude and that they are protected from forced or compulsory labour.

In its General Comment No.18 on the Right to Work, the CESCR stated that the right to work fosters independence and inclusion in the community and enhances the human dignity of persons with disabilities.[13] This is in line with Article 6 ICESCR, which provides that everyone has the right to the opportunity to earn their living by work which is freely chosen or accepted. This requires States Parties to respect the physical and mental integrity of workers in the course of their employment. Workers must also have the benefit of decent working conditions, including adequate remuneration and health and safety protection. With regard to remuneration, an acceptable income is one which allows workers to support their families (Article 7 ICESCR). It is notable that the jurisprudence of the CRPD Committee has not always been consistent with that of the CESCR. The discussion of the case law below illustrates how the CRPD Committee's interpretation of the right of persons with disabilities to employment has sometimes been the source of confusion. Whilst in its earlier case law the CRPD Committee considered that the denial of an integration subsidy to a person with a disability amounted to a violation of Article 27 CRPD, later communications have failed to uphold the right to work and employment of persons with disabilities in a similarly robust manner.

Disability-based discrimination under Article 27 CRPD

The obligations of States Parties in line with Article 27 CRPD were first considered by the CRPD Committee in the case of *Liliane Gröninger v Germany*.[14] Mrs Gröninger's case concerned her son, Erhard. Mrs Gröninger complained that Erhard's rights under Article 27 CRPD had been violated by the State of Germany. She claimed that Erhard had been the victim of discrimination. In November 2009, a complaint had duly been made about the matter to the Cologne Integration Office. Mrs Gröninger was subsequently informed that the Regional Authority had no legal means to assist Erhard in relation to the complaint of discrimination. Since 2002, Erhard had been registered with a number of employment agencies and Mrs Gröninger claimed that the methods used by the employment agencies had the systematic effect of preventing the inclusion of persons with disabilities in the workforce. She also contended that there were no legal consequences for the perpetrators of this kind discrimination since the social courts responsible for dealing with these breaches had no recourse to criminal sanctions.

Mrs Gröninger argued that the operation of the integration subsidy system had a discriminatory effect insofar as subsidies could only be claimed by employers after they had made a job offer. The system served to exclude the participation of persons with disabilities. In addition, both the duration and outcome of the applications process were uncertain. Mrs Gröninger also claimed that the integration subsidy was not available to any person whose full working capacity could not be restored within three years. Mrs Gröninger stated that Erhard had not had access to proper training or to placement services and that the employment agencies had used delaying tactics to prevent his being included in the labour market. She supported her claim with expert legal opinion to the effect that, in cases of permanent disability, participation in working life is practically impossible in accordance with the terms of the integration subsidy scheme.

The CRPD Committee concluded that the manner in which the integration subsidy scheme had been applied in Erhard's case was not in line with the State Party's obligations under Article 27(1)(h) CRPD. It was arguable that the introduction of the subsidy scheme was the only affirmative action which had been taken by the State of Germany in order to assist Erhard in his efforts to be included in the labour market. The Committee commended the wide variety of measures provided for in the State Party's legislation as well as its statement to the effect that, as a person with a disability, Erhard was entitled to assistance in relation to employment, promotion and rehabilitation, in conformity with the provisions of the Social Code. However, the Committee observed that the State Party had failed to specify which of those measures, if any, were applicable in Erhard's case.

The measures which had been taken by the State Party's authorities to assist Erhard's integration in the labour market consisted of granting him unemployment benefit, arranging counselling meetings, monitoring attendance at meetings and regulating the geographical area in which Erhard was entitled to remain. In accordance with Articles 27(1)(d) and 27(1)(e) CRPD, persons with disabilities have the right to benefit from appropriate measures to promote and increase their employment opportunities, which includes the right to access placement services and assistance in finding and securing employment. The Committee concluded that the measures taken by the responsible authorities of the State Party to assist with Erhard's integration in the labour market did not meet their obligations under Article 27(1)(d) and (e) of the Convention.

With its decision in *Gröninger*, the CRPD Committee sent a clear signal to States Parties that they must not merely pay lip service to their responsibilities regarding the employment of persons with disabilities, for example by merely introducing employment schemes or policies which are not subject to monitoring nor evaluation. Such programmes fail to target the elimination of discrimination against persons with disabilities prior to their obtaining either a job offer or the offer of a placement. The duty of States Parties is to effectively facilitate situations in which persons with disabilities might demonstrate their skills to potential employers. Disabled persons cannot not do so if employers and employment agencies do not provide them with the necessary reasonable accommodation.

Reasonable accommodation and discrimination

More recently, in its General Comment No.23 on the right to just and favourable conditions of work, the CESCR stated that workers with disabilities require specific measures to be undertaken if they are to enjoy the right to just and fair working conditions on an equal basis with others.[15] The CESCR stipulated that persons with disabilities should not be segregated in sheltered workshops and that they must benefit from an accessible working environment. Reasonable accommodation in the workplace should therefore include both making adjustments and the introduction of flexible working arrangements.

The adoption of reasonable accommodation measures by employers is essential to facilitate the employment of persons with disabilities. However, it is also important to recognise that many persons with disabilities may not actually require any reasonable accommodation whatsoever in the workplace. It is for this reason that Article 27 CRPD requires States Parties to carry out research to determine the extent to which reasonable accommodation can be met through the adoption of universal design. Two further practical steps which States Parties and their authorities may take to assist the inclusion of persons with disabilities in the workplace are to make job advertisements and applications available in accessible format and to carry out adjustments in the workplace to enable greater accessibility and inclusion. Such measures are prerequisites, if persons with disabilities are to enjoy the benefits of work on an equal basis with others.

In *Marie-Louise Jungelin v Sweden*, the CRPD Committee further clarified the obligations of States Parties to provide reasonable accommodation.[16] However, the CRPD Committee reached a different conclusion regarding the extent of the right to employment of persons with disabilities than that which it had arrived at in Mrs Liliane Gröninger's case. Ms Jungelin had been visually impaired since birth. In May 2006, she applied to the Swedish Social Insurance Agency ('the Agency') to work as an assessor or investigator of sickness benefit and sickness compensation applications. In order for Ms Jungelin to perform her work, it would have been necessary for the Agency to adapt its computers and case-handling systems to meet her needs. However, the Agency informed Ms Jungelin that although she possessed the requisite skills and qualifications to perform the role, it was not possible to make the necessary adaptations to the Agency's systems in order to meet her needs. Ms Jungelin subsequently appealed to the Swedish Labour Court against the Agency's decision.

Ms Jungelin argued that the decision by the Agency to discard her application for the insurance assessor position constituted a violation of her rights under Articles 5 and 27 of the Convention. She contended that she had been discriminated against during the Social Insurance Agency's recruitment process because the Agency had discarded her application rather than properly assessing the option of making the necessary support and adaptation measures, which included making adjustments to the Agency's computer system for users requiring screen readers and Braille display. Ms Jungelin stated that her requirements were neither unreasonable nor disproportionate.

She claimed that the Swedish Labour Court did not properly consider the expert witness and other opinions available to it. She further maintained that she had failed to take account of the fact that employers have an obligation to implement appropriate adjustments in the workplace to accommodate the needs of employees with disabilities. Moreover, the Swedish Labour Court did not take into consideration the fact that any adjustment to the Agency's computer systems would benefit not only Ms Jungelin, but would also be of benefit to other visually-impaired employees in future. Ms Jungelin argued that the State Party had failed to take appropriate steps to prevent discrimination on the basis of disability in matters concerning employment, including conditions of recruitment and hiring. Nor had the State Party ensured that reasonable accommodation was provided for persons with disabilities.

The Committee recalled States Parties' obligations under Article 27 of the Convention (Article 27(a), (e), (g) and (i) CRPD). It held that States Parties enjoy a margin of appreciation when assessing the reasonableness and proportionality of accommodation measures. It is generally the role of the domestic courts to evaluate the facts and evidence in a particular case. A State Party will be afforded a margin of appreciation unless it is found that its evaluation was clearly arbitrary, or amounted to a denial of justice. Given that the Swedish Labour Court had reached its conclusion based upon an assessment of the reasonableness and proportionality of the required accommodation measures, the CRPD Committee could not conclude that Ms Jungelin's rights had been breached under Articles 5 and 27 of the Convention. The CRPD Committee further noted that the Swedish Labour Court had thoroughly and objectively assessed all the evidence submitted by both Ms Jungelin and the Agency.

In *Jungelin*, the CRPD Committee appeared to argue that to require the Social Insurance Agency to adopt support and adaptation measures which were recommended by the Swedish Ombudsman in Ms Jungelin's case would have amounted to an undue burden on the Agency. The CRPD Committee held that Ms Jungelin did not provide evidence to support a conclusion that the assessment conducted by the Agency was manifestly arbitrary or amounted to a denial of justice. It follows from the Committee's decision in *Jungelin* that complainants before the Committee now have the burden of proving that reasonable accommodation measures do not constitute an undue or disproportionate burden on an employer. This is a departure from the Committee's previous position, which placed the onus upon employers to prove that the reasonable accommodation being requested constituted an undue or disproportionate burden. As a consequence of this departure from the Committee's previous position, six members of the Committee gave a dissenting minority view in Ms Jungelin's case:

> In the light of the above and taking into account all the information provided by the parties, we consider that the Committee should have determined that the judgment of the Labour Court reflects a wide interpretation of the notion of 'undue burden', severely limiting the possibility for persons with disabilities of being selected for positions requiring the adaptation of the working environment to their needs. We believe that the Labour Court's assessment of the requested support and adaptation measures, made in accordance with the 1999 Act, upheld the denial of reasonable accommodation,

resulting in a *de facto* discriminatory exclusion of the author from the position for which she applied. The Committee should have considered such assessment as not consistent with the general principles set forth in preambular paragraphs (i) and (j) of the Convention, and amounting to a violation of articles 5 and 27 of the Convention.[17]

The dissenting minority opinion in *Jungelin* was based upon the general principles of the Preamble and Article 5 CRPD. The minority held that Articles 5 and 27 CRPD, when applied to the facts of Ms Jungelin' case, revealed a prima facie case of discrimination. Whilst the majority of Committee members had found that the domestic court's assessment was both reasonable and objective in law, domestic case law from other States Parties suggested that a denial of reasonable adjustment measures may constitute discrimination.

In *Standard Bank of South Africa v CCMA and Others*, the Labour Court of South Africa considered whether the decision of the Commission for Conciliation, Mediation and Arbitration (CCMA) which had found in favour of the third respondent, Mrs Ferreira, was reasonable.[18] At issue was the denial of reasonable accommodation by the Standard Bank of South Africa ('the bank') to its employee Mrs Ferreira, who had injured her back in a motor collision whilst on duty, and who was subsequently dismissed by the bank a few years after the accident.

Ms Ferreira argued that the bank had failed to engage an occupational therapist to consult with her and to report on the redesign of her workstation. It had also failed to supply her with either a comfortable chair or a headset, to enable her to operate the telephone comfortably. It had also refused to allow Ms Ferreira to work on its computers, nor did it consider her for a half-day working position. Finally, she claimed that the bank had failed to make reasonable adjustments to her workstation.

The Labour Court held that the bank's duty to provide reasonable accommodation stemmed from its overriding obligation not to discriminate in the workplace. It followed from this that the bank had a legal obligation to accommodate Ms Ferreira in order to ensure that she could continue to work. There was also a reverse onus upon the bank to ensure that it did not compel Ms Ferreira to terminate her employment or encourage her to do so. However, the facts of the case suggest that the bank did, in fact, encourage Ms Ferreira to leave its employment.[19] In failing to provide Ms Ferreira with reasonable accommodation, the bank made it difficult for her to continue working. It also encouraged or compelled her to terminate her employment by seeking early retirement. She was dismissed when she failed to do so. The court found that the bank had discriminated against Ms Ferreira. It had failed to accommodate her, and nor did it discharge its onus of proving that the suggested amendments would cause unjustified hardship to the bank.

It is notable that the decision in *Standard Bank of South Africa v CCMA* predated the adoption of the CRPD. However, the court in that case nonetheless ruled that the denial of reasonable accommodation constituted discrimination. It should be highlighted that the Labour Court of South Africa took the lead from the CRPD Committee with regard to its analysis of reasonable accommodation. A similar lead, though in a different context, was also secured by the UK House of Lords regarding discrimination against persons with disabilities in the context of employment.

In *Relaxion Group plc v Rhys-Harper (FC); D'Souza v London Borough of Lambeth; Jones v 3M Healthcare Limited and three other actions*, the House of Lords had to determine whether an Employment Tribunal (the tribunal) had jurisdiction to hear discrimination complaints which arose following the termination of employment contracts.[20] After the defendants' employment contracts had been terminated, their employer refused to issue them with a reference. Given that the discriminatory acts alleged by the defendants had occurred after the termination of their employment contracts and that the alleged acts did not have a sufficiently close connection with their employment relationships, it was argued by the defendants that the allegedly discriminatory acts were beyond the scope of anti-discrimination legislation, and therefore outside the jurisdiction of the tribunal. The House of Lords held that the applicable legislation provided that when two individuals entered into an employer-employee relationship, the employee would expect to be protected against discrimination by the employer in view of all the benefits arising from that relationship. The employment relationship was the feature which elicited the employer's responsibility not to discriminate. That responsibility could not be deemed to be restricted only to the duration of the period of employment if there were incidents of the employment which fell to be dealt with after the employment had ended.

In April 2015, the French *Défenseur des droits* (Rights Defender) had to examine whether the denial of reasonable accommodation to an employee with a physical disability amounted to discrimination.[21] From the date of her initial employment in 2006 until 2012, the claimant had continuously asked her employer to provide her with reasonable adjustment measures, to no avail. Article L.5213 of the *Code du travail* (French Labour Code) places an obligation on employers to take appropriate steps to enable their employees to gain access to and retain a job corresponding to their qualifications, unless such measures would entail a disproportionate or undue burden on the employer. Article L.5213 stipulated that the non-provision of reasonable accommodation may amount to discrimination.

The Rights Defender held that the employer had failed to provide the employee with reasonable measures in relation to working hours and the supply of equipment. The employer had not responded favourably to the employee's requests concerning the rescheduling of her working hours, in order to allow her to attend her physiotherapy sessions. Moreover, he did not provide an ergonomic chair adapted to her disability, which was recommended by the work doctor. Similarly, the recommendation of the doctor to allow the employee to work part-time was opposed by the employer, who considered that the job of managing a client portfolio could only be effected on a full-time basis. Whilst the Rights Defender recognised this argument as a legitimate one, it could not agree that the sharing of a customer portfolio between several part-time employees was a disproportionate and undue burden on the employer. The Rights Defender therefore found that the employer had repeatedly failed to comply with his obligation to provide reasonable adjustment measures to the claimant with disabilities and recommended that the employer should compensate the claimant for the damage suffered as a result of the discrimination.

As the above case law illustrates, national courts have been quite proactive in recognising that the denial of reasonable accommodation to persons with disabilities which would have enabled them to work on an equal basis with others amounted to discrimination. The decisions of the national courts above are in line with the spirit and principles enshrined in the Convention, whereby States Parties must take all measures to ensure that persons with disabilities are able to retain their jobs and participate in return-to-work programmes (Article 27(1)(k) CRPD, 2007). However, some States Parties have been very slow to safeguard and promote the right to work and employment.[22]

In April 2013, the CRPD Committee received a formal request from a number of disabled persons' organisations (DPOs), alleging that serious and systematic violations of the Convention were occurring in the UK, especially in the context of the Government's austerity measures. In accordance with Article 36 CRPD and Rule 84 of its Rules of Procedure, the Committee has the power to carry out an inquiry into allegations of grave or systematic violations of the Convention. The Committee used its powers to hold an inquiry into the cumulative impact of legislation, policies and measures adopted by the UK on social security schemes, work and employment. The Committee found that:

> Evidence indicates several flaws in the processes related to the Employment and Support Allowance. In particular, the Committee notes that, despite several adjustments made to the Work Capability Assessment, the assessment has continued to be focused on a functional evaluation of skills and capabilities, and puts aside personal circumstances and needs, and barriers faced by persons with disabilities to return to employment, particularly those of persons with intellectual and/or psychosocial disabilities. In the initial period covered by the present report, evidence indicates a significant percentage of assessments were overturned by tribunals.[23]

According to the UK Inquiry Report, despite the training provided by the UK to its assessors and decision-makers, there remained a persistent lack of awareness of disability rights and the needs of persons with disabilities, in particular those of persons with intellectual or psychosocial disabilities. There was also evidence of a lack of reasonable accommodation relating to the assessment process and a lack of availability of accessible information about the assessment process.

Quotas

It was following the First World War that the use of quota schemes for the employment of persons with disabilities first emerged. Initially, such schemes were reserved for war veterans with disabilities and small employers were exempted from participation. After the Second World War, the use of quota schemes was extended to include civilians with disabilities and they were increasingly adopted by countries across the world. Quota schemes are among the most effective affirmative action measures for enhancing the integration of persons with disabilities into mainstream employment. According to the ILO, there are three types of quotas scheme.[24] First, there are binding quotas, the breach of which is backed up with enforcement actions. Second, there are binding quotas, the breach of which is not backed up with sanctions. Third, there are non-binding quotas, based upon a recommendation, for example from government. Many countries have introduced a three per cent quota scheme, based upon the employment of one per cent of blind persons, one per cent of deaf persons and one per cent of persons with physical disabilities.[25] However, such reasoning completely fails to take into account the right of persons with disabilities to employment and also reflects a general assumption that persons with psychosocial or intellectual disabilities are not able to engage in employment.

There are two main methods of applying quota systems. Some quota systems observe strict adherence to the legally stipulated percentage, regardless of the merits and qualifications of persons with disabilities in individual cases. Alternatively, a more flexible application may be adopted, taking account of both the quota and the merits and qualifications of persons with disabilities on an equal basis with non-disabled job applicants. It is submitted that both methods of application are materially flawed. A system based upon strict adherence to a legally stipulated quota perpetuates and legitimises negative stereotypes of disabled workers, whilst a system which considers the merits and qualifications of applicants may often fail to take sufficient account of the requirement to provide reasonable adjustment. This is necessary in order to promote the inclusion of workers with disabilities in the labour market. Furthermore, both systems sometimes lose sight of the need for States Parties to invest in the education and training of persons with disabilities. They do not address the need to review prevalent economic models to enable persons with disabilities to access work and employment.

In *A.F. v Italy*, the CRPD Committee considered whether Italian employment law, which was held by a national court to be non-discriminatory, amounted to a violation of Mr AF's rights under Article 27 CRPD.[26] According to Article 3(a) of Italian Law No.68/1999, at least seven per cent of the workforce recruited by public employers with a workforce of over fifty persons should be persons with disabilities. Article 7(2) of Italian Law No.68/199 further stipulated that public employers should reserve up to half of their positions to be filled in accordance with Article 3(a) through the competitive recruitment of persons with disabilities.

On 17 February 2007, Mr AF submitted a complaint to the Regional Administrative Court of Bologna. Mr AF requested the suspension and cancellation of the Public Examination for a university job on the grounds that it violated Article 7(2) of Law No.68/1999. On 7 May 2007, the Administrative Court rejected his complaint. It noted that the University of Modena and Reggio Emilia ('the University') was entitled to operate within the scope of an agreement which it had signed with the unemployment office of the Province of Modena on 20 December 2005. In line with the agreement, the University was bound to respect the seven per cent quota for employment of persons with disabilities, in accordance with Article 3(a) of Italian Law No.68/1999. However, the agreement did not guarantee the selection and appointment of Mr AF by the University.

On 4 June 2008, Mr AF appealed the decision of the Administrative Court before the Council of State, the highest Italian Administrative Court. On 4 December 2009, the Council of State dismissed Mr AF's appeal, The Council of State noted that a 50 per cent reserve quota for the employment of persons with disabilities did not apply to all public competitive examinations and that the aim of the reserve quota was to attain a general quota for the employment of persons with disabilities working in public entities, without reference to the kind of employment positions concerned. The Council of State also noted that the University had not failed to respect the 50 per cent reserve quota 'as 50 per cent of one post equalled zero'.

Mr AF claimed that the public examination organised in 2006 by the University failed to comply with the 50 per cent quota to be reserved for persons with disabilities as required by Law No.68/1999, thereby violating Article 27 CRPD. He argued that the University's interpretation of the 50 per cent general quota requirement was incorrect and that the correct application of the quota should either have resulted in his recruitment by the University, given that he was ranked third overall in the competition and was the only person with disabilities to have taken part in it, or alternatively, in the recruitment of both himself and the person that came in first in the competition.

The CRPD Committee held that Mr AF had failed to provide evidence which would enable the Committee to conclude that the national legislation and its application amounted to a violation of his individual rights under the Convention.[27] In the Committee's view, the Council of State had thoroughly and objectively assessed all the elements submitted by both Mr AF and the University before reaching its conclusion that Mr AF's non-selection was not discriminatory. Mr AF did not provide the Committee with any evidence that would have enabled it to conclude that the decision of the Council of State was manifestly arbitrary or that it amounted to a denial of justice. In the circumstances, the Committee concluded that the Council of State's decision was based upon objective and reasonable considerations. It is clear from the Committee's decision in Mr AF's case that it favoured a more flexible approach to the application of quota systems.

One question which remains unanswered from the ruling in *A.F. v Italy* is how to address the ongoing failure to give persons with disabilities the chance to obtain qualifications and training on an equal basis with others. One possible solution would be to seek an employers' contribution in the form of a levy to bear the cost of a qualifications and training programme for persons with disabilities. It is noteworthy that Mr AF did not benefit from affirmative action on the part of the Italian authorities in respect of his employment opportunities. It should also be emphasised that regardless of the occasionally flawed application of quota systems during the past decades, they have certainly been progressively assisting persons with disabilities to access education, training and employment.

Conclusion

It is an established general principle of international law that those who complain of rights violations under the Optional Protocols to international treaty bodies must substantiate the alleged violation with evidence. This point was reiterated by the CRPD Committee in *Jungelin v Sweden*. It is important for international human rights committees to be consistent in their application of such general principles and they should not venture into matters of domestic sovereignty, including the evaluation of facts by independent domestic courts. However, in refusing to re-evaluate the facts in *Jungelin*, the CRPD Committee effectively sacrificed Ms Jungelin's right to reasonable accommodation at the expense of consistency and predictability in international law. A comparison may be made with the case of *X v Tanzania*, where the civil right to freedom against torture was considered by the Committee, which held that there was a non-delegable duty on the part of States Parties to introduce legislation to ensure compliance with the provisions of the CRPD by both state and non-state actors. It is submitted that the duty to provide reasonable accommodation should have been treated by the CRPD Committee with a rigour similar to how the duty to legislate was upheld in *X v Tanzania*. Whilst the Committee is to be credited for shifting traditional perceptions of civil and economic rights, it has not been sufficiently proactive in seeking to combat discrimination against persons with disabilities in the workplace. It is therefore incumbent upon the Committee to either reverse its decision in *Jungelin* or to formulate a General Comment on Article 27.

The principles of participation, non-discrimination and accessibility for persons with disabilities underpin the development of fully-inclusive state policies. Employment is at the heart of each principle. While the CRPD has been adopted by many countries around the world, no State Party has as yet succeeded in implementing strategies and policies for the successful employment of persons with disabilities. However, most States Parties display an awareness of the importance of employment for the full inclusion of persons with disabilities in society. A successful employment strategy for persons with disabilities requires a cross intergovernmental approach which synergises action across state agencies and departments, in seeking to address the barriers which currently inhibit the employment of persons with disabilities. A successful employment strategy also requires the support of local services providers whose collaboration in delivering joined up services to support persons with disabilities in securing the right to work is essential. The state and the private sector must work in tandem to ensure the inclusion of persons with disabilities in the workplace to uphold their right to work in line with the CRPD.

Summary of Concluding Observations and Recommendations

In accordance with General Comment No.23 of the CESCR, States Parties must ensure respect for the right of workers to just and favourable conditions of work in the event that they are unable to realise it for themselves. States Parties have a role in creating an 'enabling' labour market environment, for example by adapting the workplace to accommodate persons with disabilities in the public sector and providing equipment in accordance with their needs. States Parties should also provide incentives for the private sector to do likewise. They should establish non-contributory, social security programmes for certain categories of workers, such as workers in the informal economy, to provide benefits and protection against accidents and disease in the workplace.

According to the OHCHR, while the reasons for low labour force participation by persons with disabilities are multifaceted, two of the main problems are a generally negative attitude towards persons with disabilities, and pervasive negative stereotypes surrounding them.[28] Persons with disabilities are considered as being in some way 'unsuitable' to participate in working life on an equal basis with others. Such attitudes and stereotypes contribute to discrimination against persons with disabilities in the field of employment, and contribute to their marginalisation. Today, many persons with disabilities around the world still experience the denial of their right to work, as provided for in Article 27 CRPD. The OCHR identified a wide range of efforts undertaken by States Parties to promote employment of persons with disabilities. Nevertheless, such efforts often focus on creating jobs or training opportunities in separate settings and fail to respect the principle of inclusion provided for in the Convention. States Parties must cease to rely upon sheltered employment schemes, and instead they must promote equal access for persons with disabilities in the open labour market. More importantly, States Parties have an obligation to raise employers' awareness of their duty to employ persons with disabilities. Employers in both public and private sectors are obliged to take positive steps to create a working environment that is welcoming to workers with disabilities. This includes a duty to ensure that public-sector workplaces are accessible to persons with disabilities. States Parties should also impose accessibility requirements on private-sector employers, including a duty to eliminate barriers preventing access to the workplace for persons with disabilities on an equal basis with others. States Parties must take immediate action to adopt employment legislation prohibiting disability-based discrimination, and to place the obligation to provide reasonable accommodation on a legislative footing. They should also engage in consciousness-raising camp to promote awareness of the concept of reasonable accommodation. States Parties should also adopt appropriate marketing frameworks to secure an increase in the proportion of persons with disabilities who are in mainstream employment.

Employment of persons with disabilities: a marketing framework

In order to effectively promote the inclusion of persons with disabilities in mainstream employment, States Parties must revisit their strategies. The adoption of an employer-focused marketing framework is one important means of addressing the lack of employment opportunities in both public and private sectors for persons with disabilities. However, it is the public sector that must lead the way in ensuring that the quota for employment of persons with disabilities is respected on all statutory bodies.

The causes of the under-representation of persons with disabilities are numerous, and include pervasive negative cultural stereotypes, problems of 'self-identification' amongst persons with disabilities and a general lack of information regarding the right of persons with disabilities to be included in the workplace. State Parties should adopt an incentivised approach towards achieving compliance with international norms for the employment of persons with disabilities, and they should identify an appropriate process to achieve that goal. According to Thaler et al, a number of strategies may be considered, including efforts to challenge negative stereotyping of persons with disabilities, and the introduction of education and information campaigns.[29] Persistent campaigning on key issues in order to change the status quo; a technique referred to as 'nudging' may also be instrumental in achieving change. Thaler et al have stated that:

> All behaviour is a function of the person or the situation, and so to change behaviour, you the person or the situation. Situational influences are stronger than personal influences. When we change perceptions and stereotypes we change attitudes. When we educate and inform, we change knowledge. When we use incentives, we are changing motivation.[30]

The promotion of the inclusion of persons with disabilities in mainstream employment not only entails the prohibition of discrimination but it also requires States Parties to take affirmative action in the areas of access to the labour market and the provision of reasonable accommodation.

In order to uphold Article 27 CRPD, States Parties need to adopt targeted social policies to combat an array of problems facing persons with disabilities, including unemployment and inequality of opportunities. If States Parties are serious about the inclusion of persons with disabilities in mainstream employment, the introduction of an Equality and Diversity Policy within the human resources strategies of all public and private organisations would be one important means of effecting change.

Notes

1 The Equality Act 2010 is the current UK legislation in force; repealing the 1995 Act.
2 OHCHR, Thematic Study on the Work and Employment of Persons with Disabilities, 17 December 2012, A/HRC/22/25, para.8.

3 CRPD Committee, Concluding Observations on the Initial Report of Ethiopia, 4 November 2016, CRPD/C/ETH/CO/1, para.59.
4 CRPD Committee, Concluding Observations on the initial report of Kenya, 30 September 2015, CRPD/C/KEN/CO/1, para.47.
5 CRPD Committee, Concluding Observations on the Initial Report of Denmark, 30 October 2014, CRPD/C/DEN/CO/1, para.58.
6 CRPD Committee, Concluding Observations on the Initial Report of Canada, 8 May 2017, CRPD/C/DEN/CO/1, para.47.
7 UN General Assembly, International Year of Disabled Persons, 16 December 1976, A/RES/31/123.
8 UN General Assembly, International Year of Disabled Persons, 8 December 1981, A/RES/36/77, para.14.
9 UN General Assembly, Implementation of the World Programme of Action concerning Disabled Persons and the United Nations Decade of Disabled Persons, 8 December 1989, A/RES/44/70.
10 For example, see ILO Convention No.100 concerning Equal Remuneration (1951); ILO Convention No.111 concerning Discrimination (Employment and Occupation) (1958); ILO Convention No. 118 concerning Equality of Treatment (Social Security) (1962); UN Recommendation No. 99 concerning Vocational Rehabilitation of the Disabled (1955); and ILO Convention No.159 on Vocational Rehabilitation and Employment (Disabled Persons) (1983).
11 ILO Convention No. 159 on Vocational Rehabilitation and Employment (Disabled Persons) (1983).
12 Standard Rules on the Equalization of Opportunities for Persons with Disabilities, Rule 7 (Adopted in accordance with UN General Assembly Resolution No.48/96 adopted 20th December 1993).
13 CESCR, General Comment No.18 on Article 6 (The Right to Work), 6 February 2006, E/C.12/GC/18, para.7.
14 *Liliane Gröninger v Germany* (2014) CRPD/C/11/D/2/2010.
15 CESCR, General comment No. 23 on Article 7 ICESCR (The Right to Just and Favourable Conditions of Work), 26 April 2016, E/C.12/GC/23, para.47.
16 *Marie-Louise Jungelin v Sweden* (2014) CRPD/C/12/D/5/2011.
17 Ibid, para.6 (dissenting opinion).
18 *Standard Bank of South Africa v CCMA and Others* (JR 662/06) [2007] ZALC 98; [2008] 4 BLLR 356 (LC).
19 Ibid, para.113.
20 *Relaxion Group plc v Rhys-Harper (FC); D'Souza v London Borough of Lambeth; Jones v 3M Healthcare Limited and three other actions* [2003] UKHL 33.
21 Decision of the *Défenseur des droits* MLD-2015-080 (2015).
22 See for example, CRPD Committee, Inquiry concerning the United Kingdom of Great Britain and Northern Ireland, 2016, CRPD/C/15/R.2.
23 Inquiry concerning the United Kingdom, para.102.
24 ILO, Vocational Rehabilitation of Employment of People with Disabilities: Report of a European Conference, Warsaw-Constanin Jeziorna, 23–25 October 2003 (Geneva).
25 For example, The Disabled Persons (Employment) Act 1944 (UK).
26 *A.F v Italy* (2015) CRPD/C/13/D/9/2012.
27 Ibid, para.8.5.
28 OHCHR, Thematic Study on the Work and Employment of Persons with Disabilities.
29 Thaler, Richard H., Cass R. Sustein, Nudge: Improving Decisions about Health, Wealth and Happiness, Yale University Press, 2008.
30 Ibid.

11

INCLUSIVE INDEPENDENT LIVING

Introduction

While the post-Second World War era witnessed a shift from colonialism to the recognition of the sovereignty of nations, the twenty-first century challenge remains the sovereignty of disabled men and women over their own lives within inclusive societies. The right to self-determination, as enshrined in the UDHR, can be achieved if, and only if, independent living and being included in the community are made real. Yet, from the days of the adoption of the UDHR up until the adoption of the CRPD, all the other international human rights treaties have been silent on the concept of independent living and being included in the community. The advocates of the CRPD should therefore be credited with demanding that Article 19 be incorporated in the Convention. The concept of living independently and being included in the community is unprecedented in international law; the CRPD is the first international human rights treaty to recognise its importance and its Committee has confirmed its core elements in its most recent General Comment No.5.[1]

Article 19 is not just an aspirational social right. There is an overarching connection between Article 19 and Article 3 CRPD (General Principles) and Article 4 CRPD (General Obligations). On the one hand, Article 3 makes specific reference to both individual autonomy, including the freedom to make one's own choices, and the independence of persons, as well as to the concept of full and effective participation and inclusion in society which transcends the whole Convention. At the outset, it should be pointed out that independent living

> does not necessarily mean living alone. It should also not be interpreted solely as the ability to carry out daily activities by oneself. Rather, it should be regarded as the freedom to choose and control, in line with the respect

for inherent dignity and individual autonomy as enshrined in article 3 (a) of the Convention. Independence as a form of personal autonomy means that the person with disability is not deprived of the opportunity of choice and control regarding personal lifestyle and daily activities.[2]

On the other hand, Article 4 delineates the wide spectrum of positive obligations which are placed on States Parties in order for persons with disabilities to enjoy the full extent of their rights under the CRPD. For instance, an important distinction has to be drawn between the right to live in the community and the right to choose one's place of residence. This is because the latter is a civil and political right in the negative sense of the term, as states are under an obligation to legally prohibit discrimination in housing. However, with regard to the former, it is considered as a social, economic and cultural right in the positive sense of the term, as states are under an obligation to act and disburse funds to ensure the right of the disabled to live in the community (i.e. to take measures to the maximum of their available resources, per Articles 4(2) and 32 CRPD). International human rights law thus imposes obligations which are immediately applicable and others which may be progressively realised. There are three essential elements to Article 19 which help to tease out the implications of our understanding of the nature of the rights of choice, support and availability of community services and facilities.

Article 19(a) recognises the right of persons with disabilities to choose their place of residence, where and with whom they live, on an equal footing with others. This right is extended to their choice to live in a particular living arrangement. As a civil and political right, Article 19(a) must be immediately realised at the level of policies and legislation aiming at the protection, promotion and respect of the choice and control of persons with disabilities with regard to the decisions affecting their lives. This is contrasted with the nature of the right enshrined in Article 19(b), which is categorised as an economic, social and cultural right. Article 19(b) requires that States Parties ensure that persons with disabilities have access to a range of in-home, residential and other community support services, including any personal assistance necessary to support inclusion in the community. Full inclusion and participation in the community as an obligation can be achieved progressively by States Parties.[3]

Article 19(c), on the other hand, can be considered as a hybrid right since it reflects both categories of rights. The right to access community services and facilities (Article 9) has a social and cultural dimension given that information and communications technologies (ICTs), cinemas, theatres and other cultural, recreational, leisure and sports activities are listed under Article 30 CRPD.[4] These services and facilities must be made available to persons with disabilities on an equal basis with others for the full enjoyment of all their rights enshrined in the Convention. It follows that accessible premises may imply time and monetary constraints to be realised in practice. Nonetheless, it can also be considered as a civil and political right in the sense that access to these goods and services is required with immediate effect in the form of reasonable adjustments. Legislative and policy measures may in this respect be required to ensure the compliance of non-state actors.

The nature of States Parties' obligations under Article 19

The core elements underscored by the CRPD Committee in General Comment No.5 demonstrate how Article 19 subsumes most of the rights enshrined in other articles of the Convention. The core elements of Article 19 CRPD include the obligations of States Parties to ensure non-discrimination in accessing housing, including both income and accessibility, and adopting mandatory building regulations, thus ensuring the accessibility of new and renovated housing. For instance, in its Report on the Inquiry of the UK, the CRPD Committee observed that

> the interaction of various reforms on welfare schemes, in particular changes in housing benefits, the establishment of a cap on household benefits, changes in eligibility criteria for the 'moving around' component under the new Personal Independence Payment, tightening of criteria to access social care and the closure of the Independent Living Fund in the State party, have disproportionately affected persons with disabilities and hindered various aspects of their right to live independently and be included in the community.[5]

Austerity measures have a real and negative impact on the inclusion of persons with disabilities within mainstream society. This is why the CRPD Committee identified another core element of Article 19 as being the use of any available funding, including regional funding and funding for development cooperation, to develop inclusive and accessible independent living services. States Parties are under an obligation to develop concrete action plans to facilitate independent living for persons with disabilities within the community. This can be achieved only if steps are taken towards developing and implementing basic, personalised, non-shared and rights-based disability-specific support services and other forms of services. Legislation and policies on accessibility requirements (Article 9) are sometimes not enough in and of themselves since relevant stakeholders may not always comply with these measures. States Parties should thus ensure that non-compliance is adequately monitored and sanctioned so that persons with disabilities are not deprived of basic services.

The right to education (Article 24) and the right to work and employment (Article 27) are the other sine qua non conditions that must be satisfied by States Parties to enable persons with disabilities to participate fully, and to be included in society. In its General Comment No.4, the CRPD Committee observed that States Parties should ensure that the right to inclusive education is safeguarded and upheld for children who live in foster care or care homes and persons with disabilities who live in long-term institutional care.[6] It should be highlighted that access to education falls under what constitutes access to community-based services under

Article 19(c). The inclusion of persons with disabilities within mainstream educational settings is essential to their further inclusion in the community. The right to inclusive education will manifestly be instrumental in building the strengths, skills and competencies necessary for all persons with disabilities to enjoy, benefit from and contribute to their local communities. The right to work and employment of persons with disabilities must therefore be realised in practice so that they can participate meaningfully in the workforce. States Parties are required to provide them with individualised support measures (including personal assistance) as highlighted by Article 19(b) to facilitate their inclusion in the free and open labour market on an equal basis with others.[7] This will also have the additional advantage of phasing out sheltered employment.

The above examples show the interrelationship and interdependence between Article 19 and the other provisions of the Convention. This is why it can be described as a logical extension of all the rights enshrined in the Convention. Independent living and being included in the community 'constitute a frame for the enjoyment of several human rights: the right to adequate housing, the right to participate in public and political affairs, the right to privacy, the right to free movement, the right to vote, etc.'.[8] Even if the Committee did not have the opportunity to examine claims grounded in Article 19 in most of its case law, it is argued here that violations of other rights could in effect be interpreted as a denial of the rights to live independently and to full inclusion in society. For instance, the denial of the right to vote for persons with psychosocial disabilities would be tantamount to preventing them from effectively and fully participating in political life on an equal basis with others.[9] The right to vote is undeniably an important feature of the democratic process, so much so that participation in political life can be construed as the driving force behind socially inclusive development. In this regard, the CRPD Committee had the opportunity to examine some of the key features of Article 19 in relation to States Parties' obligations in one of its communications.

In *H.M. v Sweden*, the denial of a building permit for a hydrotherapy pool as a home-based rehabilitative measure for a person with a physical disability amounted to a violation of Article 19(b) CRPD since this ostensibly could have isolated and segregated her from the community.[10] The author argued that she would have had to enter a specialised health-care institution if she were not granted a permit to build an indoor hydrotherapy pool. The CRPD Committee held that the 'rejection of the author's application for a building permit has deprived her of access to hydrotherapy, the only option that could support her living and inclusion in the community'.[11] The State Party, as a consequence, clearly violated her rights under Article 19(b) CRPD.

It should be further highlighted that one of the claims of the author fell under Article 28 CRPD (the right to an adequate standard of living and social protection) but no information was given by the CRPD Committee as to which element of Article 28 was at stake. Having already found that the State Party had violated her rights under other Articles of the Convention—i.e. Articles 5(1), 5(3), 19(b), 25 and 26—the CRPD Committee deemed it unnecessary to consider her claim under Article 28 CRPD. Perhaps the CRPD Committee could have taken this opportunity to define the nature of the right to adequate housing under that Article. This is especially so given that violations of the right to housing occur when disability is misconstrued as a medical condition, as a result of which individuals are institutionalised.[12] If H.M. had been denied the permit to build the hydrotherapy pool as the only form of rehabilitation that was available to her, she would have had no choice but to consent to be institutionalised to receive a similar treatment. However, simply granting her building permission for the construction of the pool would, at any rate, have been proportional insofar as her rights should have taken priority over the development plan of the city. Denial of the permit would have had the effect of isolating her in an institution on the basis that there she would have been provided with the relevant treatment or care. In this respect, one important objective of Article 19 is to put an end to the discriminatory practice of institutionalisation.

Institutionalisation

As has already been discussed in Chapter 5, persons with disabilities are often confined to institutions without their prior consent on the basis of their (in particular, psychosocial or intellectual) impairments. The Concluding Observations of the CRPD Committee reveal how the implementation of Article 19 is crucial in order for persons with disabilities to break free from the chains of institutionalisation. For instance, in its Concluding Observations on the Initial Report of China, the Committee was concerned about the high number of persons with disabilities living in institutions and about the fact that China maintained institutions with up to 2,000 residents.[13] This was in addition to the existence of leper colonies, where people with leprosy lived in isolation. These institutions were in clear violation of Article 19. However, in relation to Canada, the CRPD Committee commended the steps taken by different provinces in the State Party towards deinstitutionalisation; in particular, the province of Ontario, which closed its last residential institution for persons with 'developmental' disabilities in 2009.[14] It follows that the question of independent living and being included in the community cannot be dissociated from the process of deinstitutionalisation.

An institution has been described as

> any place in which people who have been labelled as having a disability are isolated, segregated and/or compelled to live together. An institution is also any place in which people do not have, or are not allowed to exercise control over their lives and their day-to-day decisions. An institution is not defined by its size.[15]

Persons with disabilities are, most of the time, confined to these institutions against their will. States Parties often take the erroneous view that institutionalisation is the only solution for persons with disabilities who are considered to be incapable of living outside segregated settings or where personal services and support are too costly.[16] Persons with severe forms of psychosocial or intellectual disabilities, in particular those with communication impediments, 'are often assessed as being unable to live outside institutional settings'.[17] From the moment that a medical assessment is employed to institutionalise persons with disabilities, the defunct medical model of disability is smuggled through the back door, to such an extent that their rights are relegated to the background.

The motivations of States Parties to continue to have recourse to institution-alisation are sometimes framed around the fact that they are required to take mea-sures to the maximum of their available resources with regard to economic, social and cultural rights in accordance with Article 4(2) CRPD. They argue that dein-stitutionalisation would require time and resources to be progressively realised. However, this does not mean that States Parties' obligations under the Conven-tion only require them to phase out institutionalisation. First, the wording of Article 4(2) CRPD makes it clear that the rights contained in the Convention must not only be progressively realised but that, crucially, they are to be 'fully' realised given that the obligations of States Parties are immediately applicable according to international law. Second, it should be highlighted that Article 19 also requires States Parties to refrain from building new institutions or to allow old institutions to be renovated beyond the most urgent measures necessary to safeguard residents' physical safety.[18] Third, institutionalisation is quite simply a discriminatory prac-tice against persons with disabilities, a practice which States Parties are under an obligation to eradicate.

The case of *Olmstead v L.C.* is an example of where a domestic court found that undue institutionalisation amounted to disability-based discrimination.[19] The US Supreme Court had to determine whether the unjustified isolation of two women with developmental disabilities and mental illness through unnecessary and unjusti-fied institutionalisation constituted discrimination on the basis of disability under Title II of the Americans with Disabilities Act (ADA). The two women were com-mitted with their consent to a public psychiatric hospital. At the end of their medi-cal treatment, the mental health professionals who attended to them concluded that they should be moved to a community-based programme. Nevertheless, they were confined to that institution for several more years.

The two plaintiffs contended that they had failed to receive 'minimally adequate care and freedom from undue restraint'.[20] Title II of the ADA specifically 'protects qualified individuals with disabilities from discrimination on the basis of disability in services, programs, and activities provided by State and local government enti-ties'. The US Supreme Court held that their unjustified isolation amounted to disability-based discrimination insofar as 'institutional placement of persons who can handle and benefit from community settings perpetuates unwarranted assump-tions that persons so isolated are incapable or unworthy of participating in com-munity life', and also because 'confinement in an institution severely diminishes the everyday life activities of individuals, including family relations, social contacts, work options, economic independence, educational advancement, and cultural enrichment'.[21]

It should be pointed out that *Olmstead v. L.C.* was decided in 1999. The judicial activism of the US Supreme Court in that case consequently empowered disabled persons in the US with the right to demand a broad range of community services and facilities compared to those provided in institutional settings. However, the US Supreme Court did not acknowledge that inclusion in the community was an unqualified right for persons with disabilities. This was understandable given that would have been similar to asking the US Supreme Court for the moon, as the human rights-based model of disability was still at a nascent stage at the time.[22] A rights-based approach to living independently and being included in the community primarily ensures that the rights of persons with disabilities are protected, promoted and respected on an equal basis with others. Persons with disabilities, therefore, have the right to participate freely in society as full and active members. The right to legal capacity (Article 12) is on that account perhaps the most important precondition to enable persons with disabilities to exercise their rights to independent living and to their inclusion in the society.

Legal capacity

Inasmuch as legal capacity is a prerequisite for persons with disabilities to restore sovereignty over their own lives, a gap still exists as to how they exercise this right. Article 19 points the way as to how this choice can be exercised when persons with disabilities are provided with the right to legal capacity on an equal basis with their non-disabled counterparts. Article 19 thus reinstates the 'power of persons with disabilities to decide about their own lives, while the right to independent living paves the way for persons with disabilities to choose how to live their lives'.[23] This view is equally emphasised by the CRPD Committee in its General Comment No.1, which acknowledges that the right to equal recognition before the law is essential for persons with disabilities to have the opportunity to enjoy their rights, as contained in Article 19.[24]

In *CC and KK v STCC*, the UK Court of Protection in the High Court of Justice had to examine whether an 82-year-old woman who was physically paralysed since childhood and who recently developed Parkinson's disease and vascular dementia lacked the capacity to determine her care needs and residence and whether she was consequently unjustifiably deprived of her liberty.[25] In relation to the issue of capacity, the Court of Protection reiterated that the applicable domestic legislation on mental health law (the Mental Capacity Act 2005)[26] should be interpreted so

> that a person must be assumed to have capacity unless it is demonstrated that she lacks it. The burden lies on the local authority to prove that KK lacks capacity to make decisions as to where she lives. A disabled person, and a person with a degenerative condition, is as entitled as anyone else to the

protection of this presumption of capacity. The assessment is issue-specific and time-specific. In due course, her capacity may deteriorate. Indeed that is likely to happen given her diagnosis. At this hearing, however, the local authority has failed to prove that KK lacks capacity to make decisions as to where she should live.[27]

If brought before the CRPD Committee, the case would have fallen squarely within the ambit of Article 19(a) CRPD and Article 12 CRPD claims, since it entails the choice of the elderly woman with disabilities between institutionalisation in home care or independent living. Even if the UK court found in favour of the woman on the issue of capacity (note, however, that it nonetheless held that she had not been deprived of her liberty), it is submitted here that the reasoning is based on an incorrect interpretation of what amounts to capacity under international disability law. While the UK court has rightly interpreted the domestic legal framework to give effect to the intention of the legislature, it would have been interesting to know whether it would have taken the subsequent jurisprudence of the CRPD Committee—which takes the distinction between 'mental capacity' and 'legal capacity'—into consideration.[28] It should be highlighted that the rights-based approach to disability points to how the right to legal capacity should never be denied on the basis of the mental, intellectual and/or psychosocial disabilities of a person.

In its General Comment No.1, the CRPD Committee further maintained that 'the human rights-based model of disability implies a shift from the substitute decision-making paradigm to one that is based on supported decision-making'.[29] Persons with disabilities must have

> opportunities to develop and express their will and preferences, in order to exercise their legal capacity on an equal basis with others. This means that persons with disabilities must have the opportunity to live independently in the community and to make choices and to have control over their everyday lives, on an equal basis with others, as provided for in article 19.[30]

The exercise of legal capacity is thus a prerequisite for the community-based approach where supported decision-making and raising awareness about the right to different support services are promoted. It becomes self-evident, then, that Article 19 can be fully realised only if all the other educational, economic, social, cultural, civil and even political rights enshrined in this norm are fulfilled. This includes the right to adequate housing.

Access to adequate housing

Access to housing has a direct impact on the possibility of persons with disabilities living in the community on an equal footing with others. It entails not only having a roof over one's head; while a roof is certainly required for a normal healthy life, the right to housing goes beyond this basic physical consideration. Other considerations such as privacy, personal space, security and protection from intemperate weather are equally as important. The right to adequate housing has its origins in Article 25(1) UDHR as a component of the right to a correct standard of living. The ICESCR reproduces this right in its Article 11(1) and provides that 'States Parties to the present Covenant recognize the right of everyone to an adequate standard of living for himself and his family, including adequate [. . .] housing, and to the continuous improvement of living conditions'. The CESCR acknowledged in its General Comment No.4 that the human right to adequate housing is fundamental and central to the enjoyment of all economic, social and cultural rights.[31] In a recent communication, it had the opportunity to examine the nature of this right and the obligations of States Parties under Article 11(1) ICESCR.

In *I.D.G. v Spain*, the CESCR had to determine whether the author's right to housing was violated by the State Party as a consequence of a mortgage enforcement process.[32] The author maintained that she was not given the opportunity to legally oppose the foreclosure procedures in relation to the defaults on her mortgage payments since she had not been duly and properly notified of the application. The CESCR found that Spain had violated her right to housing under Article 11(1) ICESCR insofar as States Parties 'must ensure that the persons whose right to adequate housing may be affected by, say, forced evictions or mortgage enforcements have access to an effective and appropriate judicial remedy'.[33] In the case of the author, effective judicial remedy could only have been guaranteed if all appropriate steps had been taken to notify her personally about the foreclosure procedures so that she had knowledge and time to prepare for a defence.

I.D.G. v Spain provides an interesting analysis of the scope of States Parties' obligations under the ICESCR in relation to the right to housing. The CESCR recalled that Article 2 ICESCR imposes various obligations which have an immediate effect so that States Parties must take measures to ensure the enjoyment of the rights established in the ICESCR 'by all appropriate means including particularly the adoption of legislative measures'.[34] This requirement includes the adoption of measures in order to ensure access to effective judicial remedies for the protection of the rights enshrined in the ICESCR. These measures should equally be extended to access to affordable and acceptable housing. The Third Party Intervention in the communication—endorsed by the CESCR—argued that effective judicial protection of the rights contained in the ICESCR involves the obligations of States Parties to contemplate all possible alternatives to eviction, to ensure the greatest possible security of tenure, to provide for adequate and reasonable notice in cases of eviction, to ensure that evictions do not render persons vulnerable to other human rights violations, and to provide adequate compensation for violations.[35] It should be remembered that one fundamental principle of the rule of law is that there cannot be a right for which no remedy is available to protect it. However, notwithstanding remedies, persons with disabilities are more often than not denied the right to housing itself.

The Special Rapporteur on Adequate Housing has observed that 'access to adequate and accessible housing are central to a life of dignity, autonomy, participation, inclusion, equality and respect for diversity'.[36] Persons with disabilities, especially those with psychosocial and/or intellectual impairments, are more at risk of being denied access to housing. Denial of access is more often than not based on the disability of the person and thus amounts to de facto discrimination. In her report, the Special Rapporteur however noted that, in relation to *H.M. v Sweden*, the CRPD Committee took a positive step in extending the remedy beyond the author's individual circumstances, recommending that the State Party should ensure that 'its legislation and the manner in which it is applied by domestic courts is consistent with the State party's obligations under the Convention'.[37] This, she argued, is an illustration of the way in which reasonable accommodation claims can give rise to individual as well as systemic and/or legislative remedies. However, as will be particularly evident in the ensuing discussion, the right to housing of persons with disabilities is still largely misunderstood at the domestic level.

In *Lior Levy et al v State of Israel*, the Israeli High Court of Justice had to determine whether five young persons with physical and intellectual disabilities had a right to live in the community.[38] The five plaintiffs had lived in their respective family homes all their lives and requested the Israeli Ministry of Social Affairs to furnish them with housing support in their local communities so that they could move out to a house of their own choice. The Ministry of Social Affairs refused to place them in an apartment of their choice and instead proposed to move them in a 24-room hostel where they would be provided with all the services they required. The High Court of Justice could, however, not adjudicate on all the subject matters of the case since the Ministry subsequently decided to adopt a new policy which recognises the rights of persons with severe disabilities in need of extensive support services to be eligible for community placement. This was subject to the condition that their medical and behavioural requirements are met in the community.

However, it is not apparent who should have decided and assessed what and how these medical and/or behavioural needs were to be construed. The High Court of Justice nevertheless held that the 24-room hostel did qualify as housing or placement in the community. Special attention should, nonetheless, be drawn to the fact that the plaintiffs argued that placement in a hostel with 24 unfamiliar persons (akin to life in an institution) was inconsistent with their right to live in the community. The High Court of Justice held that the hostel was a proportionate and reasonable solution for the plaintiffs. It is submitted here that this is in clear violation of Article 19 CRPD as well as of Article 11(1) ICESCR.

Conclusion

In view of the above discussion, Article 19 can be regarded as the unifier of all the rights enshrined in the international bill of rights (i.e. the UDHR, ICCPR and

ICESCR). In this respect, the CRPD Committee holds the view that Article 19 is the connecting bridge between the two sets of rights. As it encompasses elements of both sets of rights, it reflects the all-inclusive approach of the interrelation, interdependence and indivisibility of all human rights. Article 19 is thus 'one of the widest ranging and most intersectional articles of the Convention and has to be considered as integral to the full implementation of the Convention'.[39]

Living independently and being included in the community, as embodied in Article 19 sets out the right of persons with disabilities to choose where and with whom they want to live. It connotes the real meanings that are given to such words as autonomy, will and preferences. It means exercising freedom of choice and control over decisions affecting one's life with the maximum level of self-determination and independence within society.[40] Independent living and being included in the community are the ultimate laudable goal and the very essence of the Convention. During the public reading of General Comment No.5 on Article 19, many members of the Committee referred to it as the 'soul' of the Convention.

Summary of Concluding Observations and Recommendations

The OHCHR has made some recommendations with regard to the proper and effective implementation of Article 19.[41] It noted that Article 19 marks a paradigm shift from the medical to the human rights-based approach to disability. This model requires that persons with disabilities, without exception, be guaranteed their right to live independently and be included in the community. However, the likelihood of some groups—for instance, persons with psychosocial or intellectual disabilities—being excluded and segregated is a living reality which States Parties are under an obligation to eradicate. Ensuring that the right to legal capacity of persons with disabilities is upheld is a crucial component of the realisation of the right to independent living and being included in the community, as this would enable them to have control over their lives.

The OHCHR was also concerned about forced institutionalisation, which is in clear violation of the CRPD as it is a form of deprivation of liberty based on the existence of an impairment. The right of persons with disabilities to legal capacity plays a key role in the furtherance of deinstitutionalisation, as it ensures that they are able to exercise choice and control over their lives on an equal basis with others, with access to supported decision-making when needed. It should be highlighted that deinstitutionalisation requires a systemic transformation that goes beyond the closure of institutional settings. In order to enable social participation, such policy should provide for individualised support services as well as inclusive mainstream services, so that the will and preferences of persons with disabilities can be respected. Newer forms of institutionalisation tend to be concealed by superficial changes that do not transfer actual control from service providers to the service users as required by the human rights-based approach to disability.

In its General Comment No.4, the CRPD Committee further noted that inclusive education is incompatible with institutionalisation.[42] States Parties must engage in a well-planned and structured process of deinstitutionalisation of persons with disabilities. Such a process must address: a managed transition that sets out a defined time-frame for the transition; the introduction of a legislative requirement to develop community-based provision; the re-direction of funds and the introduction of multidisciplinary frameworks to support and strengthen community-based services; the provision of support for families; and collaboration and consultation with organisations representing persons with disabilities, including children with disabilities, as well as parents or care-givers. Pending the process of de-institutionalisation, persons in institutional care settings should be given access to inclusive education with immediate effect and be linked with inclusive academic institutions in the community.

Personal assistance is equally an effective means to ensure the right to live independently and be included in the community in ways that respect the inherent dignity, individual autonomy and independence of persons with disabilities. Personal assistance should be made available to all persons with disabilities, including those with intellectual and psychosocial disabilities. However, persons with disabilities are the best experts regarding their needs. Allocating funds directly to service users rather than service providers shifts the control and choice to persons with disabilities and ultimately improves the quality of support. Training is also important to ensure that the support provided is of adequate quality and complies with the CRPD. Effective regulatory oversight is also an important requirement to ensure that support is of adequate quality. For example, if allocating a budget for a personal assistant to a service user requires a contract of employment, the necessary support in complying with employment law should be made available to the user by the provider.

The report noted that high-quality individualised support and inclusive mainstream services may require an initial investment but, in the long term, the resultant inclusive societies, in which persons with disabilities will be able to participate fully and contribute to economic, social, political and cultural life, will undoubtedly be more cost-effective. Given the available option of 'investing to save', States Parties thus cannot hide behind resource limitations to explain their inactivity. Furthermore, austerity measures should not justify retrogressive steps as they are in clear violation of the rights of persons with disabilities.

Access to adequate housing

The Special Rapporteur on adequate housing has observed that few marginalised groups suffer such egregious violations of the right to housing as do persons with disabilities. Across the world, they are commonly homeless, institutionalised, and subjected to cruel and inhuman treatment for no reason other than their disability. They endure isolation, stigmatisation and discrimination in all aspects of housing, with regard to access, design, policy development and implementation. Their very lives are imperilled by housing and communities that are based on exclusion and uniformity rather than inclusion and diversity. Yet it is on the basis of those experiences and the claims to equal dignity and rights advanced by those affected that the disability human rights paradigm has emerged. This paradigm has the potential to breathe new life into the right to adequate housing because it underscores and amplifies the essence of that right, namely, having a place to live in dignity. It allows persons with disabilities to participate in their communities, and recognises diversity as a strength that makes households and communities thrive. If the immense potential of the integration of the disability rights paradigm with the right to housing is to be realised, states and other stakeholders will need to adopt a fundamental shift in the way in which they think about, and interact with, the human rights of persons with disabilities.

In that regard, the Special Rapporteur offers the following recommendations:

(a) In consultation with persons with disabilities and their organisations, states should:

    (i) Prioritise and recognise in domestic law the obligation to realise the right to housing of persons with disabilities to the maximum of available resources, tying this legal obligation to the commitment to ensure adequate housing for all by 2030, in accordance with target 11.1 of the Sustainable Development Goals;

    (ii) Ensure that non-discrimination provisions are based on substantive equality, recognising positive obligations to address the systemic inequality in housing experienced by persons with disabilities;

    (iii) Ensure that all persons with disabilities are able to live free from institutionalisation and that access to adequate housing, the requisite services and appropriately trained support is provided in the community;

    (iv) Ensure access to justice and effective accountability mechanisms for claims to the right to adequate housing by persons with disabilities, including when states have failed to adopt reasonable programmatic measures to realise the right;

    (v) Adopt a clear policy framework for the inclusion of all persons with disabilities in all areas of housing policy and design, ensuring that those living in poverty or homelessness, women, ethnic, religious or linguistic minorities, indigenous peoples, migrants and both young and older persons are fully included;

    (vi) Design and implement both qualitative and quantitative data collection about the housing circumstances of persons with disabilities, disaggregated on the basis of the standard survey questions of the Washington Group on Disabilities;

    (vii) Address homelessness among persons with disabilities on an urgent basis and prioritise measures to address the circumstances of those living in informal settlements and homeless encampments;

    (viii) Ensure that security of tenure and other legal protection in housing are developed and applied in a manner that recognises the distinctive needs of persons with disabilities;

(ix) Ensure that the obligation of reasonable accommodation for persons with disabilities is applied to public and private housing providers, financial actors and all aspects of the housing environment;

(x) Ensure that all persons with disabilities can exercise their right to legal capacity in any issue relating to the right to adequate housing, including to access to, and sign contracts for, credit and leases;

(xi) Ensure that the necessary support is provided to organisations of persons with disabilities to facilitate effective participation in all areas of housing policy and decision-making;

(xii) Establish an independent budgetary review mechanism to ensure that budget allocations for housing and related forms of support are consistent with the 'maximum of available resources' standard;

(xiii) Provide adequate financial and other support to persons with disabilities in a manner that ensures choice as to where to live and how support will be provided which covers the full cost of housing and related expenses;

(xiv) Adopt accessibility requirements that apply to new housing and implement a clear time-frame for ensuring accessibility within existing housing stock;

(xv) Ensure that refugees, internally displaced persons and migrants with disabilities enjoy their right to adequate housing, notably by including the relevant international human rights provisions in the forthcoming global compact on refugees and the global compact for safe, orderly and regular migration;

(xvi) Ensure that local governments implement and adhere to the right to housing in all municipal action, including urban planning, zoning, planning of transportation and the production and maintenance of housing;

(b) Courts, tribunals and national human rights institutions should:

(i) Interpret and apply domestic law in accordance with the right to adequate housing of persons with disabilities and in particular recognise that the rights to life, liberty, substantive equality and non-discrimination require governments to address homelessness, provide support for living in the community and respond to the diverse housing needs of persons with disabilities;

(ii) Ensure access to justice and effective accountability for all aspects of state obligations with respect to the right to housing of persons with disabilities, including budgetary allocations and the effectiveness of strategies and programmes;

(c) Civil society and organisations of persons with disabilities should take forward or support legal challenges to structural violations of the right to housing of persons with disabilities and seek systemic remedies.

Notes

1 CRPD Committee, General Comment No.5 on Article 19 (Living Independently and Being Included in the Community, 27 October 2017, CRPD/C/GC/5.
2 General Comment No.5 on Article 19, para.16.
3 Article 4(2) CRPD: With regard to economic, social and cultural rights, each State Party undertakes to take measures to the maximum of its available resources and, where needed, within the framework of international cooperation, with a view to achieving progressively the full realization of these rights, without prejudice to those obligations contained in the present Convention that are immediately applicable according to international law.
4 Article 30 CRPD (Participation in Cultural Life, Recreation, Leisure and Sport).
5 CRPD Committee, Inquiry concerning the United Kingdom of Great Britain and Northern Ireland, 6 October 2016, CRPD/C/15/R.2, para.95.
6 CRPD Committee, General Comment No.4 on Article 24 (The Right to Inclusive Education), 26 August 2016, CRPD/C/GC/4, para.52.
7 General Comment No.5, para.91.
8 Training Guide on the Convention on the Rights of Persons with Disabilities, Professional Training Series No.19 (United Nations 2014), p.12.
9 See *Budjoso et al v Hungary* (2013) CRPD/C/10/D/4/2011 in Chapter 7.
10 *H.M. v Sweden* (2012) CRPD/C/7/D/3/2011. For the facts, see Chapter 5.
11 *H.M. v Sweden*, para.8.9.
12 Leilani Farha (Special Rapporteur on Adequate Housing), Adequate Housing as a Component of the Right to an Adequate Standard of Living, and the Right to Non-Discrimination in this Context, 12 July 2017, A/72/128, para.15.
13 CRPD Committee, Concluding Observations on the Initial Report of China, 15 October 2012, CRPD/C/CHN/CO/1, para.31.
14 CRPD Committee, Concluding Observations on the Initial Report of Canada, 8 May 2017, CRPD/C/CAN/CO/1, para.37.
15 European Coalition for Community Living, Wasted Time, Wasted Money, Wasted Lives—A Wasted Opportunity? 2010. Available at http://community-living.info/wp-content/uploads/2014/02/ECCL-StructuralFundsReport-final-WEB.pdf, accessed 26 March 2018, p.78.
16 General Comment No.5, para.21.
17 Ibid.
18 General Comment No.5, para.49.
19 *Olmstead v L.C.* 527 U.S. 581 (1999).
20 Ibid, para.593.
21 Ibid, para.602.
22 It is to be noted however that, in 2018, the USA is still not a party to the CRPD.
23 European Foundation Centre, *Study on challenges and good practices in the implementation of the UN Convention on the Rights of Persons with Disabilities*, October 2010.
24 CRPD Committee, General Comment No.1 on Article 12 (Equal Recognition Before the Law), 11 April 2014, CRPD/C/GC/1, para.44.
25 *CC v KK and STCC* [2012] EWCOP 2136 (26 July 2012).
26 Section 1(2) of the UK Mental Capacity Act 2005:

People who lack capacity

(1) For the purposes of this Act, a person lacks capacity in relation to a matter if at the material time she is unable to make a decision for herself in relation to the matter because of an impairment of, or a disturbance in the functioning of, the mind or brain.
(2) It does not matter whether the impairment or disturbance is permanent or temporary.

(3) A lack of capacity cannot be established merely by reference to—

  (a) a person's age or appearance, or
  (b) a condition of her, or an aspect of her behaviour, which might lead others to make unjustified assumptions about his capacity.

(4) In proceedings under this Act or any other enactment, any question whether a person lacks capacity within the meaning of this Act must be decided on the balance of probabilities.

(5) No power which a person ('D') may exercise under this Act—

  (a) in relation to a person who lacks capacity, or
  (b) where D reasonably thinks that a person lacks capacity, is exercisable in relation to a person under 16.

(6) Subsection (5) is subject to section 18(3).

27 *CC v KK and STCC*, para.74.
28 See General Comment No.1 and Chapter 4.
29 General Comment No.1, para.3.
30 General Comment No.1, para.44.
31 CESCR, General Comment No.4 on Article 11(1) (Right to Adequate Housing), 1992, para.1.
32 *I.D.G. v Spain* (2015) E/C.12/55/D/2/2014.
33 Ibid, para.11.4.
34 Article 2(1) ICESCR.
35 *I.D.G. v Spain*, paras 6.1–6.5.
36 Special Rapporteur on Adequate Housing, para.1.
37 Ibid, para.60.
38 HCJ/07 *Lior Levy et al v State of Israel et al* IsrSC 2008 (3) 4561.
39 General Comment No.5, para.6.
40 Ibid, para.8.
41 OHCHR, Thematic Study on the Right of Persons with Disabilities to Live Independently and be Included in the Community, 12 December 2014, A/HRC/28/37, paras 58–66.
42 General Comment No.4, para.66.

CONCLUSION

Introduction

Chapter 1 highlighted in detail the international monitoring functions of the CRPD Committee and the procedures which must be complied with to access the Optional Protocol. The Concluding Observations on 69 countries, the associated reports and the communications are now all publicly available on the website of the CRPD. Many countries have disseminated them for implementation. They are used to alert both national and international public opinion as to the shortcomings and grave and systematic violations of the CRPD. For instance, pending the case *X v Tanzania*, a Regional Action Plan to end attacks on persons with albinism in Africa for the period 2017–2021 was adopted.[1] Another example is the recent inquiry regarding the impact of austerity measures in the UK, which led to the finding in the CRPD's report of grave and systematic violations of Articles 19, 27 and 28 CRPD.[2] In Chapter 2, the major pillars of the Convention and the principles of equality and non-discrimination have been elaborated on as they are the yardsticks to determine how States Parties comply with the international rule of law. The most recent General Comment No.6 on Article 5 fully explores the different types of discrimination, including discrimination by association. It also lays emphasis on the importance of equality under the law, a concept previously unfamiliar to other international treaty bodies. Chapter 3 emphasises the intersectional and aggravated forms of discrimination experienced by women and girls with disabilities, and we point the way forward for its elimination.

In Chapters 4 to 7, we explained how the provisions of the CRPD have been instrumental in strengthening the civil and political rights of persons with disabilities and its application to novel situations. Miscarriages of justice have been exposed to demonstrate how domestic courts should interpret disability-based discrimination in the context of legal capacity and access to justice. The use of Article 5 as the golden thread running through the whole of the Convention is an example of how domestic courts should interpret and apply standards of the CRPD. The jurisprudence of the CRPD was also compared to, and contrasted with, that of other human rights treaty bodies to show how it is possible for the other treaties to analyse disability-based discrimination cases.

Chapters 8 to 11, on the other hand, elaborated extensively on both international and domestic case law to bring home how economic, social and cultural rights have become increasingly justiciable. For example, it will be interesting in future to see how the concepts of 'universal design' or 'communication', which are enshrined in Article 2 CRPD, will be interpreted and the extent to which States Parties will be required to fulfil these obligations. Will States Parties be under an obligation to build universally-designed prisons which are accessible to all persons with disabilities? The interrelationship between civil and political rights and economic and social rights has been the primary focus in the analysis of the case law referred to in this book.

By way of conclusion, we can reflect here upon a number of pertinent themes common to all the previous chapters.

First, the ineffectiveness of the other human rights treaty bodies in analysing disability-based law and policy discourses must be highlighted. Secondly, it is clear that the CRPD Committee has been pivotal in the advancement of international public law to address this lacuna. Positive and progressive changes have been channelled through its communications, concluding observations and inquiry reports. It should further be underlined that, in many parts of the world, policy-makers have, as a result, adjusted their political manifestos. Furthermore, the judicial landscape of States Parties is constantly accommodating a new culture of judging, albeit at a slow pace. Thirdly, the CRPD Committee has created the necessary climate for change and has equipped all stakeholders—including States Parties, Disabled Persons Organisations and National Human Rights Institutions—with the required tools to be innovative. In this new era, the Convention has already been cemented for the perpetual rejection of the medical model of disability. These achievements have culminated in a fresh approach to discrimination issues: a human rights-based model of society where disabled and non-disabled people are equal in dignity.

It has been a very long journey towards the realisation of our rights. The Convention has enabled us to begin mapping our destiny. The legacy is here and is empirically verifiable for us to continue building more just and equal societies in future. Yet, for millions of disabled men and women, the dream of being equal in dignity to their non-disabled counterparts seems to be in the very distant future. Their hope that world leaders would rethink society's collective goals and that structural changes in society would take place *en amont* (upstream) in response to the voice of the CRPD Committee seems to be unrealistic. Moreover, the hope that the largest minority will determine the outcome of national and local election results, influence policy changes or effectively participate in the implementation of the Convention is unlikely to be realised in the short term.

As we have seen before, one of the major barriers to the full realisation of the human rights of persons with disabilities is the prevalence of negative stereotypical attitudes towards them. While parliaments have the power to legislate, laws alone cannot change the mind-set of the very persons who enact the best of laws. These negative attitudes lie at the heart of the perception, understanding and approach of the provisions of the CRPD. As mentioned in the preface, the role of civil society, particular DPOs, is as critical as it was decades ago. We cannot afford to be complacent and it follows that vigilance must be the order of the day. Our mottos, such as 'nothing about us without us' and 'make our rights real now' are as relevant today as they were many years ago. The shadow of the theory of the Convention as soft law is still lingering. So long as it has not completely disappeared, the struggle will never be over. While the Convention has accomplished the objective of codifying, in a single document, all the human rights of people with disabilities, its implementation and monitoring are crucial components to its effectiveness. Proper implementation and monitoring mechanisms are the key to ensuring that States Parties do not fall short of their obligations to protect, promote and fulfil all the rights of persons with disabilities.

National implementation and monitoring: the way forward

The CRPD Committee is an international treaty body and its decisions are legally binding. However, this view is diametrically opposed by sceptics who believe that international public law is not sufficiently 'hard law' and, hence, is devoid of legal validity. For instance, Professor H.L.A. Hart argued that international law is no law at all since its violation is not the subject of enforceable sanctions.[3] Today, the modern version of Hartian theory is expressed in different terminology. International public law is referred to as 'soft law'. There may be some merit in this argument insofar as states have only a moral obligation to comply with international treaties such as the CRPD. The examples which we have cited throughout this book clearly show that the discretion not to comply is being constantly fettered to such an extent that the margin of appreciation in the implementation of the CRPD by states is extremely limited. There are numerous reasons to why the soft law theory is losing ground.

At a general level, it can be safely argued that the term 'soft law' is primarily used to refer to international instruments which are not legally binding on states. These may include, for example, a memorandum of understanding between states, minimum principles agreed between governments. We agree with the UK Independent Mechanism's submission to the UK Human Rights Joint Committee which states that

> As a matter of international law the CRPD, in its totality, is binding international law—i.e. 'hard' law. It is an international treaty which has been entered into by State Parties and is subject to the law of treaties and the

principle of *pacta sunt servanda*. That is the principle, codified in the Vienna Convention on the Law of Treaties, that States enter into international agreements and implement those obligations in good faith.[4]

This argument is further strengthened by the fact that the UK has ratified the Convention by an Act of Parliament.[5] It should be highlighted that the UK is a dualist state where international treaties must be transplanted into the domestic legal order by an Act of Parliament. Since parliamentary sovereignty is the organising principle of the British constitutional landscape, the Convention therefore forms an integral part of its domestic law which is binding on domestic courts. Moreover, there is a long-established principle of common law that international law prevails over domestic law unless there are express statutory provisions to the contrary. In civil law countries which have entrenched constitutions, the Convention is de facto incorporated within the domestic system upon signature and ratification of the said treaty. Alternatively, there are constitutional provisions in other countries—for example Article 25 of the German Constitution (Basic Law)—which expressly stipulates that international treaties have equal status with constitutional law upon accession.

Another salient aspect of the CRPD is the obligation on states to set up national monitoring mechanisms for the implementation of all its provisions. The adoption and inclusion of Article 33 (National Implementation and Monitoring) in the CRPD is a major breakthrough in international law. The Article was adopted by a consensus of states, DPOs and civil society. The obligation to monitor implementation at domestic level is a unique feature of the CRPD in contrast to other treaty bodies, such as CEDAW and CRC, which do not have a similar provision. The only other exception is the Optional Protocol to the Convention against Torture, which imposes an obligation upon ratifying states to set up a preventive mechanism against torture, cruel and degrading treatment and other forms of punishment.

The CRPD is, however, the first international human rights treaty to take a Montesquieuan approach to its monitoring and implementation at national level. These two functions are separated insofar as implementation is the responsibility of the State Party's government, while protection, promotion and monitoring call for the leadership of national entities established in line with the Paris Principles and the participation of persons with disabilities and their representative organisations.[6] The Convention specifically requires that the two functions should not be assigned to one single entity. As mentioned in Chapter 2, one exigency of the rule of law requires States Parties to ensure the independence and integrity of the monitoring framework. This means that monitoring institutions vested with jurisdiction to monitor compliance and evaluate progress must be free from political interference. As we shall see, the scope of Article 33 further curtails the margin of appreciation of states in the implementation of the Convention. It could be plausibly argued that the soft law theory, even when exposed with all its eloquence, is losing ground at both international and domestic levels.

The scope of Article 33 CRPD

Article 33(1) provides that

> States Parties, in accordance with their system of organization, shall desig-
> nate one or more focal points within government for matters relating to the
> implementation of the present Convention, and shall give due consideration
> to the establishment or designation of a coordination mechanism within gov-
> ernment to facilitate related action in different sectors and at different levels.

The Convention requires States Parties, in accordance with their domestic system
of governments, to set up one or more focal points to implement the provision of
the Convention. In so doing, the state should establish a coordinating mechanism
at different levels of their government to facilitate the implementation of corresponding disability policies. For instance, the National Action Plan 2007 of Mauritius provides for a steering committee which is chaired by the Minister of Social
Security.[7] The steering committee in turn has set up at least ten sub-committees
composed of persons with disabilities and their representative organisations, as well
as government officials of all the ministries. The term of reference of each sub-
committee is clearly defined and the committee is presided over by a person with
disabilities. The sub-committees formulate observations and recommendations and
regularly report to the steering committee. In this regard, the steering committee
may be considered as the focal point. Given the relatively small size of Mauritius in
terms of population (1.3 million), the steering committee is also the coordinating
mechanism as it networks both with government and civil society.

The role of the focal point is to gather the maximum information possible from
civil society, formulate policy such as national action plans, and make recommendations to all appropriate government ministries. It is strongly recommended
by the CRPD Committee that the focal point should include representatives of
all the ministries as this facilitates the mainstreaming of disability issues. This also
allows the focal point to respond to recurrent and real gaps in the implementation
of legislation and policies. The focal point is also a forum which is responsible
for awareness-raising with the required budget allocation, in conformity with
Article 8 CRPD.

Other countries with huge territories – for instance, the UK, South Africa,
as well as federal states such as Canada – may designate coordinating mechanisms
between the different focal points. For a long time, the focal point for coordinating mechanisms was often placed within the purview of the Ministry of Health or
Social Welfare. Focal points and coordinating mechanisms are not service providers, but rather policy-formulation forums. It is therefore strongly recommended
that the focal point be placed under the Attorney General's office or Ministry for
Human Rights in order to enhance the human rights model of disability. However, it should also be noted that Article 33(1) does not impose a one-size model
which fits all political and legal systems.

The Thematic Study on national implementation and monitoring of the CRPD highlights the importance of Article 33(1):

> Ratification of the Convention offers an important opportunity for the strengthening of existing structures where necessary or for their establishment. Where more than one focal point within government is appointed, it would seem appropriate that such focal points participate in the coordination mechanism. The mechanism should ideally be chaired by the focal point within government with the key responsibility for the implementation of the Convention. Through inter-ministerial action and participation in the mechanism, government agencies will be able to focus their activity and policy development on areas where they have an added value, avoid duplication and make the best use of limited resources.[8]

Article 33(2) provides that

> States Parties shall, in accordance with their legal and administrative systems, maintain, strengthen, designate or establish within the State Party, a framework, including one or more independent mechanisms, as appropriate, to promote, protect and monitor implementation of the present Convention. When designating or establishing such a mechanism, States Parties shall take into account the principles relating to the status and functioning of national institutions for protection and promotion of human rights.

In its Concluding Observations on the Initial Report of Luxembourg, the CRPD Committee expressed concerned about the insufficient clarity and scope of the mandates, resources and authority of the entities designated under Article 33(2), and that discrimination occurring in the private sector is not covered.[9] Similarly, the CRPD Committee was concerned that Canada had not designated an independent mechanism to monitor the implementation of the Convention, as required under Article 33(2).[10] The CRPD Committee also noted that the Directorate-General of Development for Persons with Disabilities in Honduras was not an independent monitoring mechanism in accordance with the Paris Principles.[11] Other States Parties, such as Gabon, purely and simply lack an independent monitoring mechanism.[12]

The CRPD Committee further noted that, in both Luxembourg and Canada, there was an absence of mechanisms to ensure the participation of persons with disabilities, through their representative organisations, in monitoring processes. With explicit reference to the Paris Principles, the CRPD Committee noted that both States Parties should adopt measures which include no government representatives, that they have an adequate budget for the functioning of independent monitoring mechanisms, and that they operate in close consultation with organisations of persons with disabilities. In relation to Luxembourg, the Committee explicitly recommended that the independent monitoring mechanism has the mandate to cover cases of discrimination in the public and private sectors to extend its protection. With regard to Canada, the CRPD Committee strongly encouraged the State Party to formally appoint the Canadian Human Rights Commission as the independent monitoring mechanism under Article 33 of the Convention.

The key salient features that must be complied with within the purview of Article 33(2) include: first, the independence of the monitoring framework established by law or even by the Constitution. Second, a clear mandate must be formulated to promote, protect and evaluate the implementation of the Convention. The terms of reference may impose an obligation upon the monitoring mechanism to constantly carry out research on policies and legislation which are not in conformity with the CRPD. Third, the monitoring mechanism must be vested with the required budgetary allocation to investigate complaints, mediate between the aggrieved person and the discriminator, and be capable of providing the aforementioned person with effective remedies. Fourth, adherence to the Paris Principles provides for a system of check and balance which holds the Government accountable for its acts and omission. Fifth, Article 33(3) expressly requires States Parties to ensure the meaningful participation of persons with disabilities and their representative organisations in their monitoring framework. In this respect, over and above compliance with the Paris Principles, States Parties are called upon to ensure that the composition of its monitoring framework reflects the diversity and plurality of its society. The monitoring framework with quasi-judicial jurisdiction should additionally reflect current public opinion.

In other words, national institutions responsible for the monitoring of the implementation of the Convention should not suffer from any democratic deficit or budgetary constraint. The criteria for members to serve on the national monitoring institutions should be transparent and the success of the monitoring depends largely on its integrity and independence. Existing national human rights institutions have the potential to be designated to protect, promote and monitor implementation as required under Article 33(2).

Concluding remarks

Article 33 CRPD has set the bar very high, but at the same time it has left a margin for states to choose their own system of monitoring mechanism. It is hoped that, irrespective of the domestic legal system chosen, disability laws and policies will be applied in a consistent and predictable manner which can result in the mainstreaming of the rights of citizens with disabilities across States Parties. The 'soft law' theory will continue to lose ground and the theory of the traditional set of rights will be combated at both domestic and international level. As the Committee recharges its batteries for a General Comment No.7 on Articles 33(3) and 4(3), States Parties would be better equipped to grasp the crucial importance of the monitoring role of representative organisations of persons with disabilities. As Stig Langvad, disability activist and eminent member of the CRPD Committee puts it: 'I can be proud of the drafting history of the Convention because for the first time, we meaningfully participated with States for the formulation and adoption of a Convention for persons with disabilities.' This statement is equally true today but in a different era, when we call upon states and DPOs to participate together in its implementation. Three decades ago, it would have been very difficult to foresee the adoption of a Convention on the rights of persons with disabilities which would bring us back our dignity and our sense of belonging to the large human family. Today, it is a reality which raises hope and a common destiny for men and women to stand up for justice and equality. With the combined and concerted efforts of all stakeholders, we should be prepared to combat retrogression of our rights and advance towards more independence and inclusion. People with disabilities should also bear in mind that they not only have rights, but, crucially, they have the right to be right-holders.

Notes

1 Consultative Forum—Action on albinism in Africa, 17 to 19 June 2016—Dar es Salaam (United Republic of Tanzania).
2 CRPD Committee, Inquiry concerning the United Kingdom of Great Britain and Northern Ireland, 2016, CRPD/C/15/R.2.
3 HLA Hart, *The Concept of Law*, Oxford University Press, 1961, Chapter 10.
4 UK Independent Mechanism, cited in UK Human Rights Joint Committee, Implementation of the Right of Disabled People to Independent Living, 23rd Report, 6 February 2012.
5 UK Parliament, The European Communities (Definition of Treaties) (United Nations Convention on the Rights of Persons with Disabilities) Order (8 June 2009).
6 The Paris Principles (UN Resolution 48/134 of 20 December 1993) elaborates on the principles relating to the status of national institutions for the promotion and protection of human rights.
7 Coomara Pyaneandee, *National Policy Paper and Action Plan on Disability: Valuing People with Disabilities*, 2007.
8 OHCHR, Thematic Study on the Structure and Role of National Mechanisms for the Implementation and Monitoring of the Convention on the Rights of Persons with Disabilities, 22 December 2009, A/HRC/13/29, para.36.
9 CRPD Committee, Concluding Observations on the Initial Report of Luxembourg, 10 October 2017, CRPD/C/LUX/CO/1, para.58.
10 CRPD Committee, Concluding Observations on the Initial Report of Canada, 8 May 2017 CRPD/C/CAN/CO/1, para.57.
11 CRPD Committee, Concluding Observations on the Initial Report of Honduras, 4 May 2017, CRPD/C/HND/CO/1, para.69.
12 CRPD Committee, Concluding Observations on the Initial Report of Gabon, 2 October 2015, CRPD/C/GAB/CO/1.

BIBLIOGRAPHY

Aguilar, Catalina Devandas (Special Rapporteur on the Rights of Persons with Disabilities), Sexual and Reproductive Health and Rights of Girls and Young Women with Disabilities, 14 July 2017, A/72/133.

Amnesty International, 2014, World Day Against The Death Penalty: Protecting People with Mental and Intellectual Disabilities from the Use of Death Penalty, https://www.amnesty.org/download/Documents/4000/act510052014en.pdf, accessed 26 March 2018.

CEDAW Committee, Concluding Observations on the Combined Seventh and Eighth Periodic Reports of Colombia, 29 October 2013, CEDAW/C/COL/CO/7-8.

CEDAW Committee, General recommendation No.18 (Disabled Women), 1991, INT_CEDAW_GEC_4729_E.

CEDAW Committee, General Recommendation No.19 (Violence against Women), 1992.

CEDAW Committee, General Recommendation No.24, Article 12 CEDAW (women and health), 1999.

CEDAW Committee, General Recommendation No.25 on Article 4(1) (Temporary Special Measures), 2004.

CEDAW Committee, General Recommendation No.30 (Women in Conflict Prevention, Conflict and Post-Conflict Situations), 2013.

CEDAW Committee, General Recommendation No.35 (Gender-Based Violence against Women), 26 July 2017, CEDAW/C/GC/35.

CEDAW Committee, Statement of the Committee on the Elimination of Discrimination against Women on Sexual and Reproductive Health and Rights: Beyond 2014 ICPD review, 10–28 February 2014.

CEDAW Committee, Statement on the Situation in Gaza, July 2014.

Center for Reproductive Rights, Organizations in several countries reject decision of the Colombian Constitutional Court allowing for sterilization of minors with disabilities without their consent, 18 March 2014. Available at https://www.reproductiverights.org/press-room/Organizations-in-several-countries-reject-decision-of-the-Colombian-Constitutional-Court, accessed 26 March 2018.

CERD Committee, General Recommendation No.25 (Gender Related Dimensions of Racial Discrimination), 20 March 2000.

CERD Committee, General Recommendation No.27 (Discrimination against Roma), 2000.

CESCR, General Comment No.14 on Article 12 ICESCR (The Right to the Highest Attainable Standard of Health), 2000, E/C.12/2000/4.

CESCR, General Comment No.18 on Article 6 (The Right to Work), 6 February 2006, E/C.12/GC/18.

CESCR, General comment No.23 on Article 7 ICESCR (The Right to Just and Favourable Conditions of Work), 26 April 2016, E/C.12/GC/23.

CESCR, General Comment No.4 on Article 11(1) (Right to Adequate Housing), 1992.

Cohen, Adam, *Imbeciles: The Supreme Court, American Eugenics, and the Sterilization of Carrie Buck*, Penguin 2016; Roberta Capko, 'Involuntary Sterilisation of Mentally Disabled Women', *Berkley Women's Law Journal* (2013) 8 (1).

Consultative Forum—Action on albinism in Africa, 17 to 19 June—Dar es Salaam (United Republic of Tanzania).

CRC Committee, General Comment No.9 (The Rights of Children with Disabilities), 27 February 2007, CRC/C/GC/9.

CRPD Committee considers the Initial Report of Belgium, 19 September 2014, available at http://www.ohchr.org/EN/NewsEvents/Pages/DisplayNews.aspx?NewsID=15073& LangID=E, accessed 26 March 2018.

CRPD Committee, Comments on the Draft General Comment No.36 of the Human Rights Committee on Article 6 of the International Covenant on Civil and Political Rights, para.1 (on file with the author).

CRPD Committee, Concluding Observations on Initial Report of Lithuania, 11 May 2016, CRPD/C/LTU/CO/1.

CRPD Committee, Concluding Observations on the Initial Report Latvia, 10 October 2017, CRPD/C/LVA/CO/1.

CRPD Committee, Concluding Observations on the Initial Report of Montenegro, 22 September 2017, CRPD/C/MNE/CO/1.

CRPD Committee, Concluding Observations on the Initial Report of Luxembourg, 29 August 2017, CRPD/C/LUX/1.

CRPD Committee, Concluding Observations on the Initial Report of Ethiopia, 4 November 2016, CRPD/C/ETH/CO/1.

CRPD Committee, Concluding Observations on the Initial Report of Bosnia and Herzegovina, 2 May 2017, CRPD/C/BIH/CO/1.

CRPD Committee, Concluding Observations on the Initial Report of Qatar, 2 October 2015, CRPD/C/QAT/CO/1.

CRPD Committee, Concluding Observations on the Initial Report of Armenia, 8 May 2017, CRPD/C/ARM/CO/1.

CRPD Committee, Concluding Observations on the Initial Report of Peru, 16 May 2012, CRPD/C/PER/CO/1.

CRPD Committee, Concluding Observations on the Initial Report of Denmark, 30 October 2014, CRPD/C/DNK/CO/1.

CRPD Committee, Concluding Observations on the Initial Report of Costa Rica, 12 May 2014, CRPD/C/CRI/CO/1.

CRPD Committee, Concluding Observations on the Initial Report of the Republic of Korea, 29 October 2014, CRPD/C/KOR/CO/1.

CRPD Committee, Concluding Observations on the Initial Report of the Islamic Republic of Iran, 10 May 2017, CRPD/C/IRN/CO/1.

CRPD Committee, Concluding Observations on the Initial Report of Canada, 8 May 2017, CRPD/C/CAN/CO/1.

CRPD Committee, Concluding Observations on the Initial Report of Hungary, 22 October 2012, CRPD/C/HUN/CO/1.

CRPD Committee, Concluding Observations on the Initial Report of Ukraine, 2 October 2015 CRPD/C/UKR/CO/1.

CRPD Committee, Concluding Observations on the Initial Report of Lithuania, 11 May 2016, CRPD/C/LTU/CO/1.

CRPD Committee, Concluding Observations on the Initial Report of Bolivia, 4 November 2016, CRPD/C/BOL/CO/1.

CRPD Committee, Concluding Observations on the Initial Report of Honduras, 4 May 2017, CRPD/C/HND/CO/1.

CRPD Committee, Concluding Observations on the Initial Report of Guatemala, 30 September 2016, CRPD/C/GTM/CO/1.

CRPD Committee, Concluding Observations on the Initial Report of Cyprus, 8 May 2017, CRPD/C/CYP/CO/1.

CRPD Committee, Concluding Observations on the Initial Report of Sweden, 18 September 2012, CRPD/C/SWE/1.

CRPD Committee, Concluding Observations on the Initial Report of Belgium, 28 October 2014, CRPD/C/BEL/CO/1.

CRPD Committee, Concluding Observations on the initial report of Kenya, 30 September 2015, CRPD/C/KEN/CO/1.

CRPD Committee, Concluding Observations on the Initial Report of China, 15 October 2012, CRPD/C/CHN/CO/1.

CRPD Committee, Concluding Observations on the Initial Report of the Republic of Moldova, 18 May 2017, CRPD/C/MDA/CO/1.

CRPD Committee, Concluding Observations on the Initial Report of Gabon, 2 October 2015, CRPD/C/GAB/CO/1.

CRPD Committee, Concluding Observations on the Initial Report of Tunisia, 13 May 2011, CRPD/C/TUN/CO/1.

CRPD Committee, Concluding Observations on the Initial Report of Spain, 19 October 2011, CRPD/C/ESP/CO/1.

CRPD Committee, General Comment No. 1 on Article 12 (Equal Recognition Before the Law), 11 April 2014, CRPD/C/GC/1.

CRPD Committee, General Comment No. 2 on Article 9 (Accessibility), 2014, CRPD/C/GC/2.

CRPD Committee, General Comment No. 3 on Article 6 (Women and Girls with Disabilities), 2016, CRPD/C/GC/3.

CRPD Committee, General Comment No. 4 on Article 24 (Right to Inclusive Education), 2016, CRPD/C/GC/4.

CRPD Committee, General Comment No. 5 on Article 19 (independent living and being included in the community), 2017, CRPD/C/GC/5.

CRPD Committee, Guidelines on Article 14 (The Right to Liberty and Security of Persons with Disabilities), September 2015.

CRPD Committee, Inquiry concerning the United Kingdom of Great Britain and Northern Ireland, 2016, CRPD/C/15/R.2.

CRPD Committee, General Comment No. 6 on Article 5 (Equality and Non-Discrimination), CRPD/C/GC/5.

de Beco, G., 'Article 33(2) of the UN Convention on the Rights of Persons with Disabilities. Another Role for National Human Rights Institutions?', (2011) 29 (1) *Netherlands Quarterly of Human Rights* 84–106.

Duguner, Theresia, 'A New Human Rights Model of Disability' in V. Della Fina et al. (eds), *The United Nations Convention on the Rights of Persons with Disabilities: A Commentary* (Springer, 2017).

Duke Initiative for Science & Society, Iran: Premarital Genetic Testing Mandatory, 13 February 2017. Available at http://scipol.duke.edu/content/iran-premarital-genetic-testing-mandatory, accessed 26 March 2018.

ECOSOC, Safeguards Guaranteeing Protection of the Rights of those Facing the Death Penalty, 25 May 1984, Resolution 1984/50.

European Centre for Law and Justice, 'The Right to Life is not the Right to Kill', 2017, https://eclj.org/abortion/un/protgez-toute-vie-humaine, accessed 26 March 2018.

European Coalition for Community Living, Wasted Time, Wasted Money, Wasted Lives— A Wasted Opportunity? 2010. Available at http://community-living.info/wp-content/uploads/2014/02/ECCL-StructuralFundsReport-final-WEB.pdf, accessed 26 March 2018.

European Disability Forum and European Parliament, 'Hearing on Ending the Forced Sterilisation of Women and Girls with Disabilities', 5 December 2017, http://www.edf-feph.org/5-december-hearing-ending-forced-sterilisation-women-and-girls-disabilities accessed 26 March 2018.

European Foundation Centre, *Study on challenges and good practices in the implementation of the UN Convention on the Rights of Persons with Disabilities*, October 2010.

Fuller, Lon L., *The Morality of the Law*, Yale University Press, 1964.

Hart, HLA, *The Concept of Law*, Oxford University Press, 1961.

HRC, Concluding Observations of the Sixth Periodic Report of the Russian Federation, 24 November 2009, CCPR/C/RUS/CO/6.

HRC, Concluding Observations on Report of Netherlands, 2009.

HRC, Concluding Observations on the Fourth Periodic Report of Ireland, 19 August 2014, CCPR/C/IRL/CO/4.

HRC, Draft General Comment No. 36 on Article 6 ICCPR (Right to Life) available at http://www.ohchr.org/Documents/HRBodies/CCPR/GCArticle6/GCArticle6_EN.pdf, accessed 26 March 2018.

HRC, General Comment No.34 on Article 19 (Freedoms of Opinion and Expression), 12 September 2011, CCPR/C/GC/34.

HRC, General Comment No. 35 on Article 9 (Liberty and Security of the Person), 16 December 2014, CCPR/C/GC/35.

HRC, General Comment No.6 on Article 6 (The Right to Life), 30 April 1982.

HRC, General Comment No.25, Article 25 (The Right to Participate in Public Affairs, Voting Rights and the Right of Equal Access to Public Service), 12 July 1996, CCPR/C/21/Rev.1/Add.7.

Human Rights Watch, 'Treated Worse than Animals, Abuses against Women and Girls with Psychosocial or Intellectual Disabilities in Institutions in India', 3 December 2014. Available at https://www.hrw.org/report/2014/12/03/treated-worse-animals/abuses-against-women-and-girls-psychosocial-or-intellectual, accessed 26 March 2018.

Hynes, Aine (2017) 'Assisted Decision-Making (Capacity) Act 2015 – Update on Implementation' Irish Mental Health Lawyers Association Annual Conference 2017, available at: https://www.ucc.ie/academic/law/docs/mentalhealth/conferences/2017/11.05-A.Hynes-08Apr2017.pdf, accessed 26 March 2018.

ILO Convention No.100 concerning Equal Remuneration (1951).

ILO Convention No.111 concerning Discrimination (Employment and Occupation) (1958).

ILO Convention No.118 concerning Equality of Treatment (Social Security) (1962).

ILO Convention No.159 on Vocational Rehabilitation and Employment (Disabled Persons) (1983).

Kiai, Maina Report of the Special Rapporteur on the Rights to Freedom of Peaceful Assembly and of Association, 14 April 2014, A/HRC/26/29.

Leilani Farha (Special Rapporteur on Adequate Housing), Adequate Housing as a Component of the Right to an Adequate Standard of Living, and the Right to Non-Discrimination in this Context, 12 July 2017, A/72/128.

Manjoo, Rashida, Report of the Special Rapporteur on Violence against Women, its Causes and Consequences, 3 August 2012, A/67/227.

Marrakesh Treaty to Facilitate Access to Published Works for Persons Who Are Blind, Visually Impaired, or Otherwise Print Disabled, adopted in 2013 by the World Intellectual Property Organization.

Méndez, Juan E. Report of Special Rapporteur on Torture and Other Cruel, Inhuman or Degrading Treatment or Punishment, 1 February 2013, A/HRC/22/53.

Mental Health Units (Use of Force) Bill 2017–19, available at https://services.parliament.uk/bills/2017-19/mentalhealthunitsuseofforce.html, accessed 26 March 2018.

Morgon Banks, Lena and Sarah Polack, *The Economic Costs of Exclusion and Gains of Inclusion of People with Disabilities: Evidence from Low and Middle Income Countries*, International Centre for Evidence in Disability, London School of Hygiene & Tropical Medicine.

Muñoz, Vernor, The Right to Education of Persons with Disabilities—Report of the Special Rapporteur on the Right to Education, 19 February 2007, A/HRC/4/29.

Newcomen, Nigel (UK Prisons and Probation Ombudsman) January 2017, Independent investigation into the death of Ms Sarah Reed a prisoner at HMP Holloway on 11 January 2016, available at http://www.ppo.gov.uk/app/uploads/2017/07/L250-16-Death-of-Ms-Sarah-Reed-Holloway-11-01-2016-SID-31-40.pdf, accessed 26 March 2018.

NGO Submission to the CEDAW Committee Pre-Sessional Working Group for Nigeria October 2016 available at https://womenenabled.org/pdfs/WEI%20and%20Nigeria%20Partners%20CEDAW%20Review%20Submission%20June%2012%202017.pdf accessed 26 March 2018.

Nowak, Manfred, Interim Report of the Special Rapporteur of the Human Rights Council on Torture and other Cruel, Inhuman or Degrading Treatment or Punishment, 28 July 2008, A/63/175.

OHCHR, Equality and Non-Discrimination under Article 5 of the Convention on the Rights of Persons with Disabilities, 9 December 2016, A/HRC/34/26.

OHCHR, Report of the Special Rapporteur on the Rights to Freedom of Peaceful Assembly and of Association on his Mission to the Republic of Korea, 15 June 2016, A/HRC/32/36/Add.2.

OHCHR, Thematic Study on Participation in Political and Public Life by Persons with Disabilities, 21 December 2011, A/HRC/19/36.

OHCHR, Thematic Study on the Right of Persons with Disabilities to Education, 18 December 2013, A/HRC/25/29.

OHCHR, Thematic Study on the Right of Persons with Disabilities to Live Independently and be Included in the Community, 12 December 2014, A/HRC/28/37.

OHCHR, Thematic Study on the Structure and Role of National Mechanisms for the Implementation and Monitoring of the Convention on the Rights of Persons with Disabilities, 22 December 2009, A/HRC/13/29.

OHCHR, Thematic Study on the Work and Employment of Persons with Disabilities, 17 December 2012, A/HRC/22/25.

Pyaneandee, Coomara, *National Policy Paper and Action Plan on Disability: Valuing People with Disabilities*, 2007.

Report on Forum on Disability Inclusion and Accessible Urban Development, Co-organized by DESA and UN-Habitat, supported by the African Disability Forum, 28 to 30 October 2015, UN Convention Center, Nairobi, Kenya. Available http://www.un.org/disabilities/documents/2015/report-desaforum-disability-inclusion-Nairobi.pdf, accessed 26 March 2018.

Secretariat for the Convention on the Rights of Persons with Disabilities and UNDESA, Accessibility and Disability Inclusion in Urban Development.

Shakespeare, Tom, 'Disabled People's Self-Organisation: A New Social Movement?', 8:3 *Disability, Handicap and Society* 1993.

Standard Rules on the Equalization of Opportunities for Persons with Disabilities, Rule 7 (Adopted in accordance with UN General Assembly Resolution No 48/96 adopted 20th December 1993).

Stone-MacDonald, Angie, 'Cultural Beliefs and Attitudes about Disability in East Africa', *Review of Disability Studies: An International Journal 8:1* 2014, available at http://www.rdsjournal.org/index.php/journal/article/download/110/367, accessed 26 March 2018.

Thaler, Richard H., Cass R. Sustein, Nudge: Improving Decisions about Health, Wealth and Happiness, Yale University Press, 2008.

The Paris Principles (UN Resolution 48/134 of 20 December 1993) elaborates on the principles relating to the status of national institutions for the promotion and protection of human rights.

Training Guide on the Convention on the Rights of Persons with Disabilities, Professional Training Series No. 19 (United Nations 2014).

UK Disability History Month, War and Impairment: The Social Consequences of Disablement (2014). Available at http://ukdhm.org/v2/wp-content/uploads/2014/09/UK-Disability-history-month-2014-Broadsheet.pdf, accessed 26 March 2018.

UK Independent Mechanism, cited in UK Human Rights Joint Committee, Implementation of the Right of Disabled People to Independent Living, 23rd Report, 6 February 2012.

UK Parliament, The European Communities (Definition of Treaties) (United Nations Convention on the Rights of Persons with Disabilities) Order (8 June 2009).

UN General Assembly, 6th Resolution Calling for a Universal Moratorium on Executions, 19 December 2016, A/RES/71/187.

UN General Assembly, Draft Resolution addressing the impact of multiple and intersecting forms of discrimination and violence in the context of racism, racial discrimination, xenophobia and related intolerance on the full enjoyment of all human rights by women and girls, 28 June 2016, A/HRC/32/L.25.

UN General Assembly, Implementation of the Convention on the Rights of Persons with Disabilities and the Optional Protocol thereto: Situation of Women and Girls with Disabilities, 13 November 2017, A/C.3/72/L.18/Rev.1.

UN General Assembly, Implementation of the World Programme of Action concerning Disabled Persons and the United Nations Decade of Disabled Persons, 8 December 1989, A/RES/44/70.

UN General Assembly, International Year of Disabled Persons, 16 December 1976, A/RES/31/123.

UN General Assembly, International Year of Disabled Persons, 8 December 1981, A/RES/36/77.

UN Recommendation No. 99 concerning Vocational Rehabilitation of the Disabled (1955).

UNICEF, Children with Disabilities, available at http://www.unicef.cn/en/child-protection/children-with-disabilities/, accessed 26 March 2018; See also Jessie Li, Pulitzer Center

Project China: Students With Disabilities, available at https://pulitzercenter.org/proj ects/china-children-education-disabilities, accessed 26 March 2018.

United Nations Declaration on Human Rights Education and Training, 19 December 2011, A/RES/66/137.

United Nations General Assembly Resolution (2001) A/RES/56/168.

United Nations General Assembly, 'Declaration on the Elimination of Violence Against Women', December 1993, A/RES/48/104.

Walton, Oliver, *Helpdesk Research Report: Economic Benefits of Disability-Inclusive Development*, Governance and Social Development Resource Centre, 6 September 2012.

INDEX